LANGUAGE IN SOCIETY 31

The Development of African American English

Language in Society

GENERAL EDITOR
Peter Trudgill, Chair of English Linguistics,
University of Fribourg

ADVISORY EDITORS
J. K. Chambers, Professor of Linguistics,
University of Toronto

Ralph Fasold, Professor of Linguistics,
Georgetown University

William Labov, Professor of Linguistics,
University of Pennsylvania

Lesley Milroy, Professor of Linguistics,
University of Michigan, Ann Arbor

The Development of African American English

Walt Wolfram and Erik R. Thomas

In collaboration with
Elaine W. Green, Becky Childs,
Dan Beckett, and Benjamin Torbert

Blackwell
Publishers

WITHDRAWN FROM
J. EUGENE SMITH LIBRARY
EASTERN CONN. STATE UNIVERSITY
WILLIMANTIC. CT 06226-2295

© Walt Wolfram and Erik R. Thomas 2002

Editorial Offices:
108 Cowley Road, Oxford OX4 1JF, UK
Tel: +44 (0)1865 791100
350 Main Street, Malden, MA 02148-5018, USA
Tel: +1 781 388 8250

The right of Walt Wolfram and Erik R. Thomas to be identified as the Authors of this Work has been asserted in accordance with the UK Copyright, Designs and Patents Act 1988.

All rights reserved. No part of this publication may be reproduced, stored in a retrieval system, or transmitted, in any form or by any means, electronic, mechanical, photocopying, recording or otherwise, except as permitted by the UK Copyright, Designs and Patents Act 1988, without the prior permission of the publisher.

First published 2002 by Blackwell Publishers Ltd, a Blackwell Publishing company

Library of Congress Cataloging-in-Publication Data has been applied for.

ISBN 0-631-23086-6 (hardback); ISBN 0-631-23087-4 (paperback)

A catalogue record for this title is available from the British Library.

Set in 10 ½ on 12pt Ehrhardt
by Graphicraft Limited, Hong Kong
Printed and bound in Great Britain
by MPG Books Ltd, Bodmin, Cornwall

For further information on
Blackwell Publishers, visit our website:
www.blackwellpublishers.co.uk

Contents

List of Figures

List of Tables

Series Editor's Preface

This book is an example of the linguistic study of language in society at its best. Wolfram, Thomas, and their associates have produced a superb work in what we might perhaps call linguistic archaeology. By dint of highly professional fieldwork in a hitherto uninvestigated enclave community, and by virtue of careful and detailed quantitative analyses of a wide variety of linguistic variables, they have been able to develop a highly insightful window on to the past. This window, which depends crucially on the tendency for isolated communities to retain conservative linguistic features (although it is of course always much more complicated than that), has helped the authors to answer, in a balanced, nuanced, and ideologically neutral way, some vexed questions – some of them also treated by other books in this series – about the history of African American English. Importantly, the authors have also been able to generalize from the findings produced in this single small community at one point in time to social and linguistic events which span the Americas, and the Atlantic Ocean, and to issues with a time depth of three hundred years or more. They have also been able to shed light on the equally fascinating question as to where ongoing developments in contemporary African American English are currently taking this important variety. Throughout the whole work, moreover, we find treatments of theoretical issues of interest to all who work in the area of linguistic variation and change. This is an in-depth study of a small area of the United States which most readers will never have heard of. But it is also a wide-ranging exercise in sociohistorical linguistics with the widest possible theoretical and methodological implications.

Prof. Peter Trudgill
Chair of English Linguistics
University of Fribourg

Preface

No topic in modern sociolinguistics has engendered more interest than African American Vernacular English. Furthermore, this interest has not been restricted to the sociolinguistic research community. As evidenced by sporadic national controversies that have played out in the media over the past several decades, the public at large has also been captivated by the socio-political and educational implications attendant to this language variety. In this book, we address some of the major issues related to the historical and contemporary development of the speech of African Americans, based on empirical data from a unique enclave dialect situation that has existed for almost three centuries now in coastal North Carolina. Though the specific sociolinguistic situation is limited, it has much to tell us about the general development of African American speech in the past and the present. Our goal is to follow the data as they lead us to conclusions that sometimes confirm the results of other studies while, at other times, challenge the conclusions of other studies.

The fact that African American Vernacular English has undergone so many name changes over the past four decades speaks symptomatically of the controversy associated with the recognition of this variety. Over the last half century this variety has been assigned the following labels, listed here in approximate chronological sequence: *Negro Dialect, Substandard Negro English, Nonstandard Negro English, Black English, Vernacular Black English/ Black English Vernacular, Afro-American English, Ebonics, African American Vernacular English, African American Language, Ebonics* (again), and *Spoken Soul*. In choosing to use the term *African American Vernacular English (AAVE)* in this book, we underscore our focus on the ethnolinguistic status of AAVE as a significant vernacular variety of American English. Our definition clearly suffers from a structural linguistic and sociolinguistic bias in that it focuses, for the most part, on "nonmainstream" linguistic traits that both set this variety apart and unite it with other vernacular varieties. This is, of course, only one of the perspectives on African American speech and, admittedly, a limited one. The focus is not intended to minimize or trivialize important issues of definition related to the construct African American English, including the right of self-definition, but simply to set forth the sociolinguistic focal point of this study. Accordingly, we concentrate on some of the structural forms that have been at the heart of the debate over the linguistic history of AAVE while also considering some traits that traditionally have been overlooked in this controversy.

In all respects, this book resulted from a team effort by the members of the North Carolina Language and Life Project at North Carolina State University. This collective effort is recognized in the authorship of the book, which acknowledges the primary authorship of Walt Wolfram and Erik R. Thomas, along with the full participation of key team members in all phases of the research. Wolfram took the lead in writing chapters 1–3, 5, 7, 9, and 10, and Thomas was responsible for writing chapters 4, 6, and 8, although all the chapters reflect contributions by both authors. While Wolfram and Thomas were responsible for the writing and various phases of the analysis, critical fieldwork and analysis were undertaken by a number of staff members. Elaine W. Green and Becky Childs coordinated most of the fieldwork for this project, along with Erik Thomas and Benjamin Torbert. Green, in particular, conducted by far the largest number of interviews. Other fieldworkers who conducted interviews include Sherise Berry, Tracie M. Fellers, Barbara E. Hunter, Natalie Schilling-Estes, Jason G. Sellers, Byinna Warfield, Tracey Weldon, and Marge Wolfram. Four tapes recorded in 1981 by the late Rebecca Swindell were provided to us by the Hyde County Historical and Genealogical Society. The analysis of consonant clusters in chapter 7 was carried out by Becky Childs, with supplemental analysis by Walt Wolfram. Walt Wolfram and Daniel Beckett were responsible for the analysis of postvocalic *r* vocalization, copula absence, past tense *be* regularization, and third person -*s* reported in chapter 9. Elaine Green also conducted part of the analysis of *weren't* regularization and copula absence that was integrated into chapter 5, and did genealogical analyses for a number of African American families who were a part of this study. Bridget L. Anderson conducted about half of the acoustic vowel measurements discussed in chapter 6; Thomas conducted the other half. Jeffrey Reaser and Amy Gantt worked on the listener perception experiments reported in chapter 10. Dede A. Addy conducted an analysis of invariant *be* that was incorporated into chapter 5 and chapter 10 under a Carnegie Mellon mentoring fellowship. Bridget L. Anderson, Daniel Beckett, Rebecca Childs, Caroline Fleming, Amy Gantt, Christine Mallinson, Maureen F. Matarese, Jaclyn Ocumpaugh, Jeffrey Reaser, and Benjamin Torbert typed transcripts that were used in the intonational analysis in chapter 8. The essential role of the entire team of researchers is happily acknowledged, including colleagues who had a more indirect role in this research project. In this regard, we give special thanks to our colleague David Herman, who provided an insightful, Hermanskijan perspective on a number of emerging ideas in this study.

Local Hyde County historian, R. S. Spencer, Jr., provided invaluable assistance in compiling the history chapter. Thanks in large part to him, the Hyde County Historical and Genealogical Society is one of the most active historical organizations in North Carolina, and much of our historical account has been gleaned from two of its publications: Selby et al. (1976) and the periodical *High Tides*. T. J. Mann cheerfully assisted us in contacting residents and provided encouragement when we needed it most – at the outset of our study. Special thanks also to Dorothy Collins, James Thomas Burrus, and Jarrett Spencer for their help in coordinating contacts and interviews with many of the younger members of the Hyde County community, and for simply hanging out and sharing pizza with fieldworkers along the way. As with any field-initiated sociolinguistic study, we are forever indebted to all of the kind people of Hyde County who tolerated our seemingly inane intrusions into their everyday world.

Special thanks to a number of people who read parts of the manuscript and commented on it, including Guy Bailey, John Baugh, Ron Butters, Kirk Hazen, Cathleen Hellier, David Herman, Bill Labov, Michael Montgomery, Shana Poplack, John Rickford, Natalie Schilling-Estes, Daniel Schreier, Sali Tagliamonte, James Walker, and especially the students enrolled in the Language Variation Research Seminar in the spring of 2001 who read and commented on the manuscript in progress. Our greatest indebtedness is, of course, reserved for our spouses, Barbara Hunter and Marge Wolfram. They have given the most – in time, patience, and support throughout this venture and through all of our varied sociolinguistic adventures. To be perfectly honest, sometimes we don't know how they do it, but we are simply thankful that they do.

We gratefully acknowledge support from National Science Foundation research grants BCS 99-10224 and SBR-96-16331, as well as funding from the William C. Friday Endowment and from a Faculty Research and Professional Development grant (both at North Carolina State University), to carry out this research. Naturally, these funding agencies are not responsible for the contents or the opinions expressed in this book.

Walt Wolfram, William C. Friday Professor
North Carolina State University

Erik R. Thomas
North Carolina State University

March 2001

1

Introduction

1.1 The Status of African American English

The synchronic and diachronic status of African American Vernacular English (AAVE) has now been scrutinized more than that of any other vernacular variety in the history of American English. In fact, a survey (Schneider, 1996:3) of published research on dialects of American English from the mid-1960s through the mid-1990s indicates that AAVE has had more than five times as many publications devoted to it as any other variety of English and more publications than all other varieties of American English combined. Given the level of attention, it is therefore somewhat surprising to find Singler's (1998) appraisal of historical research on AAVE highlight the paucity of data about earlier African American speech.

> A vexing problem in determining the age of particular AAVE features has been the general absence of data about earlier stages. Moreover, the data that have been available have often been suspect because of the circumstances under which they were gathered, because of questions as to whether or not the speakers were actually speaking AAVE, and the like. (Singler, 1998a:227)

Despite periods of apparent consensus among sociolinguists, data on the origin and early development of AAVE are still quite limited, and debate over its genesis continues to be intense after almost half a century of inquiry.

The debate over the evolution of AAVE is hardly limited to its origin and early development. At the same time, there is continuing debate about its more recent development, particularly in relation to other vernacular varieties of English. Is AAVE changing in ways that make it more distinct from other vernacular varieties of English – the so-called *divergence hypothesis* (Labov, 1985; Fasold, 1987) – or is it aligning more closely with other varieties of

English? Arguments over the development of AAVE in the twentieth century are as contentious as the debate over its earlier history, even though the empirical data to address questions of language change in the twentieth century would seem to be more readily accessible than data related to earlier African American speech. Obviously, issues concerning the development of AAVE are not limited to the simple accumulation of data; they concern the reliability of the sources of data, the methods of analysis, and the interpretations of the results derived from different studies.

Our goal is to address some of the major issues in the historical and current development of AAVE by examining in detail a unique enclave dialect situation that we have uncovered in Hyde County, North Carolina, located along the coast of the Atlantic Ocean by the Pamlico Sound. Although the empirical study focuses on a single, long-standing biracial enclave situation in a remote geographical location, the implications for the more general origin and early development of AAVE are far-reaching. The data allow us to consider fundamental issues in the reconstruction of AAVE such as the effect of regional dialects on the earlier speech of African Americans, the role of persistent substratal influence from earlier language contact situations between Africans and Europeans, the nature of intracommunity language variation in earlier AAVE, and the trajectory of language change in earlier and contemporary African American speech. All of these issues are central to the resolution of the debate over the past and current development of AAVE.

1.2 A Unique Database

Data from two sources have fueled the re-examination of the earlier history of AAVE in the last couple of decades. First, there has been a significant expansion in uncovering written documentation representing earlier African American speech. Although previous accounts of earlier African American speech (Stewart, 1967, 1968; Dillard, 1972) often included citations from written records by African Americans and observations about African American speech, the detailed analysis of different types of written texts have challenged the textual reliability of some earlier written records, and correspondingly, the view on the early development of African American speech. One important type of data that came to light in the 1980s was a set of written records and audio recordings of ex-slaves. These include an extensive set of ex-slave narratives collected under the Works Project Administration (WPA) (Schneider, 1989) in the 1930s, letters written by semiliterate ex-slaves in the mid-1800s (Montgomery et al., 1993; Montgomery and Fuller, 1996), and other specialized collections of texts, such as the Hyatt texts – an extensive set of interviews conducted with black hoodoo doctors in the 1930s

(Hyatt, 1970–8; Viereck, 1988; Ewers, 1996). All of these records seemed to point to the conclusion that earlier AAVE was not nearly as distinct from postcolonial Anglo-American English varieties as earlier hypotheses had proposed, namely, those hypothesizing a protocreole origin for AAVE (Stewart, 1967, 1968; Dillard, 1972). Although emerging written documentation on earlier African American English has raised essential issues related to reconstructing African American speech (see chapter 2), we have little to add to this discussion, since we have uncovered no written records from earlier African Americans in Hyde County.

The second type of database that inspired the re-examination of the historical development of earlier African American speech came from the investigation of black expatriate varieties of English. For example, in the 1820s, a group of blacks migrated to the peninsula of Samaná in the Dominican Republic, living in relative isolation and maintaining an apparent relic variety of English up to the present day (Poplack and Sankoff, 1987; Poplack and Tagliamonte, 1989; Poplack, 1999). A significant population of African Americans also migrated from the United States to Canada in the early 1800s, and some have lived to this day in relative isolation in Nova Scotia. The examination of the English varieties spoken by blacks in these areas by Shana Poplack and Sali Tagliamonte (1991), and their team of researchers (Poplack, 1999; Poplack and Tagliamonte, 2001) has led to the conclusion that these insular varieties were quite similar to earlier European American varieties, again raising important challenges to the hypothesis that a protocreole language was implicated in the origin and early development of African American English. The validity of such evidence is premised on three assumptions: (1) that the transplant language variety of the expatriates was an authentic reflection of a vernacular variety typical of many African Americans at that time; (2) that such communities would be relatively conservative in their language change in their new settlement communities; and (3) that these communities would remain relatively unaffected by the influence of surrounding communities and immune to changes taking place in contemporary AAVE. There are important questions that have been raised with respect to each of these issues, not unlike the kinds of questions we must confront in our study of Hyde County.

The community we examine here falls squarely within the tradition of enclave dialect studies, though it is a different kind of situation in that it involves a long-standing, relatively isolated biracial community in the rural Southern United States. Although expatriate transplant communities such as those studied by Poplack, Tagliamonte, and their team of researchers at the University of Ottawa (e.g., Poplack, 1999) may seem, at first glance, to hold more potential for examining the state of earlier African American speech than the coastal North Carolina Hyde County community because of greater physical dislocation and obvious social detachment from cohort communities of European Americans in the USA, we would argue that enclave situations in the USA may offer equally compelling insight. In the community we examine here, there is comparable geographic remoteness and social detachment though the physical dislocation may not be nearly as great as that involved in expatriate situations. There is, however, continuity within the community for a much longer time frame than that found for transplant situations, since the community is now almost three centuries old.

As we will see in our detailed description of Hyde County in chapter 4, it is one the oldest European American and African American settlement communities in North Carolina. Europeans settled there at the turn of the 1700s, and shortly thereafter African Americans were brought to the area. After a period of growth in the early 1700s, the area became an isolated enclave located in terrain that was 85 percent marshland. This setting, which has maintained an African American population of between a quarter and a half of the overall population of Hyde County throughout its history, provides an ideal setting for examining several critical issues regarding the historical development of African American speech. For one, it offers a sociolinguistic context involving a long-term, relatively insular, biracial situation featuring a distinctive European American variety. The Outer Banks dialect described in a number of recent publications (e.g., Wolfram and Schilling-Estes, 1995, 1997; Wolfram, Hazen, and Schilling-Estes, 1999) is found in this mainland setting as well as in the Outer Banks. The location of Hyde County and the approximate extent of the Pamlico Sound dialect area are given in figure 1.1.

The historical continuity of the African American community in the Hyde County region – almost three centuries old now – also provides an important perspective on the possible genesis and early development of AAVE. For example, the family genealogies of many of the current European American residents date back to the earliest residents of the area.

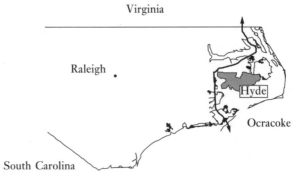

Figure 1.1   Location of Hyde County and the traditional Pamlico Sound dialect

Although comparable genealogies do not exist for African Americans, oral histories and emerging genealogies (see chapter 4) point to a parallel historical continuity. This observation is confirmed by the large number of shared surnames found among African Americans and European Americans in Hyde County – naming practices that reflect the tradition of the antebellum South when slaves were assigned their owners' surnames. The relatively stable census figures of Hyde County over two centuries of official census records also reflect the fact that there has been limited in-migration into Hyde County.

Finally, this situation offers insight into how African American speech is presently developing with respect to local European American vernacular varieties of English, as well as to varieties spoken by African Americans elsewhere. Through the application of the apparent time construct, we can see how the residents of Hyde County have been changing their speech during the twentieth century. By comparing the trajectories of language change for African Americans and European Americans both in relation to each other and in relation to external norms we can provide answers to the prominent debate about ethnolinguistic accommodation and diversity in the twentieth century.

1.3 The Hyde County Corpus

Since 1997, the staff of the North Carolina Language and Life Project has interviewed 144 lifetime residents of Hyde County, comprising 92 African Americans and 52 European Americans, as part of an ongoing sociolinguistic investigation. The age range of the speakers spans a century in apparent time, including those born as early as the 1890s to those born in the 1990s. Subjects for this study were chosen following the social network procedure of locating a friend of a friend (Milroy, 1987) and a family tree social network in which different members of extended families were selected for interviewing (Green, 1998). The use of the family tree procedure in selecting subjects was related to an effort to trace genealogies for some of the long-standing African American families in the community. The family tree sample offers the obvious advantage of comparing speech across different generations within the same family, while the social network sample offers the advantage of a broader representation of socially connected speakers within the community.

Some of the interviews followed the format of the traditional, conversationally based sociolinguistic interview (Labov, 1966; Wolfram and Fasold, 1974), while other interviews followed Green's (1998) genealogical inquiry interviewing procedure that focused on discussions of family lineage. Both interviewing techniques led to extended conversations and significant amounts of casual speech data, although there may have been some consequences in terms of the conversational themes and the occurrence of particular structural features due to the differential topic focus in the interviews. For example, the two techniques precluded a systematic investigation of lexical variants, including such local terms as *pone bread* "cornbread made with molasses (treacle)," *juniper* "Atlantic white-cedar (*Chamaecyparis thyoides*)," and *shivering owl* "screech owl."

Our analysis is based on data from the conversational portion of the interview, which typically lasted 60–90 minutes. A few of the speakers in our corpus were interviewed several times over the course of our fieldwork, so that we have three to four hours of conversation for these speakers. Both European American and African American interviewers of different ages and both sexes conducted interviews, although we do not consider the effects of interviewer variables such as ethnicity, sex, and age in the current analysis. Subjects were interviewed in their homes, at work, or at various meeting places where they spend their leisure time. Our goal was to interview subjects in a social setting in which they were most comfortable and relaxed. Generally, one or two members of our research team conducted the interviews, sometimes with one participant but in some cases with more than one subject. In some cases, a community member also accompanied the fieldworker, especially for interviews with members of the African American community. The majority of conversations are three-way conversations rather than dyads, following the model we established in the earlier study of Ocracoke (Wolfram, Hazen, and Schilling-Estes, 1999:6). We found that most participants felt more comfortable in a three-way conversation than they did in a one-on-one question and answer format.

Although we ended up with a convenience sample of Hyde County that followed social network and family network relations, attention was given to the representation of different age levels in our sample. We also sought to have adequate representation of men and women for both ethnic groups and different age groups, although we do not examine the role of gender in a systematic way as a part of this study (see Beckett, 2001). Therefore, our sample includes speakers who represent all ages for both ethnic groups. Such a generational distribution is critical for the goals of this study as they relate to language change and ethnolinguistic alignment in apparent time.

1.4 Data Analysis

The analytical procedures generally fall in line with the current methods used in quantitative sociolinguistics, with a couple of notable exceptions.

For morphosyntactic structures, discussed in chapter 5, a sample of diagnostic structures was first selected for detailed examination. The representative variables selected here include two morphosyntactic patterns typically associated with the Pamlico Sound regional variety, past tense leveling to *weren't* (e.g., *It weren't me*) and 3rd plural *-s* marking (e.g., *The dogs barks*), and two features commonly associated with the core morphosyntactic structures of AAVE, copula/auxiliary absence (e.g., *She nice*) and 3rd sg. *-s* absence (e.g., *The dog bark*). In comparing patterns of variation and change for a sample of AAVE-exclusive structures and distinctive Pamlico Sound morphosyntactic structures across different generations of African American and European American speakers, we hope to ascertain the ways in which the vernaculars were aligned at an earlier period in their history and how this alignment is changing. Accommodation to distinct Pamlico Sound morphosyntactic features by African Americans would show that they were sensitive to regionalized dialect norms. On the other hand, the persistence of dialect features associated exclusively with the African American speech community would give us insight into the maintenance of long-term ethnolinguistic distinctiveness.

The morphosyntactic analysis is based on a subsample of 49 speakers: 35 African American speakers divided into four age groups of speakers (12 young, aged 14–23; 6 middle-aged, aged 32–43; 6 senior, aged 55–70; and 11 elderly, aged 77–102) and 14 European American speakers divided into an elderly (6, aged 77–92) and a young (8, aged 15–27) group. The age delimitation for the four different groups of African American speakers follows the clustering of generational age groups in our sample of speakers (elderly = 77–91; senior = 55–70; middle = 32–43; young = 14–23) rather than the arbitrary, chronologically based increments sometimes found in studies of apparent time (e.g., 21–40, 41–60, etc.). To some extent, divisions between age groups also correspond to some significant historical events. For example, the two oldest groups of speakers represent speakers born during or before World War II, an event sometimes correlated with significant language shifts in the South (Bailey et al., 1991, 1993). Speakers in the two oldest age groups also attended segregated schools, whereas the two younger groups of speakers were educated during or after school integration took place (see chapter 4) in the Hyde County schools.

Because European American speakers serve primarily as a baseline group for comparison with the African American speakers in this study, samples of European Americans tend to be more limited in this study. As noted above, only 14 European Americans divided into two age groups – elderly speakers and younger speakers – were used in the morphosyntactic comparison and analysis of diagnostic consonants. Fewer European Americans than African Americans were used for the vowel analysis as well. It should also be noted that the European Americans selected for the morphosyntactic analysis were limited to those classified as primary speakers of a vernacular version of Pamlico Sound English, based on independent linguistic criteria and background sociodemographic data. Judgments of vernacularity were made on the basis of sociodemographic background information as well as independent linguistic variables. All speakers in the sample who used negative concord and/or vernacular irregular verb patterns such as participial past tense forms (*I seen it*) or bare root past irregular forms (*Yesterday they come there*) were considered to be vernacular for the selection of this sample.

For the morphosyntactic analysis and the impressionistically based analysis of phonological variables (namely consonants), each instance of the diagnostic structure was extracted for the subsample of speakers, and the incidence of variants for each variable was tabulated for each speaker in the sample. However, in many cases, our analysis is based on summary descriptive data figures given for aggregate groups classified on the basis of ethnicity and age. Following the tradition of current quantitative sociolinguistics, we subjected these figures to VARBRUL analysis (Cedergren and Sankoff, 1974; Young and Bayley, 1996). VARBRUL is a probabilistic-based, multivariate regression procedure that shows the relative contributions of different factors to the overall variability of fluctuating forms. Factor groups may consist of independent linguistic constraints, such as following phonological environment, or external social ones, such as age group or social affiliation. The weighting values range from 0 to 1; a value of greater than .5 favors the occurrence of the variant, while a value of less than .5 disfavors its occurrence in a binomial analysis.

One of the limitations of VARBRUL analysis is its reliance on aggregate data that typically ignores the role of individual variation. But the relation of the individual to the group in sociolinguistics is hardly a settled issue. Thus, we also consider profiles of individual speakers to examine the role of the individual and group in sociolinguistic variation. In fact, one full chapter (chapter 9) is dedicated to the examination of the role of the individual variation in Earlier African American English, and much of our analysis of vowels focuses on individuals rather than groups. In this way, we hope to balance the analysis by considering both group and individual dynamics.

Chapters 6 and 7 treat variation in vowels and consonants, respectively, with chapter 8 devoted to intonation. The vowel analysis in chapter 6 comprises three parts. The first part consists of a general discussion of the vowel variants that make the dialect of Hyde County and the rest of the Pamlico Sound area distinctive. This discussion centers on a set of representative vowel formant plots. A detailed discussion of the acoustic measurement techniques, selection of tokens, and so forth used to produce these plots is provided. Next, we provide a historical survey of Hyde County vowels that compares our data with records from the *Linguistic Atlas of the Middle and South Atlantic States* (LAMSAS). The historical survey attempts to project backward to reconstruct what Hyde County vowel configurations, both African American and European American, were like around 1800. In our estimation, the evidence from LAMSAS and from historical information about eastern North Carolina – especially about Hyde County, as described in chapter 4 – is adequate to make these conjectures. However, we do not feel that we can project back before 1800 with much confidence. Finally, we embark on a detailed acoustic analysis of twentieth-century developments in Hyde County vowel configurations. This analysis is based on a sample of 49 Hyde Countians, comprising 27 African Americans and 22 European Americans, who represent the entire range of ages interviewed for the study. It focuses on three vowels for which adequate numbers of tokens were available in the recordings: /ai/, as in *tide*; /au/, as in *out*; and /o/, as in *coat*. Using a linear regression analysis of the normalized mean formant values for these speakers, we show how African American and European American vowel configurations in Hyde County are changing with respect to each other and note the implications of these developments. Taken together, chapter 6 provides an overview of Hyde County vowels over a 200-year period, which allows us to reach broader conclusions about the long-range relationship of AAVE with European American vernaculars than most other studies have been able to do.

Our analysis of consonants (chapter 7) involves both a general qualitative profile of the phonological traits of African American and European American Pamlico Sound English and the detailed quantitative examination of two consonant variables, namely syllable-coda consonant cluster reduction and postvocalic *r*-lessness. The former variable is probably the most analyzed phonological variable in current quantitative sociolinguistics, but this replication offers insight into its historical role and current development within an insular biracial enclave situation. The other consonant variable we examine, postvocalic *r*-lessness, is also well represented in the sociolinguistic literature, including regional and ethnic varieties of English, but the regional pattern of postvocalic *r* in Hyde County is quite distinctive, thus making it particularly diagnostic in terms of the examination of historical and current ethnolinguistic alignment.

In contrast to the heavily studied variables of chapter 7, chapter 8 examines one of the most sparsely studied variables, intonation. We concentrate on one intonational variable, the frequency of high pitch accents. The ethnic alignment appears to be as strong for intonation in Hyde County as for other variables. However, the paucity of research on African American intonation prevents us from drawing any conclusions about the past state of AAVE intonation. Our inquiry in chapter 8 opens up at least as many questions as it resolves.

While our analysis hardly covers the entire spectrum of diagnostic structures for African American English and Pamlico Sound English, it includes a fairly representative set of diagnostic phonological and grammatical features. In this respect, it is somewhat different from some of the current analyses of insular African American situations that tend to focus exclusively on a single feature or a restricted set of AAVE structures. Our investigation shows that an authentic picture of earlier African American speech can emerge only if a wide array of dialect structures is considered, including overall profiles of vowel systems, consonants, and prosody, along with diagnostic morphosyntactic variables. While selective, single-structure studies may reveal significant insight into a particular linguistic process and/or a dimension of an ethnolinguistic boundary, such studies may obscure or even distort our understanding of the overall relationship of African American speech to other varieties. We also complement some of our objective findings with results obtained from a speaker identification task. It is essential to keep both the objective and subjective dimensions in mind as we attempt to capture a clear picture of change and variation in earlier and contemporary African American English.

1.5 Beyond Hyde County

On the one hand, it may seem presumptuous to generalize about the earlier and the contemporary state of African American speech on the basis of a single community such as Hyde County. Certainly, we are mindful of the many cautions that must be exhibited in extrapolating from this situation to the general development of AAVE, regardless of how insightful this situation might be. On the other hand, there appear to be some unavoidable implications for the more general study of African American speech that derive from the examination of this unique sociolinguistic situation. These data allow us to address several critical issues related to the past and present evolution of African American speech in the USA.

One of the crucial issues addressed here is the accommodation of earlier African Americans to regional speechways. Few empirical situations can inform us as richly about the potential for such accommodation than the study of an African American community situated within a highly distinctive regional variety. At the same time, the persistence of long-term ethnolinguistic distinctiveness is a critical issue for reconstructing the history of African American speech. Recent studies of African American speech (Labov, 1998; Poplack, 1999) have suggested that the distinctiveness of AAVE is primarily a twentieth-century phenomenon, but our evidence suggests that this view may be somewhat exaggerated. In fact, our study suggests that, in many instances, earlier African American speech was more likely a mixture of regional traits shared with their European American cohort speech and some persistent substrate features reflective of the earlier contact history between Africans and Europeans. Finally, our study addresses the issue of contemporary change, and the so-called divergence issue. Much has been made of the independent changes taking place within AAVE that are distancing it from comparable European American English vernacular varieties (Dayton, 1996; Labov, 1998). While there is selective support for some of these assertions, the most compelling evidence suggests that the crux of contemporary ethnolinguistic divergence may, in fact, lie in the development of a supraregional AAVE norm that entails the abandonment of, or resistance to, local regional norms. In this context, the results of our study are hardly limited to the small Hyde County community that is the focus of this study. Our findings should impact the core understanding of the earlier and present-day development of African American speech throughout North America in general.

2

Issues in the Development of African American English

In order to understand the broader significance of our study, it is necessary to set forth the kinds of issues that frame the examination of language change in African American speech, ranging from the origin and early evolution of African American English to its recent development in the latter half of the twentieth century. Given the unique type of sociolinguistic situation we consider here as our empirical base, it is also necessary to consider issues related to the construct "enclave dialect community." As noted in chapter 1, corpora from enclave communities have provided a critical database for re-examining the historical development of African American speech, so that the implications of our discussion of this construct extend well beyond the Hyde County community.

2.1 Hypotheses on Earlier African American English

Over the past half century, the study of AAVE has undergone several major shifts in hypotheses about its genesis and early development. In the mid-twentieth century the *Anglicist hypothesis* – that the speech of African Americans essentially was derived directly from British-based dialects – was commonly accepted by American dialectologists, along with the conclusion that present-day African American speech was identical to that of comparable rural Southern white speech. Although the synchronic status of AAVE in relation to other vernacular varieties of American English has sometimes been linked to its historical origin, this is not necessarily the case (Wolfram, 1974a, 1987; Rickford, 1987, 1999). In fact, as we discuss later in this chapter, one of the positions currently held by some sociolinguists maintains that African American speech of the nineteenth century was identical to that of cohort European American speech but that it has since diverged

(Labov, 1998; Poplack, 1999). By the same token, of course, one might maintain that earlier African American English was quite different but has since converged with cohort European American vernaculars.

Kurath (1949) and McDavid and McDavid (1951) probably best represent the traditional dialectologist position:

> By and large the Southern Negro speaks the language of the white man of his locality or area and of his education . . . As far as the speech of uneducated Negroes is concerned, it differs little from that of the illiterate white: that is, it exhibits the same regional and local variations as that of the simple white folk. (Kurath, 1949:6)
>
> . . . the overwhelming bulk of the material of American Negro speech – in vocabulary as well as grammar and phonology – is, as one would expect, borrowed from the speech of white groups with which Negroes come in contact. Sometimes these contacts have been such that Negroes simply speak the local variety of standard English. It is also likely that many relic forms from English dialects are better preserved in the speech of some American Negro groups than in American white speech. . . . After all, the preservation of relic forms is made possible by geographical and cultural isolation. (McDavid and McDavid, 1951:12)

This hypothesis has been referred to as the Anglicist hypothesis, so-called because it maintains that the roots of AAVE can be traced to the same source as European American dialects – the dialects of English spoken in the British Isles. Briefly put, this position maintains that the language contact situation of those of African descent in the United States was roughly comparable to that of other groups of immigrants. Under this historical scenario, slaves brought with them to North America a number of different African languages, as well as some pidgin and creole varieties spoken in the African diaspora. Over the course of a couple of generations, only a few minor traces of these heritage languages remained, as Africans learned the regional and social varieties of surrounding white speakers.

In the 1960s and 1970s this position was replaced by the widespread acceptance of the *creole* (or *creolist*) *hypothesis*, which maintains that the roots of AAVE were embedded in an expansive creole found in the African diaspora, including the antebellum Plantation South (Bailey, 1965; Stewart, 1967; Dillard, 1972). A strong version of the creolist hypothesis is offered by Stewart (1968), who argues that:

> Of the Negro slaves who constituted the field labor force on North American plantations up to the mid-nineteenth century, even many who were born in the New World spoke a variety of English which was in fact a true creole language – differing markedly in grammatical structure from those English dialects which were brought directly from Great Britain, as well as from New World modifications of these in the mouths of descendants of the original white colonists. (Stewart, 1968:3)

While not all AAVE researchers accepted such a strong interpretation of the creolist hypothesis, most accepted some version of it. Fasold (1981:164) noted that "the creole hypothesis seems most likely to be correct, but it is certainly not so well established as Dillard (1972), for example, would have us to believe."

In the last couple of decades, new corpora have emerged to challenge the creolist hypothesis, leading to what may be referred to as the *neo-Anglicist hypothesis* (Montgomery et al., 1993, Montgomery and Fuller, 1996; Mufwene, 1996a; Poplack, 1999). This position, like the Anglicist hypothesis of the mid-twentieth century, maintains that earlier, postcolonial African American speech was quite similar to the early British dialects brought to North America. However, the neo-Anglicist position acknowledges that AAVE has since diverged so that it is now quite distinct from contemporary white vernacular speech. Based on recent studies of several important expatriate enclave communities, Poplack (1999:27) asserted that "AAVE originated as English, but as the African American community solidified, it innovated specific features" and that "contemporary AAVE is the result of evolution, by its own unique, internal logic." Labov (1998:119) characterizes the most recent position on the historical development of AAVE as follows: "The general conclusion that is emerging from studies of the history of AAVE is that many important features of the modern dialect are creations of the twentieth century and not an inheritance of the nineteenth."

Despite growing support for the neo-Anglicist position, it has hardly become a consensus one; disputes remain over the nature of the data (e.g., Debose, 1994; Hannah, 1997; Sutcliffe, forthcoming), the earlier language contact situation between Africans and Europeans (Winford, 1997, 1998, forthcoming), and the sociohistorical circumstances that contextualized the speech of earlier African Americans (Mufwene, 1996a; Rickford, 1997; Singler, 1998a, 1998b). If nothing else, the shifting positions on the origin and development of earlier African American speech should caution us to go slow in arriving at conclusions about its earlier status. In fact, based on empirical evidence from Hyde County, we question the conclusions of each of the primary positions that have been offered over the past half-century.

2.2 Issues in Reconstructing Earlier AAVE

The study of earlier African American speech has certainly witnessed some major advances in the past couple of decades, but the issues surrounding its development remain quite complex and, at times, the "facts" can still be quite elusive. As a context for examining data from Hyde County, we identify some of the major issues that have emerged in recent studies.

Although our analysis addresses some of these issues more than others, it is still important to consider the full range of factors that must be examined in any attempt to understand the development of African American speech over the past couple of centuries.

2.2.1 The nature of earlier written texts

Documented data on African American speech from the seventeenth through the nineteenth centuries are obviously limited to written records. The reliance upon written records is always problematic in historical linguistics, as analysts are limited to available texts written for purposes other than linguistic documentation, but the problems are compounded severely for writers of a vernacular variety. To begin with, writing would typically evoke the more formal register of a language and likely repress vernacular forms where possible. Furthermore, writing was a rare, specialized skill for early African Americans in the USA, given the prohibition against literacy imposed on slaves. Finally, earlier African Americans capable of writing would be among the most educated African Americans, and therefore the least likely to use vernacular structures that are critical for the documentation of earlier AAVE. Using first person writers as a primary basis for earlier written documentation is thus beset with problems that Montgomery (1999) identifies as follows:

1 *questions about authorship*: that is, whether documents actually are written by African Americans or were instead written by or dictated to someone else;
2 *questions about models*: that is, whether writers are using native speech patterns or literary, rhetorical forms;
3 *questions about manipulating the written code*: that is, whether the oral language patterns are obscured by the writer's ability to handle the mechanics of the written code;
4 *questions about representativeness*: whether the writer is a representative speaker of the vernacular.

While first person accounts by antebellum African Americans can be fraught with documentation and interpretation problems, this does not make them unusable. Indeed, Montgomery (1999) has shown that such records, subject to a number of constraints on selection and interpretation, can offer essential insight into the status of earlier African American speech.

First person written records by African Americans have been augmented by amanuensis accounts, court records, journalistic observations, and literary representations of dialect. One set of important written texts for earlier African American speech is the accounts of ex-slaves (Schneider, 1983, 1989,

1997) collected in the 1930s, which came to light in the 1980s, along with a limited set of audio recordings of interviews with ex-slaves (Bailey, Maynor, and Cukor-Avila, 1991; Sutcliffe, forthcoming). Written corpora include the extensive set of narratives collected under the Works Project Administration (WPA) in the 1930s (Schneider 1989), letters written by semiliterate ex-slaves in the mid-1800s (Montgomery et al., 1993, Montgomery and Fuller, 1996), letters of an exported variety written by African Americans who migrated to Sierra Leone by way of Nova Scotia (Montgomery, 1999), and other specialized collections of texts, such as the Hyatt texts, an extensive set of interviews conducted with black hoodoo doctors in the 1930s (Hyatt, 1970–8; Viereck, 1988; Ewers, 1996).

Newly uncovered written records of earlier African American language are emerging on a regular basis, but there are a number of issues that have been raised about the reliability of various written accounts. Some of the inherent paradoxes of first person accounts have been pointed out above; there are also important questions of reliability with respect to amanuensis accounts and other written accounts involving third person observation (Wolfram, 1991). Accounts that aim to capture the "literal words" of African Americans are certainly subject to a kind of stereotyping that seizes selectively on particular structures – and in some cases structures not characteristic of the normative population – that exaggerates differences, resulting in caricatures that are not faithful to actual spoken language. There is, for example, evidence that one convention in the late 1700s and early 1800s used creole features from the West Indies to present caricatures of black speech in the USA – even by writers who had never even visited the USA (Cooley, 1997).

To give an idea of the range of dialect representation for early written texts of AAVE, a sample of written accounts of the eighteenth and early nineteenth centuries is given below, based on written records graciously provided by Cathleen Hellier of the Colonial Williamsburg Foundation, and analyzed in Wolfram, Watson, Reaser, and Hellier (1999) and Wolfram (2000). First, there is an example of an amanuensis account from conversations with a slave of George Washington's brother. A small sample of the record from this account is given in (1). The document dates from the early 1800s, and, according to Hellier (personal communication), there is considerable sociohistorical documentation from family records that establishes the existence of the slave Jeremy, the speaker represented in this account, and the events recounted by Jeremy. Second, a sample of a literary sermon, which represents a kind of literary dialect, is given in (2). By the mid-1700s there was already an established literary convention representing African American English in plays, written sermons, and other written texts (Cooley, 1997). The sermons thus represent text comparable to that documented in literary works of the late eighteenth century, such as the play *The Padlock*, analyzed by Cooley (1997). Third, a sample of a couple of letters written by African American slaves is given, as represented by (3a,b). One is an early, anonymous letter from 1723 and the other is a letter by a slave named James Carter in which he recounts his sufferings. Finally, there are court records and minute books from Petersburg, Virginia, that include brief quotes of African Americans from the first decade of the 1800s. Examples of this are given in (4) below.

(1) **Sample of Amanuensis Account** (*Letters from the South,*1835 edn., orig. 1817)
"... In de morning, we started by time it was light, and got up to Colonel Snigge's to breakfast almost fifteen mile. De snow was up to our knees, and dare wornt no much of a road any how, and so we had hard work to get along, I tell you. But mass John so fond of he brodder George, and de old lady, he go foot sooner dan turn back ..."

(2) **Sample of Literary Dialect** (Bacon and Meade, *Sermons addressed to Masters and Servants*, Winchester, PA, early 1800s)
"... Toney – I no like them, they be hypocrites. By and by they will all turn back again. This religion for white men, not for negro.
Sambo – Who tell you so, Toney?
Toney – Our overseer, he say all black people will go to the devil ..."

(3) **Samples of Slave Letters**
a. James Carter's Account of his Sufferings, Caroline Co., VA, 1807
"... I ask my master if I might go with my father to look for my brother (.) he said no you must go to Dumfries after my horse (.) it appear that he had more regard for his horse then he had for my poor dead brother (.)"
b. "Releese us out of this Cruell Bondegg," letter dated 1723
"... my Riting is vary bad (.) I whope yr honour will take the will for the deede (.) I am but a poore Slave that writt itt and has no other time butt Sunday and hardly that att Sumtimes."

(4) **Sample of Court Record** (Petersburg, VA, Minute Book, 1800–11)
"... Tom a free man of colour deposed that he came home & the prisoner was not at home (.) he push the Door go in (.) She (the prisoner) some after come home – say who here – tell him go away – I say No – no go way she say he shall go away-she look for knife to kill him – he thought she Jok (.) she say again – go away – he say he woudnt go away – she take him by the Throat pull him about & cut him with the knife ..."

A comparison of vernacular grammatical, phonological, and lexical structures represented in these four types of written representations indicates a range of dialect representations in the texts, with the amanuensis and literary accounts showing the highest frequency levels of vernacular dialect forms (Wolfram, Watson, et al., 1999; Wolfram, 2000). The comparison of the amanuensis and the literary dialect samples strongly suggests that an emerging literary convention for AAVE may have influenced transcribers attempting to represent the "literal voice" of African Americans. There is support for Cooley's (1997, 2000) contention that early caricatures of African American speech in literary representation seized upon creole features (e.g., bare negative particles and undifferentiated pronoun forms) to emphasize the most different version of early African American speech.

A cursory examination of various texts underscores several important points about the use of written documents in reconstructing earlier AAVE. First, we have to recognize that there was an early, emerging literary tradition that tended to represent more extreme versions of African American speech, including some creole-like structures that may have been rare or nonexistent in the actual speech of normative black populations. This tradition also may have affected the representations in amanuensis accounts, thus casting doubt on their authenticity. For example, the analysis of the amanuensis account of conversations with Washington's servant given above shows that it aligns much more closely with the literary representations of plays and sermons than it does with the letters written by African Americans. In retrospect, it appears that some of the evidence for the creole status of earlier African American speech found in works such as Dillard (1972) may have been unduly influenced by taking such accounts at face value. It seems clear that written records, including letters, need to be confirmed by other types of historical, archival evidence, such as family records, sociohistorical circumstances, and other traditional methods of establishing the authenticity of historical documents. Some earlier written text certainly can be used in reconstructing earlier AAVE, but not without imposing strict conditions that take into account the general historical situations, the specific sociolinguistic circumstances of the author, the nature of the text, and the purposes for writing (Montgomery, 1999).

2.2.2 Spoken language data representing earlier AAVE

Until audio recording equipment became available in the 1930s, there was no possibility of recording samples of elderly African Americans who might represent the earlier state of African American speech. In terms of real time, recorded speech samples are limited to the last 75 years. The *apparent time construct* (Weinreich et al., 1968; Bailey, Wikle, Tillery, and Sand, 1991), which assumes that a speaker's dialect (at least with respect to phonology) will represent that learned as a child, allows recorded spoken language data to be extended considerably but it is still restricted in terms of the history of

African American speech. Given a sample of elderly speakers recorded in the 1930s, the most we can hope for in the apparent time assumption is a glimpse of speech from speakers born shortly before the cessation of slavery in 1865. Audio recordings of such speakers continue to be uncovered (Bailey, Maynor, and Cukor-Avila, 1991; Brewer, 1996), but the recorded data are often of questionable audio fidelity given the ediphone and telediphone cylinder equipment used for recording in the 1930s. For example, approximately half of the six hours of recordings with ex-slaves used as the basis for the analyses reported in Bailey, Maynor, and Cukor-Avila (1991) is unsuitable for detailed data extraction due to its poor recording quality. Furthermore, there are questions about the speakers in terms of their representation of vernacular speech. Some of the interviews are relatively formal, and speakers may use only their most careful styles of speech. Perhaps even more problematic is the fact that different researchers can look at the same data and reach quite contrary interpretations based on the researcher's background and perspective (Rickford, 1991; Sutcliffe, forthcoming). So the relatively rare audio recordings of speakers born in the mid-1800s hardly provide conclusive evidence for determining what the earlier state of African American speech may have been like.

In the absence of a definitive set of audio recordings of earlier speakers, researchers have turned to insular sociolinguistic situations involving transplant enclave communities of African Americans. Prominent insular situations have thus far focused on transplant communities of African American expatriates in locations such as Samaná (Poplack and Sankoff, 1987; Poplack and Tagliamonte, 1989), two communities in Nova Scotia (Poplack and Tagliamonte, 1991; Poplack, 1999), and Liberia (Singler, 1989, 1991). For example, as noted in chapter 1, in the 1820s, blacks from the United States migrated to the peninsula of Samaná in the Dominican Republic where they lived in relative isolation. It is assumed that this community maintained a relatively relic variety of English that they brought with them (Poplack and Sankoff, 1987; Poplack and Tagliamonte, 1989). A significant number of African Americans also migrated from the USA to Canada in the early 1800s, and some still live in relative isolation in Nova Scotia (Poplack and Tagliamonte, 1991; Poplack, 1999). The English varieties spoken by blacks in Nova Scotia and Samaná, as analyzed in detail by Poplack, Tagliamonte, and their team of researchers (Poplack, 1999; Poplack and Tagliamonte, 2001) appear to show a much greater similarity to postcolonial British-based English varieties in North America than a presumed creole predecessor would be expected to show, thus supporting a neo-Anglicist hypothesis.

While such studies of insular transplant communities have provided the impetus for a resurgent interest in the Anglicist hypothesis, it has not been without dispute (e.g., Rickford, 1997, 1999; Hannah, 1997; Singler, 1989, 1991, 1998b; Sutcliffe, forthcoming; Winford, 1997, 1998). Data from an expatriate black population that migrated to Liberia in the 1800s (Singler, 1989), for example, seem to support the creolist hypothesis rather than the Anglicist hypothesis, and Hannah's (1997) and Debose's (1994) alternative analyses of data from expatriate blacks in the same Samaná community studied by Poplack and Sankoff (1987) offer interpretations that are consonant with the creolist rather than the Anglicist position represented in Poplack (1999), Poplack and Sankoff (1987) and Poplack and Tagliamonte (1989, 2001). Enclave transplant communities may shed light on earlier African American speech, but these communities also must be scrutinized in closer demographic and sociohistorical detail to ensure that they constitute authentic cases of relic, vernacular-speaking speech communities. For example, Singler (1998b) points out that the Samaná community comprised primarily middle-class African Americans from the North who would not be expected to speak a vernacular variety of English to begin with. Furthermore, an examination of tapes from Samaná collected by Howard Mims and Grace Lee Mims in the 1970s (personal communication) suggests that there has been significant influence from England on this community over the years through the importation of ministers from England for the church, a central community institution. There is also evidence of influence from the USA in the earlier part of the century, so that the community may not have been as insular as originally thought.

One of the important lessons to be learned from such an examination concerns the selection of diagnostic structures for investigating earlier African American speech. A very different picture of earlier African American speech might emerge if a researcher focuses on past tense *be* regularization (e.g., *The dogs was here, It weren't me*) as opposed to 3rd sg. -*s* or copula absence. An authentic picture of earlier African American speech can emerge only if a wide array of dialect structures is considered, including overall profiles of vowel systems, as well as tense, mood, and aspect systems, and so forth. While selective, single-structure studies may reveal significant insight into a particular linguistic process, they may obscure or even distort our understanding of the overall relationship of African American speech to other varieties.

2.2.3 The sociohistorical context of earlier African Americans

One of the major considerations in reconstructing the history of earlier AAVE is establishing the sociohistorical context of the early waves of African Americans brought to the New World. This includes patterns of immigration, migration within the USA, ethnic density, and the local interactional patterns that have characterized the African American contact situation at various historical stages in its evolution. Dialectologists and sociolinguists have sometimes slighted the critical role of demographic and sociohistorical circumstances in reconstructing the genesis and development of African American speech in the United States, although more recent attention to this dimension by Mufwene (1996b), Rickford (1997) and Winford (1997) has stressed the significance of demographic ecology and the local interactional setting in framing the examination of earlier African American speech. Such investigation shows that sociohistorical contexts were quite varied in terms of the local settings and historical time frame. The study of African American English in Hyde County adds to the representative types of contexts by showing the development of speech in a biracial community where African Americans have always been less than half of the population and most slaves lived on small plantations. This situation counters, for example, that in coastal South Carolina and Georgia where African Americans largely outnumbered European Americans.

Consider the kinds of factors that need to be appealed to in establishing the sociohistorical context of the Hyde County community under examination here. First, we need to consider where the European American and African populations came from and when they settled in their present location. As we will describe in chapter 4, the European American inhabitants in Hyde County settled in the coastal region of North Carolina in the first decade of the eighteenth century, coming mostly from Virginia and Maryland. This pattern closely followed the pattern of migration on the Outer Banks communities of North Carolina (Wolfram and Schilling-Estes, 1997; Wolfram, Hazen, and Schilling-Estes, 1999). Similarly, the majority of African Americans were brought south to mainland Hyde County from Virginia and Maryland, rather than north from Charleston, South Carolina, or directly from Africa (Kay and Cary, 1995), setting them apart from those of the Sea Islands off South Carolina and Georgia, who came through the Charleston port and developed Gullah.

It is further necessary to look at the different time periods in terms of the importation of slaves from various places. For example, there were different historic periods of African importation into Virginia, Maryland, and elsewhere that support the notion of varied types of English development among early Africans Americans (Winford, 1997, 1998; Rickford, 1999). During the period from approximately 1600–90, slaves were largely imported from Barbados and typically worked with English-indentured servants on small plantations, with considerable interethnic contact taking place. This group therefore may have brought a creole-like variety with them, but they also may have lost some of the traits rapidly through their regular interaction with owners and indentured European American servants. There was also probably considerable individual variation based on the life histories of particular individuals, so that different speakers may have represented a full range along the acrolect–basilect creole continuum. During the 1690–1750 period, there was massive importation directly from Africa – about 90 percent – due to the need for cheap labor, and there was also less interaction with whites. With more blacks coming directly from Africa in large numbers, there might have been more contact-related language fossilization arising from imperfect language learning. During the next period, from 1750 to 1793, larger plantations were established in many areas of the Southeast United States, and the overseer system was established. In areas with larger plantations (over 20 slaves), there would be less contact with whites for the majority of field servants, enabling the corresponding development of more separate speech communities. In areas where the plantations were smaller, such as Hyde County (see chapter 4), the potential of distinct speech communities is more in question. Then in the period between 1793 and the Civil War, slavery was stabilized, and some of the earlier contact influence could have developed into a more uniform ethnic vernacular, even while accommodating local varieties of cohort European American communities.

Perhaps more important than the documentation of overall patterns of migration, it is necessary to establish the local sociohistorical context in terms of past and present contact ecology. As we will see in chapter 4, in the two centuries of official census figures and half century of unofficial census figures for Hyde County, the ratio of African Americans and European Americans in Hyde County has not fluctuated greatly, with approximately one-quarter to almost a half of the population being African American. It is difficult to assess precisely how many of the European American and African American families currently residing in Hyde County date back to the earliest non-Native American inhabitants, but it is noteworthy that some of the long-standing African American families share common surnames with long-standing Hyde County European American families who assigned slave names connected to the slaveholders (Sharpe, 1958:890). There are ample genealogies for the European American population in Hyde County that chart the continuity of the European American population there, but more limited genealogies for the African American population (see, for example, Spencer, 1984).

Establishing the historical context in terms of large-scale and local patterns of immigration, migration, ethnic density, and continuity is obviously a critical phase of the reconstruction process in the establishment of the earlier state(s) of African American speech. Linguistic facts related to the earlier stages of AAVE do not stand in isolation; they are the products of broad-based and localized historical contact situations that frame the reasoned explanation of how and why AAVE originated and developed as it has over the centuries.

2.2.4 Variation in earlier AAVE

Great linguistic diversity existed at the time Africans were brought to North America, both in terms of the ancestral languages of West Africa and the developing English language in the Americas. The earliest waves of slaves from Africa spoke different native languages, represented different levels of proficiency in English, and were placed into quite varied contact situations depending on their geographical location and social situation. There is thus no reason to think that there was a seamless transition to a homogenized variety of English in the United States. The question is not whether there was diversity in earlier African American speech, but the nature of the variation and the delimitation of relevant sociolinguistic, sociohistorical, and sociocultural factors that might have accounted for it.

Variation in English proficiency is amply demonstrated by advertisements for slaves that refer to levels of proficiency in English, as well as other records such as court transcripts that make reference to levels of proficiency in English by African Americans. But there were also other types of variation that emerged as African Americans lived in diverse regional and social situations in the USA. For example, there are obvious differences between earlier African Americans in the North and South, as well as differences among those who lived on large plantations with overseers versus those who lived with families owning just a few slaves, or even a single house servant. And, of course, there were emerging social divisions and status differences within the African American community itself.

One of the important issues addressed in this study is the extent to which African Americans assimilated regional speech patterns. We need to know exactly how localized contact situations might have figured in the early development of African American speech. For example, we need to know the extent to which African Americans may have participated in distinctive regional dialect norms. Our empirical examination of this long-term, historically isolated biracial community with a distinct dialect heritage demonstrates that such enclave situations provide critical insight into the role of localized dialects in the development of earlier vernacular varieties spoken by African Americans. The data seem to add support for some of the conclusions derived from the examination of expatriate black communities and the written records of African Americans from postcolonial America that show a strong similarity between postcolonial African American and European American speech. At the same time, the results challenge some of the conclusions about the overwhelming congruence of these varieties.

Related to the issue of intracommunity variation is the relationship between individual and group variation in small enclave communities (Dorian, 1994; Wolfram, Hazen, and Tamburro, 1997; Wolfram and Beckett, 2000). With the increasing trend towards quantification in variation linguistics, it is now quite common for studies simply to report data for groups of speakers as an aggregate whole, or as Chambers (1995:100) puts it, as an "undifferentiated mass." When the assumed homogeneity of a particular group is challenged, it is typically replaced with what Chambers (1995:100) describes as more "numerous small groups with subtle, special relationships to the whole." There are, however, important questions about individual variation in small, isolated communities where everybody knows everybody. Through examining individual variation among elderly speakers in Hyde County, as we do in chapter 8, we can determine how much individual variation may exist in insular communities in general, and, in particular, the extent of individual variation in earlier African American speech. The examination of individual elderly speakers will show that there may be considerable variation among different individuals with common demographic profiles (e.g., level of education, socioeconomic status, etc.) in small isolated communities. We thus need to scrutinize personal history and interactional relations along with constructed social group identities in examining patterns of individual variation.

The evidence suggests further that there may have been considerably more variation in the vernacular varieties spoken at an earlier period than is found in some contemporary versions of AAVE. Most sociolinguists are struck by the common core of contemporary AAVE features now found to a large extent throughout urban and rural North America, but this may not have been the case historically. Any reasonable reconstruction of earlier AAVE must take this variation into account.

2.2.5 Donor source attribution

One of the most persistent and elusive issues in the debate over earlier AAVE concerns the attribution of donor sources for its distinctive dialect traits. Where did the structures come from originally and how did they develop in subsequent phases of African American speech? There are several possible explanations. First, it is possible that the distinctive structures of the variety could have been adopted from the distinctive input English varieties, that is, from the regional and social varieties brought by the various English settler groups from the British Isles. Of course, one cannot assume that such structures would remain in an unmodified "relic" state, given the nature of language change through independent development or contact-induced change. A second possibility is that the distinctive structures of AAVE may have come about through the diffusion from dialect forms found in the emergent regional varieties in the United States. For example, the affinity of AAVE with regional Southern rural varieties of European American English is no accident given the historic concentration of large numbers of African Americans in this region. A third possibility is that distinctive features may have derived from an earlier language-contact situation in which forms that arose in language contact were fossilized and maintained as an integral part of the dialect structure of AAVE. There is, of course, a wide range of language effects that might derive from a language contact situation, from the imperfect learning of English by African slaves who acquired English as a nonnative language to the extreme systemic language mixture of creolization (Winford, forthcoming). The attribution of structures in AAVE to an earlier language contact situation is far more complex than the simplistic dichotomy between the creolist versus Anglicist positions that the AAVE origin debate has sometimes been reduced to (Winford, 1997, 1998, forthcoming). In reality, the discussion of language contact scenarios as a basis for the emergence of distinctive AAVE structures must start with the realistic recognition that "trying to sort out the linguistic results of language contact plunges us immediately into a region of enormous complexity" (Thomason, forthcoming).

Finally, there is the possibility of independent innovation, in which system-internal changes have guided AAVE on a course that has caused it to diverge from other varieties of English in the past and/or the present. Here again, however, the processes may be complex and may bring together aspects of independent innovation along with language contact and diffusion in the molding of distinctive dialect structures. Language change does not come in neat, compartmentalized packages, and the sources of dialect development identified here are not necessarily mutually exclusive.

There are obviously a number of issues that need to be confronted in assigning donor sources for the structures of AAVE. A tentative list of the issues includes the following:

- *The internal reconstruction issue* – determining the earlier status of the variety vis-à-vis its current status;
- *The contact issue* – determining the nature of contact accommodation and restructuring, recognizing universal and/or specific transfer strategies;
- *The constraint issue* – determining structural and nonstructural effects on the development of structures;
- *The transition issue* – determining progressive stages of adoption and accommodation in the development and acquisition of structures;
- *The explanation issue* – formulating principled cognitive constraints and universal production and processing strategies that account for language change and development.

Claims about donor sources in AAVE involve methodological, descriptive, and explanatory issues. For example, Rickford (1985) and Montgomery (1989) address some of the methodological issues when they assert that the analyst must attend carefully to the form and meaning of diagnostic features, specify the linguistic environment in which the feature occurs, tabulate the frequency with which the feature occurs, consider the interrelation of the feature to other features in the grammar, and document that the sociohistorical demographic information demonstrates a historical connection between the groups speaking the varieties.

There are also issues related to the kinds of data that might be admissible in making claims about an earlier state of a language variety. Mufwene (1996a, 1999) has suggested that there is a *founder effect* in which structural peculiarities of an area are predetermined by the characteristics of the vernaculars spoken by the population that founded the English-speaking settlement. Although Mufwene originally applied this principle to creole studies, it has been expanded (Mufwene, 1999) to the study of dialects in general and AAVE in particular, but only given certain constraining conditions. For example, it might be assumed that the existence of linguistically marked dialect features found in the speech of the oldest group of recorded speakers reflects an earlier dialect feature if a group of speakers has been living in ethnographic circumstances of long-standing community stability and relative isolation. This assumption is, in fact, the basis for conclusions about the earlier state of AAVE that guide the interpretation of data from enclave African American transplant communities and the isolated community of African Americans in Hyde County.

With respect to the explanation of structural adoption in language contact, Mufwene (1991) points to markedness principles rooted in factors such as regularity or invariance of forms, statistical dominance, semantic transparency, perceptual saliency, and simplicity, and Winford's (forthcoming) contact linguistic model appeals to general or "universal" cognitive constraints based on ease of perception and production (that is, learnability). Winford's model is not unlike Mufwene's markedness model in that "constraints which appeal to economy, semantic transparency, perceptual salience and the like fall into this category" (Winford, forthcoming). Meanwhile, Thomason and Kauffman (1988) categorize constraints that effect adoption into typological (typologically similar features will be acquired more easily than those that are different), naturalness (more marked features are less likely to be transferred), and implicational constraints (structural feature X, e.g., affixation, is dependent upon feature Y, e.g., lexical borrowing). However, as Winford (forthcoming) notes, "the task of determining how cognitive, structural and non-structural factors interact to determine the linguistic outcomes of various contact situations is still very much in its infancy." Linguistic factors that affect the adoption of structures obviously include markedness, economy, semantic transparency, and saliency; sociolinguistic considerations include social valuation and frequency; sociohistorical issues include migration, contact ecology, and population demographics.

Finally, we should mention the *matrix language turnover model* proposed by Myers-Scotton (1998; Myers-Scotton and Jake, forthcoming) to explain the morphosyntactic dimensions of language accommodation in language contact situations. Briefly put, this model proposes that many instances of language influence involve a shift from one dominant, or matrix language, to another, and that not all morphemes have the same freedom of appearance in either monolingual or bilingual production. Accordingly, it is proposed (Myers-Scotton, 1998; Myers-Scotton and Jake, forthcoming) that "content morphemes" carrying thematic roles are more likely to resist adoption than "system morphemes," which do not carry thematic roles.

Our discussion of different structural traits in the following chapters will show the confluence of structural and nonstructural principles in ascribing donor influence as they reveal the differential pattern of selective adoption. When the full array of factors is considered, it appears reasonable to conclude that earlier English of coastal African American speakers in North Carolina indicated a kind of language selectivity that clearly supports a constrained version of the so-called "cafeteria principle" (Dillard, 1970) in which the putative dialect appears to reflect the retention of selected structures from founder dialects and vestiges of the original contact situation. The formative dialect of the area included selected items from an earlier contact variety, localized grammatical features attributable to British dialect retention, and restructured interdialectal items that resulted from the adaptation of contact-based and British-origin dialect structures. More important than the specific attribution of donor sources for particular structural features is the appeal to a set of structural and nonstructural principles that might guide donor dialect attribution. Only as such principles are developed and tested will some of the outstanding controversies over the earlier status of AAVE be resolved. The application of such principles not only benefits the study of AAVE; it should also benefit the fields of historical linguistics, sociolinguistics, and contact linguistics. The establishment of solid documentation, rigorous extraction, and principled explanation is hardly limited to the study of AAVE.

2.3 African American English in the Twentieth Century

As noted in chapter 1, the controversy over the development of AAVE is not confined to its genesis and early development. In many respects, its trajectory of change in the twentieth century has been just as controversial as the debate over its earlier history. Two types of emerging data fueled the controversy over the more recent development of AAVE. One was the research on the relationship of African American and European American

English in the nineteenth century that suggested that these varieties may have been much more closely aligned than had been assumed previously. If, in fact, African American speech was much like other postcolonial English varieties spoken in the USA, then the apparent differences between present-day AAVE and cohort European American vernacular varieties must have been a more recent development.

The second strand of research that ignited the controversy over the more recent development of AAVE came from data offered by William Labov and his team of researchers investigating AAVE in Philadelphia in the mid-1980s (e.g., Ash and Myhill, 1986; Myhill and Harris, 1986; Graff et al., 1986; Dayton, 1996). Compared with his own research conducted two decades earlier in New York City (Labov et al., 1968; Labov, 1972a), it appeared that AAVE was actually diverging from other vernacular dialects of English because of its internal development rather than converging with surrounding vernaculars. As Labov put it (1985:1), "their [African American residents of Philadelphia] speech pattern is becoming more different from the speech of whites in the same communities." Support for his position came from Bailey and Maynor (1987, 1989), and Dayton (1996), coupled with the historical evidence that emerged from the study of enclave dialect situations by Poplack, Tagliamonte, and their team of researchers at the University of Ottawa (Poplack, 1999), as well as analyses of the expanding database of written documentation (e.g., Schneider, 1989; Montgomery and Fuller, 1996; Montgomery et al., 1993), and audio-recordings of ex-slaves (Bailey, Maynor, and Cukor-Avila, 1989). Cumulatively, these emerging analyses led Labov (1998:119) to his conclusion that "many important features of the modern dialect are creations of the twentieth century and not an inheritance of the nineteenth."

There are two primary issues related to the recent assertions: (1) whether or not the distinct linguistic properties of AAVE are indeed primarily a development of the twentieth century as opposed to a variety inherited from the nineteenth century, and (2) whether AAVE is currently diverging from cohort European American vernacular varieties of English. On one level, these questions may seem inexorably related, but there is an important sense in which they are independent. For example, it is possible to maintain that contemporary AAVE may be diverging from cohort vernacular African American English varieties, but that its structural essence was rooted in an earlier history that was, in its own right, substantially different from cohort white vernacular varieties. In fact, this seems to be Rickford's position (1992, 1999), as he offers evidence for more recent divergence in AAVE while maintaining that some of the structures of AAVE were apparently rooted in a creole predecessor quite different from British-derived dialects of English spoken by European Americans in colonial America (Rickford, 1998, 1999).

The so-called *divergence hypothesis*, which maintains that AAVE is evolving independently in ways that increase its difference from other vernacular dialects of English, has evoked considerable interest on both a popular and a scholarly level. On a popular level, the divergence of AAVE was seen as a reflection of the social and economic plight of African American underclass brought about by increasing de facto segregation and the widening socio-economic gap between mainstream American society and lower-class minority groups. As Labov (1985:3) noted:

> Our results can be seen as signals of the dangerous drift of our society towards a permanent division between black and white: the linguistic research gives us an independent and objective measure of this drift.

In fact, the senior author first learned about the divergence hypothesis in the mid-1980s from a nightly national newscast on CBS, which framed the linguistic differences as an alarming indication of the extent of the growing social problems between black and white culture. The scholarly debate heated up in a panel discussion in 1986 at an annual meeting of the New Ways of Analyzing Variation conference, published as an issue of *American Speech* (Fasold et al., 1987). The controversy has led to a number of subsequent books and research articles on this topic (e.g. Butters, 1989; Bailey and Maynor, 1987, 1989; Rickford, 1991).

As indicated in Fasold et al. (1987), the linguistic details involved in language change can be quite complex, with a range of language change trajectories characterizing divergence and/or convergence. Consider, for example, the possible options for divergence and convergence detailed in figure 2.1. The paths of change may originate at different points and take a variety of paths that are unidirectional or bidirectional.

It is also possible for trajectories of change to shift at various points over history. Thus, the position on the history of AAVE most approximating Rickford's (1999:255) reconstruction of AAVE seems to be best represented by figure 2.2, which shows an earlier period of diversity, a period of convergence, and then a subsequent period of divergence.

The issue of divergence versus convergence is further complicated by the fact that it is quite possible for particular structures, or structures on one level of language organization, to show convergence at the same time that other structures indicate divergence. In fact, the description of Hyde County in the subsequent chapters will reveal several different permutations of language change trajectories. These include divergence from formerly shared dialect features in which change was initiated within the African American community (e.g., postvocalic *r*-lessness as discussed in chapter 7), change initiated by the European American speech community that differentiates it from the African American community (e.g., past tense *weren't* in

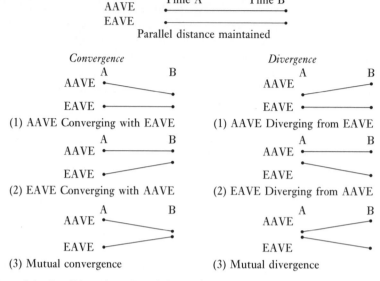

Figure 2.1   Possible trajectories of change for AAVE and cohort European American Vernacular English (EAVE) (adapted from Wolfram, 1987:41)

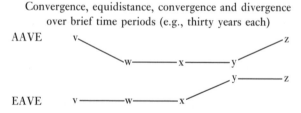

Figure 2.2   Change over time in AAVE and EAVE (adapted from Rickford, 1987:59)

chapter 4), and cases of parallel change (e.g., vowels in chapter 6). These empirical data suggest that overall assessments of AAVE as "diverging" or "converging" are oversimplistic and reductive as caricatures of language change. At the same time, there are clearly instances in which particular structures change in ways that align or differentiate African American and European American vernacular varieties. We also cannot deny the overall effect of the particular changes as they are evaluated in terms of their broader sociolinguistic implications on developing ethnolinguistic relations.

Although issues related to the earlier development of African American speech will probably remain embedded in speculation because of the limitations of data for reconstruction and often incomplete sociohistorical facts, there is more hope of resolving some of the controversies over the development of African American English in the twentieth century. Certainly, the data seem more accessible, though the interpretation of results may still be arguable. The study of language change in Hyde County has much to add to this phase of the study of AAVE, as we examine how the African American speech communities and European American communities have changed in both obvious and subtle ways.

3

Defining the Enclave Dialect Community

3.1 Introduction

As noted in chapter 2, so-called *enclave dialect communities* – groups of speakers who have been set apart for significant periods of time from more widely dispersed, socially dominant, groups – have provided essential evidence for revising the historical reconstruction of AAVE over the past couple of decades (Poplack, 1999; Poplack and Sankoff, 1987; Poplack and Tagliamonte, 1989, 1991, 2001). The significance of these communities for reconstructing AAVE is based on the assumption that these dialect situations will remain relatively immune to changes diffusing throughout the wider population and that linguistic change will be conservative, thus providing a window into the earlier state of the language. While studies of such "peripheral" dialects have provided essential data for dialect reconstruction, there has been little critical examination of the construct "enclave dialect community" and its sociohistorical corollary, "historical isolation." Most dialectologists and sociolinguists are content to set forth the sociohistorical circumstances related to the particular community under investigation and assume that this description satisfies a tacit set of sociological and historical conditions for classifying the community as historically isolated and the associated dialect as an enclave variety. As more studies of such situations emerge, however, it seems apparent that there is a need to consider the general sociohistorical and sociocultural circumstances that give rise to isolated speech communities, and a corresponding need to examine more closely the type and extent of language variation across different situations. Is there a common set of historical circumstances that unite these situations? Are there particular linguistic traits that characterize isolated speech communities? And are there underlying sociolinguistic principles that typify dialect maintenance and change in these situations? In this chapter, we consider the kinds of sociohistorical and sociocultural conditions that lead to the establishment of the enclave speech communities and propose some general sociolinguistic principles that might account for their sociolinguistic configuration in relation to one another and in relation to other language varieties.

3.2 Historically Isolated Speech Communities

What are the social and historical circumstances that give rise to historically isolated speech communities? Although practically all descriptive studies of such situations provide the specific details of historical migration and settlement that led to the disconnection of the particular community from more widespread, dominant populations, sociolinguists have not proposed a general set of physical, historical, demographic, sociocultural, and sociolinguistic conditions associated with such communities. On the one hand, it might be assumed that the circumstances of historical isolation are self-evident and that there is no need to engage in a general account of this condition. However, these circumstances are often far from obvious, even in the most transparent cases where a substantive community is transplanted from one physical and cultural setting to another, remote geographical location. On the other hand, it might be assumed that each situation is so particularized that, in fact, there are no common principles that unite different circumstances. Both of these assumptions seem unjustified. As we shall see, there appear to be some unifying conditions that characterize different historically isolated speech communities. At the same time, these conditions are also quite fluid and may exist in different permutations.

Montgomery (2000) points out the failure of linguists to critically examine the notion of "historical isolation," the basis for the establishment of dialect enclaves in dialect reconstruction.

> While often invoking the concept of isolation, linguists have yet to define it in a way that is sociologically respectable (based on valid, measurable criteria), or anthropologically sensitive (involving analysis of the community on its own terms and based on community perceptions and behavior – what is remoteness for the investigator may not be perceived as such by residents) . . . In sum, we can see that American linguists may have recognized several types of isolation, but have done little to examine it critically or explore its many dimensions. (Montgomery, 2000:45)

Montgomery's challenge warrants consideration; there is an obvious need to consider the general sociohistorical and sociocultural circumstances that give rise to enclave speech communities and the particular linguistic traits that might characterize such communities.

3.2.1 Geography

Perhaps the most obvious physical trait associated with historically isolated dialect situations is a set of ecological constraints that result in geographic remoteness. Geographical factors typically play a significant role in cases of historical isolation, not because of topography per se, but because bodies of water, mountains, and other features of the terrain often serve to foster separation and hence create sociocultural and communication discontinuities that promote linguistic divergence. Although enclave speech communities are often characterized by geographical separation from other groups, the speech community may be concentrated in a particular locale within a more expansive region or dispersed throughout a region. For example, the island of Ocracoke, located on the Outer Banks of North Carolina, is 14 miles long, but the entire residential population lives within a square mile at the southern end of the island. By the same token, in mainland Hyde County, the site of the study reported here, a different residential distribution pattern is manifested in which residents often live in clusters of three to ten homes separated from other clusters of homes by several miles.

A survey of isolated speech communities featured in recent sociolinguistic studies (e.g., Dorian, 1981, 1994; Poplack and Sankoff, 1987; Poplack and Tagliamonte, 1989, 1991; Poplack, 1999; Wolfram and Schilling-Estes, 1995; Schilling-Estes, 1997; Schilling-Estes and Wolfram, 1999; Shores, 1984, 1985, 2000) suggests that geographical factors have played a prominent role in their formation, though the type and extent of the topographic constraints vary. Islands such as Smith Island (Schilling-Estes, 1997; Schilling-Estes and Wolfram, 1999) and Tangier Island (Shores, 2000), located in the Chesapeake Bay off of the Maryland and Virginia coastline, and Ocracoke Island on the Outer Banks of North Carolina, are not accessible by land, and mainland Hyde County is 85 percent marshland so that boats were used for primary travel at earlier stages in its history. Other areas in which enclave dialects have existed, such as the Appalachian communities of West Virginia and the western Carolinas (Hall, 1942; Wolfram and Christian, 1976; Montgomery, 1989; Montgomery and Hall, forthcoming), were at one point difficult to access because of mountainous terrain. Still other communities were located in remote areas where outsiders had little economic or social incentive to visit, as is apparently the case for the African American communities of Nova Scotia (Poplack and Tagliamonte, 1991).

Although physical boundaries play a role in the delimitation of historical isolation and the associated enclave dialect community, the notion of "place" obviously is not limited to an objective, physical entity (Johnstone, forthcoming). Topography may play a role in the formative status of a historically isolated situation, but it is hardly a sufficient condition. There are islands, mountains, and rivers implicated in many other speech communities (for example, Manhattan Island in New York City) but these objective physical factors have hardly created the kinds of cultural and linguistic discontinuities analogous to those associated with enclave dialects.

Obviously, community size is a factor in historical isolation, and most of the enclave dialects examined in the recent sociolinguistic literature are relatively small communities, sometimes consisting of just a couple of hundred people. But here again, size is not a necessary defining condition. In fact, the Lumbee Indian community in Robeson County, North Carolina, which has a number of traits characteristic of enclave dialects (Wolfram and Dannenberg, 1999; Dannenberg, 1999; Schilling-Estes, 2000a), has a population of over 50,000 people. Geographical remoteness and community size are often relevant attributes of enclave communities, but these are often quite relative traits rather than absolute conditions.

3.2.2 Economy

One of the factors that enters into the maintenance of isolated communities is the potential for economic autonomy. In fact, one of the reasons that fishing communities are implicated so often in historically isolated situations is the combination of geographic location and the potential for economic self-sufficiency (Dorian, 1981, 1994). Likewise, economic conditions tend to play a prominent role in shifts in insularity and the eventual emergence of a community from isolation (e.g., Wolfram and Schilling-Estes, 1995; Schilling-Estes, 1997; Schilling-Estes and Wolfram, 1999). Without the ability to maintain an independent livelihood, communities are highly vulnerable to wider influences. In fact, economic constraints are often cited as the most essential reason for the endangerment and ultimate death of the language varieties associated with historically isolated groups (Grenoble and Whaley, 1998).

3.2.3 Historical continuity

A critical component of enclave dialect situations, especially with reference to earlier African American English, is time depth. Most enclave communities endure extended periods of time during which they do not sustain regular contact with more widespread, dominant populations. However, the time dimension, like other factors, is quite relative. There must at least be enough time for the establishment of linguistic separation from mainstream population groups, but the time frame can actually be quite compressed. Linguistic change that leads to divergence or convergence needs only a couple of generations to take effect.

In an overview of Mid-Atlantic and Southern coastal enclave dialect communities in the USA, Wolfram and Schilling-Estes (forthcoming) noted that the time depth for some communities often extended a couple of centuries, in most cases dating from the late 1600s and 1700s. Each of the communities examined went through extended periods – in some cases a century or more – in which a substantial number of community members did not have regular, sustained contact with outside groups. At the same time, it must be recognized that isolation exists on a continuum and that groups do not necessarily follow a direct path from greater to lesser insularity. Due to various economic and social factors, communities may become more or less isolated through their history. As we note in chapter 4, the coastal area of mainland Hyde County became a major logging area and doubled its population during a short period before 1900, only to recede to its earlier population levels in the twentieth century. The logging industry brought jobs for African Americans that reduced the incentive to leave the area in search of economic opportunity.

Historical continuity seems to be an important feature of enclave speech communities in general and especially for those critical for the reconstruction of Earlier African American English. While different historical events may have brought people to the region and there may have been significant out-migration over the years, there is a recognized core of members that has been a part of the community for generations. In fact, continuous family residency is often a fundamental defining trait of community membership in enclave dialect situations.

The factor of historical continuity has obvious implications for patterns of in- and out-migration. In most enclave situations, there is limited in-migration, though there may be considerable out-migration by residents for various economic and social reasons. Obviously, communities like Hyde County and the Samaná and Nova Scotia situations examined in Poplack (1999) have undergone considerable out-migration at various periods in their history while maintaining their isolated, enclave status. In fact, one of the reasons that a community such as Hyde County could maintain a relatively small but stable population level over two centuries is the continuous flow of some of the residents out of the county. At the same time, isolated communities may also be subjected to periods of in-migration. Sustained in-migration might eventually end the insular status of the community but communities can obviously endure periodic in-migration as well as out-migration as they sustain their insular status.

3.2.4 Social relations

We may point to physical and historical conditions in defining isolation, but separation is more than a physical condition or the lack of communicative interaction with other groups. Social relations and sociocultural definition are also integral to the delimitation of historically isolated speech communities. One of the recurrent trends of the enclave communities examined in the sociolinguistic literature is their social subordination in relation to widely dispersed, so-called "mainstream" regional and national groups. Even when such groups have control of local governing institutions and enjoy some measure of economic prosperity, they may remain vulnerable to more powerful regional, state, and national institutions that have ascribed them marginalized, "nonmainstream" status. Indeed, the dichotomy between mainstream and nonmainstream groups is socially constructed in such a way to ensure an asymmetrical social hierarchy. Accordingly, the dialect differences associated with these nonmainstream communities are socially stigmatized and consonant with the *principle of linguistic subordination* (Lippi-Green, 1997), in which the speech of a socially subordinate group is interpreted as inadequate by comparison with socially dominant groups.

The traditional speech of enclave communities is viewed as "backward" and unsophisticated by comparison with other varieties, as are the cultural lifestyles of the people in these communities. Although such communities are sometimes romantically viewed as preserving a "purer" form of English such as "Shakespearean" or "Elizabethan" English (Montgomery, 1998), this is ultimately attributed to the community's backward, nonprogressive ways. Therefore, such lifestyles and their associated dialects are treated as marginal and negatively valued in society – even if they are "purer." Certainly, the cultural centers ascribing social status are never located in such regions.

With the residential concentration of the local population, we might expect that high-density, multiplex social networks (Milroy, 1987) are more likely to be found in isolated dialect communities than they would be in larger, more metropolitan areas. Although this is true in most cases, there may, however, be different configurations of these relations. For example, in Hyde County, with residential clusters often separated by miles, there appear to be subcommunities typified by dense networks. However, such networks apparently are not essential to the definition of such speech communities, and do not, in fact, even typify all of the situations of historic isolation (e.g., Schilling-Estes, 2000a).

3.2.5 Group identity

Enclave communities often develop a strong, positive sense of group identity related to the phenomenological notion of "place." As Johnstone (forthcoming) notes:

> Regions have come to be seen as meaningful places that individuals construct
> as well as select as reference points. Identification with a region is identification
> with one kind of "imaged community." . . . The process by which individuals
> ground their identities in socially constructed regions is seen as analogous to,
> or the same as, the process by which people construct, claim, and use ethnic
> communities. (Johnstone, forthcoming)

In this connection, we observe that there is a strong sense of "at-homeness"
associated with the sense of localized place as discussed in Johnstone, and
the notion of home may be symbolically associated with the local dialect.

Related to the sense of localized identity, the distinction between "insiders"
and "outsiders" is often codified as a primary social boundary. Quite typically, there are indexical labels that place local community members in
opposition to all "others." Furthermore, the local construction of "us"
versus "them" may be perpetuated in the postinsular state of the community as well and therefore help maintain some dialect distinctions when
the physical barriers promoting isolation are reduced or eliminated. It
must be kept in mind that increasing levels of contact do not necessarily
entail increasing assimilation (whether linguistic or cultural) among groups.
Andersen (1988) points out that it is not uncommon for communities
that are becoming more open in terms of increasing contacts with the
outside world to remain attitudinally (and linguistically) closed; nor is it
unusual for relatively closed communities to be attitudinally open, whole-
heartedly embracing the cultural and linguistic innovations that happen to
come their way. Thus, Andersen maintains that a distinction be drawn
between *open* versus *closed* communities and *endocentric* versus *exocentric*
ones (1988:74–5), with the former distinction referring to levels of contact
with the outside world and the latter to the degree to which a community is
focused on its own internal norms versus outside norms. In addition, increasing levels of contact may actually serve to sharpen dividing lines among
groups, as residents of formerly closed communities set up psychological –
and, often, linguistic – barriers against the encroachment of the outside
world.

3.2.6 The social construction of enclave status

While it may be possible to set up an inventory of physical and social traits
for enclave dialect communities such as those identified here, there are
many qualifications that need to be made about these attributes. It thus
seems theoretically and methodologically questionable to establish an invariant
set of physical, social, and psychological attributes characterizing an enclave
community. As observed in Wolfram and Schilling-Estes (forthcoming),

particular situations represent different configurations of these traits. Perhaps the most constant attributes are those related to identity and norming, but they, in turn, are connected to various historical circumstances and physical conditions. It might be possible to objectify these traits and arrive at an objectifiable and quantitative "index of insularity" but subjective evaluations by community members and investigators would ultimately serve as the basis for such a quantitative index. At their base, *historical isolation* and *enclave speech community* are socially constructed notions, negotiated by those within and outside the community. Montgomery (2000), however, points out that perceptions of isolation by insiders and outsiders may not necessarily coincide and that the "isolation" label imposed by outsiders – including linguists – may not be shared by insiders. Nonetheless, constructed identity appears to play an important role in the development and maintenance of the community and its language, as witnessed by the fact that these communities may reshape and perpetuate dialect distinctiveness during less insular periods, just as they maintain dialect distinctiveness during periods of greater isolation.

It is also essential to recognize that insularity is a relative notion and that, accordingly, the conception of an enclave community is "more of a popular – and social science – fiction than a sociohistorical fact" (Schilling-Estes, 2000a:144). Contact and connections pervade society, and cultures do not come in neatly packaged, independent entities. Similarly, so-called enclave dialect communities have linkages and interrelationships with other communities, and their interrelatedness is reflected in their dialect configurations. In this connection, we note that it is not unique dialect structures *per se* that typically define enclave dialect communities, but a constellation of structures. Very few of the dialect structures found in a given enclave community are unique to that variety; the vast majority of structures are found in other dialects as well, so that it is the combination of structures rather than individual structures that sets enclave communities apart. In this respect, Hyde County is no different from other enclave dialect situations that have provided essential evidence for reconstructing the history of AAVE.

Although we can establish some general traits that often correlate with enclave dialect situations, we ultimately rely on the description of local history as a basis for justifying the claim that the Hyde County sociolinguistic situation provides important evidence for reconstructing earlier African American speech. In chapter 4, we offer a profile of the history of Hyde County in support of its designation as a historically isolated region. This, in turn, justifies our claim that this setting offers important insight into the historical development of African American speech. Our investigation should also show how enclave communities develop and reconstruct their linguistic identities over time, both in terms of their local identity and in terms of identities that extend beyond their immediate community. As we see in the ensuing chapters, one of the most dramatic changes that has taken place in the speech of Hyde County African Americans is the shift toward the adoption of widespread AAVE norms, despite the enduring geographical dislocation of the community.

3.3 Language Change in Enclave Communities

Like other language varieties, enclave dialects are dynamic rather than static entities undergoing constant change. Despite the romantic notion that enclave dialects develop in consummate isolation, no dialect of English stands completely apart from contact with other communities and these enclave dialects are vulnerable to the adoption of language forms from external groups. There is always some type of interaction with other groups, though there are, of course, vast differences in the regularity and intensity of the contacts (e.g., Schreier, 2001). Accordingly, intracommunity and extracommunity contact must be factored into an understanding of isolated dialect situations, not only in their formative stages but also as they reconfigure themselves at various points over time, including their development into postenclave varieties.

Although the potential for internally motivated innovation must be admitted, most dialectologists and sociolinguists rely on a version of the founder principle combined with the relic assumption in describing the linguistic composition of historically isolated dialect situations. Under the founder principle (Mufwene, 1996a, 1999) as discussed in chapter 2, it is maintained that the distinctive structural traits of a given dialect are predetermined by the varieties spoken by the population that first brought the language to the region. For example, we assume that the primary dialect group that brought English to Southern Appalachia (Montgomery, 1989), the Scots Irish, was responsible for its formative dialect traits, or that the variety of English spoken by the original group of expatriate blacks from Philadelphia left an indelible imprint on the English dialect established in the transplant community of Samaná in the Dominican Republic (Poplack and Sankoff, 1987). Under *the relic assumption*, it is presumed that dialect forms will be quite conservative with respect to language change and thus will remain relatively intact after the dialect's formative period.

It is not difficult to find support for both the founder principle and the relic assumption in enclave dialects. For example, the existence of the Southern Appalachian verbal concord pattern which attaches -*s* to verbs occurring with plural noun phrase subjects (e.g., *The dogs barks*) has been attributed to the Scots-Irish immigrants who brought this form with them when they settled the region (Montgomery, 1989). The form was a characteristic dialect trait in the Ulster region of Ireland at the time of the emigration, and therefore it is assumed that the primary population group in the area simply imparted this linguistic trait in the formative stage of the dialect. In a similar way, it seems reasonable to assume that the absence of copula in the speech in black expatriates in Samaná or Nova Scotia (Walker, 1999; Hannah, 1997) was brought to the locale by the original speakers when they migrated there.

There is also certainly empirical evidence for the conclusion that peripheral dialects can be conservative in linguistic change by comparison with linguistic change taking place among wider sociospatial population groups. For example, the use of *a*-prefixing (e.g., *She's a-huntin' and a-fishin'*) has been documented in virtually all of the isolated dialect communities surveyed in Wolfram and Schilling-Estes (forthcoming), as well as rural dialect areas in New England (Kurath, 1949), in the Midwestern USA (Allen, 1973–6), and in the American South (Pederson et al., 1986–92). Further, this structure has been amply documented in earlier English throughout the British Isles (Trudgill, 1990:80). In the meantime, *a*-prefixing has virtually vanished in the dialects found in the contemporary cultural centers of the Unites States, the large metropolitan areas. It thus appears that the maintenance of *a*-prefixing is legitimately attributable to a founder effect and linguistic conservatism.

Similarly, the use of initial *h* in *hain't* for *ain't* and *hit* for *it* has been found across a sample of enclave communities (Wolfram and Schilling-Estes, forthcoming) as well as a wide range of other rural varieties even as it has disappeared in other major dialects of contemporary North America. Like *a*-prefixing, the syllable-onset *h* in these forms is well documented in earlier varieties in the British Isles and in an array of rural dialects in the United States. Furthermore, as a marked linguistic feature, it would be unlikely for it to emerge independently in a number of different dialect settings. Thus, cases such as *a*-prefixing and initial *h* in *(h)it* and *(h)ain't* appear to qualify as genuine instances of conservatism with respect to the founder dialects of American English.

While recognizing the role of the founder effect and conservative language change, however, it is necessary to set forth several important qualifications on their application – on a local level as it relates to a particular enclave dialect community, and on a more general level in terms of the dynamics of language maintenance and change. On a practical level, the application of the founder principle assumes that we know the structural traits of the original donor varieties and that these may be distinguished reliably from features that derive from other sources, including parallel, independent development and diffusion. It assumes further that we have a clear understanding of dialect lineage during earlier time periods. For isolated dialect communities where dialect histories sometimes go back several centuries, ascertaining genuine founder effects can be an elusive methodological challenge.

On a descriptive-theoretic level, we cannot simply assume that so-called relic forms will remain static in their linguistic composition. The empirical investigation of isolated dialect communities shows that these dialect communities exhibit both selective retention and differential rates of change. This development is readily illustrated by the case of perfective *be* (e.g., *I'm been there* for *I've been there* or *You're lost some weight* for "You've lost some weight") in enclave dialects (Wolfram, 1996; Dannenberg, 1999). The history of English indicates that the semantic territory for *be* once overlapped with that now covered by perfect forms, and that well into the seventeenth century there was widespread use of both auxiliary *have* and auxiliary *be* for intransitive perfect forms and motion verbs (Rydén and Brorström, 1987). However, although the use of perfective *be* is amply documented in representative enclave dialects (Sabban, 1984; Wolfram, 1996; Dannenberg, 1999; Tagliamonte, 1997), it cannot simply be assumed that it has remained intact in its structural and functional form. For example, in Lumbee English, unlike a number of other dialects on the coastal United States (Wolfram and Schilling-Estes, forthcoming), the use of perfective *be* is still a robust, productive form, even among younger Lumbee speakers. At the same time, the form has undergone some independent development that now distinguishes its use in Lumbee English from other varieties where it is still productive (Sabban, 1984; Kallen, 1989; Tagliamonte, 1997). For one, there is an important constraint related to the form of the co-occurring subject, so that perfective *be* is now strongly favored with first person singular forms over other subject types. Thus, a construction such as *I'm been there* is much more likely to occur than *You're been there* (Dannenberg, 1999), even though both may occur. It has also become more structurally restricted in Lumbee English, so that it is now limited to contracted finite forms such as *I'm been here* versus **I am been here*. Meanwhile, it has expanded its tense and aspect parameters so that it currently applies to some simple past constructions (e.g., *I'm forgot the food yesterday*) as well as perfect constructions. Thus, there are changes in the structural and functional parameters of the form that distinguish its use in Lumbee English, not only from dialects where its use has receded, but also from other varieties where it is still in use.

Though the perfective use of *be* might qualify as a "relic" form given the traditional definition of such items, it must be understood that such items are hardly static structurally or functionally. Indeed, these forms may undergo independent developments within a particular dialect community that sets the community dialect apart from other enclave dialects in subtle but important ways. In fact, we have to ask whether the term "relic" is even a useful linguistic designation. If we assume that the label "relic" refers to earlier forms selectively preserved intact, then there are few forms that qualify. If, on the other hand, we admit that these forms are subject to change just like "nonrelic" features, then we are hard put to show how change in relic forms differs from other types of language change, apart from the fact that relic forms involve changes in forms that have receded in varieties of the language considered "mainstream." Ultimately, the label "relic form" seems to be a designation that necessarily takes into account social relations and social valuation rather than language change *per se.*

Some changes in enclave dialects also involve parallel independent development, or "drift" due to the operation of general processes of analogy and a universal tendency to move towards unmarked forms (Keiser, 2001). For example, a survey of various enclave dialects along the mid-Atlantic and Southern coast of the United States in Wolfram and Schilling-Estes (forthcoming) shows the uniform tendency to expand the regularization of once-irregular plurals (e.g., *two sheeps*), the regularization of past tense forms (e.g., *They growed up*), and the adoption of negative concord (e.g., *They didn't do nothing*), along with the stopping of syllable-onset, interdental fricatives (e.g., [dɪs] "this"). These general traits are shared not only by these isolated communities but by a host of other vernacular communities of English in the United States and elsewhere. As Chambers (1995:242) points out, "certain variables appear to be primitives of vernacular dialects in that they recur ubiquitously all over the world." These developments are simply part of the natural processes that guide changes quite independently of diffusion or language contact. More than anything, analogical pressures to regularize and generalize linguistic processes distinguish socially subordinate dialect communities, including enclave communities, from the prescribed standard English norm which is, according to Chambers (1995:246), "more strictly tightly constrained in its grammar and phonology" due to the social pressures to resist some natural linguistic changes. The essential unifying dimension of such changes seems to be the alignment of varieties that are less loosely constrained by prescriptive social norms of "correctness" than those of the dominant social groups.

Although enclave dialect communities may be conservative with respect to some changes, they are not uniformly and invariably conservative. In fact, they may be innovative and change rather rapidly in some cases. Schilling-Estes and Wolfram (1999), based on a moribund dialect in the Chesapeake Bay of Maryland, provide evidence that peripheral varieties existing in closed, concentrated communities may show rapid, accelerated change with respect to some marked dialect features. Andersen (1988) also observes the role of independent innovation for peripheral dialects based on the empirical examination of a number of different European dialect situations:

... there are internally motivated innovations which arise independently of any external stimulus. These too have an areal dimension and may appear to spread merely because they arise in different places at different times. (Andersen, 1988:54)

Andersen not only admits the vitality of internally motivated change in peripheral dialect areas; he asserts that peripheral varieties existing in closed, concentrated communities may show the "ability to sustain exorbitant phonetic developments" (1988:70). Such a claim certainly counters the relic assumption that enclave dialect communities will necessarily be conservative in their patterns of change and rarely favor innovation. Furthermore, Bailey, et al. (1993) have demonstrated that innovation can spread contra-hierarchically, that is, from rural areas to urban centers. Thus, it is quite possible for a peripheral dialect to be at once both conservative and innovative in language change.

The unqualified application of the founder principle and relic assumption is empirically unwarranted. The real methodological and descriptive challenge for the study of enclave dialects is, in fact, sorting out the layers of founder effects and distinguishing instances of conservatism from innovation. No simple set of assumptions about a unilateral founder effect and conservatism will suffice; instead, questions of attribution in enclave dialects must be grounded in an in-depth understanding of the particular structures of the founder dialect as they have been subjected to or resisted language change.

3.4 Sociolinguistic Principles in the Configuration of Isolated Dialects

Based on our previous discussion, we may offer a tentative set of general principles that apply to the sociolinguistic configuration of enclave dialects. These principles are offered more as a set of preliminary hypotheses that need to be tested against a more expansive sample of communities rather than a definitive set of sociolinguistic axioms.

Principle of Dialect Exclusion
Discontinuities in regular communication networks with outside groups impede isolated dialect communities from participating in ongoing dialect diffusion taking place in more widely dispersed and socially dominant population groups. This exclusion is, of course, relative rather than absolute given the interconnectedness of dialect communities. Nonetheless, the relative exclusion may give rise to the selective retention and/or independent language change that leads to dialect divergence.

Principle of Selectivity in Change
Speakers of isolated dialects may selectively retain and develop putative dialect structures in ways that result in divergence, even when the varieties are the product of a common founder variety. Furthermore, such dialects may show conservatism in change for some dialect structures while indicating accelerated change for others. In part, the rate of change may relate to the linguistic status of the structure, but change may also be a function of the social role of the structure as well. For example, linguistic structures that carry symbolic social value are more likely to show accelerated rates of change than other dialect structures (Schilling-Estes and Wolfram, 1999).

Principle of Regionalization
The retention of founder effects selectively together with internally based, independent language change may lead to divergence both from other enclave dialects and from more broadly based regional dialect communities, leading to the regional demarcation of particular enclave communities.

Principle of Social Marginalization
The social relegation of enclave communities to nonmainstream social status naturally leads to a marginalized, subordinate sociolinguistic status for the speakers of such varieties. In keeping with principle of linguistic subordination, the linguistic structures associated with these varieties will therefore be socially disfavored.

The Principle of Vernacular Congruity
Natural linguistic processes that involve analogical leveling, regularization, and generalization may lead to parallel dialect configurations in quite disparate isolated dialect communities. Such changes may thus unite enclave dialects with one another and with other socially subordinate vernacular dialects.

The Principle of Intracommunity Variation
Speakers living in small, relatively self-contained communities may show considerable intracommunity variation. Some of this variation may correlate with localized, intracommunity social and ethnic boundaries (Wolfram, Hazen, and Tamburro, 1997), but some may also be a product of "patterned individual variation" (Dorian, 1994) in which particular speakers simply retain divergent language patterns within the community apart from any obvious social boundaries. Small homogeneous communities can tolerate considerable long-term language variation among speakers (Dorian, 1994; Wolfram and Beckett, 2000; Beckett, 2001).

Principle of Localized Identity

Speakers of peripheral dialects often embrace dialect distinctiveness as an emblematic token of local identity. Dialect perpetuation may range from selective dialect focusing (Bailey et al., 1993) to overall dialect intensification (Schilling-Estes, 1997, 2000b; Schilling-Estes and Wolfram, 1999). Given the social construction of local identity, distinct dialect features may be perpetuated beyond the insular state of an isolated variety.

Many of these principles will be exemplified in our discussion of morphosyntactic and phonological variation in Hyde County in the ensuing chapters of this book. At the same time, some of the sociolinguistic principles offered here will no doubt have to be amplified or abandoned on the basis of a more extensive sample of enclave dialect situations. We are convinced, nonetheless, that our understanding of the interrelation of linguistic variation in its social context will advance most by extrapolating from the individual cases and postulating general principles that might apply to a broad base of enclave dialect situations. In the process of formulating these principles, we stand to gain insight, not only into the sociolinguistic construction of enclave dialects but into the social embedding of language change and maintenance in general.

4

The Social History of Mainland Hyde County

A sign along the highway leading into Engelhard in Hyde County proclaims "Welcome to Engelhard: Rooted Deep in History, Growing Toward Tomorrow." For Engelhard, and for Hyde County in general, historical links not only are an advertising draw, they are also vital for gaining an understanding of the community. This chapter therefore traces sociohistorical dimensions of Hyde County that are relevant to our explanation, in subsequent chapters, of local speechways. More archival information is available about European Americans than about African Americans from the county, especially from earlier periods, so there are some gaps in African American history; accordingly, a bias toward European American history was unavoidable. Hyde County is fortunate to have one of the most active historical organizations in North Carolina, the Hyde County Historical and Genealogical Society, and much of the following account has been gleaned from two of its publications: Selby et al. (1976) and the periodical *High Tides*.

4.1 Chesapeake Bay Origins

European settlement of northeastern North Carolina, including the region around the Albemarle and Pamlico Sounds, began as an offshoot of the Chesapeake Bay settlement area in Virginia and Maryland. For that reason, the history of Hyde County begins with the Chesapeake Bay. Although Jamestown, the first English settlement in Virginia, was established in 1607, and the first recorded permanent settlement by Europeans in present-day Hyde County did not occur for another 98 years, the sociocultural ties with the Chesapeake Bay determined the development of Hyde County to a large extent. In addition, Hyde County retained closer ties in commerce and transportation with the Chesapeake Bay region than with the rest of North Carolina until well into the twentieth century. Even today Baltimore is a key destination for Hyde County products (R. S. Spencer, Jr., personal communication).

Fischer (1989) discusses the early social developments of English settlements around Chesapeake Bay. A minority of the settlers in Virginia and Maryland were descended from English nobility, but those settlers dominated politics. The largest group, however – approximately three-quarters – came to the region as indentured servants. These servants, most of whom were illiterate, were from lower social levels, often having been unskilled, agrarian tenant laborers (Fischer, 1989:228). Almost all were between the ages of 15 and 35 (Fischer, 1989:231). Many had been forced into indentured servanthood because of debts or as punishment for petty crimes, and some by being kidnapped or even by being sold by parents or husbands[1]. A stark dichotomy between powerful planters and poor former servants evolved, and as a result the culture of the region came to be quite hierarchical. Nevertheless, according to Kulikoff (1986), there was a great deal of upward social mobility until 1680. At that point, the price of tobacco, which had become the main crop and was quite profitable, began to fall. During the period from 1620 to 1680, freed servants were readily able to buy land (usually along the frontier), start their own plantations, and hire their own servants. Fischer (1989:216), though, argues that "many men of humble origins became prosperous planters in Virginia but were never admitted into this [Virginian] higher elite."

Many aristocrats in Virginia and Maryland professed Royalist sympathies (Fischer, 1989). While the Chesapeake Bay region was being settled, hostilities between Royalists and Puritans – culminating in the English Civil War – created considerable turmoil in England, and the progress of settlement was greatly affected by developments in the home country. Early on, from 1607 until 1641, the Virginia colony barely grew at all. Horn (1979, cited in Fischer, 1989) found that the vast majority of the early settlers came from London and nearby areas. This situation changed after 1641, when Sir William Berkeley became governor of Virginia. The English Civil War broke out, lasting from 1642 until 1649, and was followed by the Commonwealth (1649–60), during which Oliver Cromwell and his fellow Puritans ruled England. Royalists in England, formerly persecutors of Puritans, found themselves persecuted. Berkeley managed to remain as governor and used the Commonwealth as a chance to recruit Royalists and others from England. As the population of Virginia grew, the demand for indentured servants did, too. Farming in Virginia and Maryland, unlike in the more northerly colonies, became focused on one cash crop: tobacco (Kulikoff, 1986). Cultivation of tobacco, being labor-intensive, created a need for agricultural labor. In contrast to the early years, however, most of the indentured servants were shipped from Bristol after 1650. These servants were predominantly from areas near Bristol, especially Gloucestershire and Somerset (Horn, 1979, cited in Fischer, 1989). Because the Royalists were also concentrated in south-western England, most of the newcomers to Virginia during this period, both nobles and servants, were from the Southwest.[2]

Indentured servanthood eventually gave way to slavery around Chesapeake Bay. For most of the seventeenth century, indentured servants from England filled the demand for labor. Kulikoff (1986) notes that a few blacks, mostly from the West Indies, were brought to Jamestown during the early and mid-seventeenth century as indentured servants, but planters preferred English (and, later, Irish) servants. During the 1680s, according to Kulikoff, two factors changed the situation in Virginia and Maryland. First, the supply of indentured servants from England evaporated. Second, tobacco prices fell but tobacco consumption in Europe did not rise, in part because wars often interrupted tobacco shipment. The result was that small planters were forced to turn to other crops, especially grain, and tobacco production became concentrated on larger plantations. The shortage of indentured servants caused planters to turn to blacks, who – because of new laws – were now treated as slaves instead of as servants. Most of these slaves were brought directly from Africa (Kulikoff, 1986:319–20). By 1700, slavery had displaced indentured servanthood as the primary form of plantation labor in Virginia and Maryland.

4.2 The Settlement of Hyde County

The movement of freed servants to the frontier continually expanded the bounds of the Chesapeake Bay settlement area. Powell (1977) states that an English settler established himself in what is now North Carolina in 1653 and that others quickly followed. By the early 1660s, much of the northern shore of Albemarle Sound was settled. In 1665, this area became part of the new colony of Carolina and thus lay outside of the jurisdiction of Virginia.

English settlement did not spread southward from Albemarle Sound as rapidly, in large part because Native Americans occupied the region between the Albemarle and Pamlico Sounds, including present-day Hyde County. Bath, the first English-sanctioned community on the Pamlico Sound, was established in 1706 by a group of French Huguenots from Virginia (Powell, 1977:29). English settlers had lived in the vicinity for over a decade before that, however. Hyde County extended westward nearly to Bath from its establishment in 1705 (originally as Wickham Precinct) until 1819, when lands west of the Pungo River were transferred to Beaufort County (Corbitt, 1950:125–6). A map of Hyde County is provided in figure 4.1.

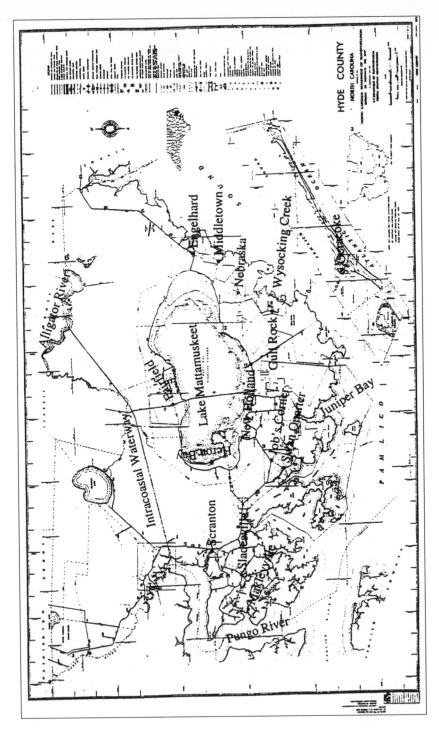

Figure 4.1 Map of Hyde County

Some sources on the history of Hyde County state that the date of its earliest European settlement is unknown (e.g., Simmons, 1907), while Kretzschmar et al. (1994:349) assert that it was "[w]ell settled by 1710." Kretzschmar et al.'s date may be based on the settlement of the western part that was later annexed to Beaufort County. Nonetheless, excellent research on colonial court records and wills reported in Spencer et al. (1988) and Williams (1988a, 1988b) provides a clearer picture of when English settlement reached the different parts of present-day Hyde County. Deeds described by Williams (1988a) show that the portion of Hyde County that was later transferred to Beaufort County was probably settled by 1702. European settlers continued to filter eastward, and the earliest deeds to land on the east side of the Pungo River (around present-day Scranton and Sladesville), which is still part of Hyde County, date from 1704 or 1705. One of those deed-holders, Benjamin Sanders or Sanderson, was apparently living there by then. By 1711, at least 11 people held deeds to land on the east side of the Pungo. Some, unlike Sanders(on), may have been absentee landlords, but there may also have been a few squatters, so the exact extent of European settlement at that point is uncertain.

Although a small fort, called Fort Point, had been established on the north shore of Lake Mattamuskeet (Harris, 1995:53), further English settlement of Hyde County seems to have been limited to squatting for nearly another generation. Much of the county was occupied by Algonkian-speaking Native Americans. As Selby et al. (1976:3.7) and Harris (1995) describe, these groups joined the Iroquoian-speaking Tuscaroras in an uprising against European American settlers from 1711 to 1715. The uprising was quelled and captured warriors were enslaved. Some of the remaining Tuscaroras left for New York and the rest were confined to a reservation near the Virginia border. The remnants of the Algonkian tribes – not only from Hyde County but from all of eastern North Carolina, including the Outer Banks – as well as some Iroquoian-speaking Corees were gathered into the newly established Mattamuskeet Reservation in 1715. This reservation encompassed much of present-day eastern Hyde County, including the communities of Engelhard, Middletown, Nebraska, and Gull Rock, though it was part of Currituck County until 1745. Its inhabitants came to be called the Arro(w)musket Indians. An official land survey in 1727 was necessary to expel European American squatters from the reservation.

In spite of the survey, pressure from whites soon compelled the Arromuskeets to sell tracts within their reservation. According to Selby et al. (1976:3.13) and Spencer et al. (1988), the first such sale that was recorded was in 1731, to Henry Gibbs, progenitor of many contemporary Hyde Countians. Williams (1983) states that Gibbs had arrived there in 1723. More and more tracts were sold, and by 1792, the Arromuskeets had sold the entire reservation. Some of them left the county, while others intermarried with European Americans or African Americans; according to Selby et al. (1976:3.8) and Harris (1995), several Hyde County families can still trace their ancestry to these intermarriages.

The dates of European settlement in eastern Hyde County are clouded both by the fact that this area had been part of Currituck County, for which many early records were lost (Spencer et al., 1988), and by the presence of squatters. Available evidence suggests that its settlement was later than that of the western end of the county, however. Local tradition places English settlement of this area as early as the 1650s (Selby et al., 1976:3.15), but there seems to be no substantiation for such an early date. As mentioned above, the first recorded sale of lands in the Mattamuskeet reservation took place in 1731, but Europeans had been encroaching on the Arromuskeets for some years before that. Spencer et al. (1988) report numerous other transactions involving reservation land throughout the 1730s, 1740s, and 1750s, and even though some landowners did not live in the county, it seems clear that European American settlement was becoming solidly established. Spencer (1987) reports that Mount Pleasant Ridge, now called Gull Rock, was settled by European Americans in 1739.

The central part of Hyde County, around Heron Bay (at the western end of Lake Mattamuskeet) and Swan Quarter, seems to have been settled somewhat later. Deeds described in Williams (1988b) for this area date from no earlier than 1745. The northern part of the county, around Fairfield, was probably settled at about the same time, though published evidence is lacking. For some locales, settlement occurred even later. The earliest known deed for the swampy "Over the Creek" community east of Swan Quarter was dated 1786 (Williams and Williams, 1999) and that from the remote New Lands community north of Fairfield was dated 1789 (Selby et al., 1976:2.15).

The geographical origins of most of the settlers are unknown, but they have been determined for a number of early Hyde County residents; we hope that these are representative. Spencer et al. (1988) list sources for many landowners. Sources of a few others are found in Williams (1988a, 1988b) and in several genealogical studies that have appeared in *High Tides*. From these sources, it appears that there were three main sources of European American settlers. The first was Albemarle County, North Carolina (which included lands north of Albemarle Sound), especially its easternmost precinct, present-day Currituck County. The second was Norfolk County, Virginia, which bounded Albemarle County on the north. The third was the Eastern Shore of Virginia (i.e., Northampton and Accomack Counties). R. S. Spencer, Jr. (personal communication) suggests that the Eastern Shore of Maryland was also an important source for early Hyde County residents. All of these sources are coastal areas; as Powell (1989) notes, transportation in North Carolina was almost entirely by boat at the time because of vast, impenetrable swamps and a lack of roads.

Information on the number and sources of slaves in early Hyde County is much scarcer than for whites. The fact that indentured servanthood had given way to slavery in Virginia by the time Hyde County was settled by European Americans suggests that Hyde County planters either brought slaves with them when they moved to Hyde County or procured them as soon as they could afford to do so. Indeed, Benjamin Sanders(on), the first known European American settler in present-day Hyde County, is recorded as acquiring "a Negro Charles" in 1709 (Williams, 1988a:28). Powell (1989) states that there were about 900 African Americans in North Carolina in 1710, including 97 in Currituck Precinct, which extended into modern-day eastern Hyde County. Hyde County wills for the period from 1709 to 1775, published in Williams (1989), show numerous slave transfers; the earliest dates from 1719.

By 1754, Hyde County contained 183 taxable slaves (i.e., slaves at least 12 years old; Saunders, 1886–90:5.320). Populations estimated by Kay and Cary (1995:221) from colonial lists of taxables indicate that the Hyde County population was about 20 percent black in 1755 and 23 percent black in 1767. Both of these figures are lower than corresponding figures for Beaufort County, which adjoins Hyde County on the west. The overall density of the slave population in Hyde County was lower than that in most of the settled regions of Virginia and South Carolina or in much of North Carolina. Although Kay and Cary (1995) report that, in the mid-1700s, more than 60 percent of the slaves in the Pamlico-Neuse region of North Carolina (which included Hyde County) lived on plantations with 10 or more slaves, and more than 30 percent lived on plantations with at least 20, these figures are misleading. Within the Pamlico-Neuse region, slaveholdings were smaller in coastal counties such as Hyde than in more inland counties. Census data published in Clark (1895–1906) show that, in 1790, only 37 percent of Hyde County slaves lived on plantations with 10 or more slaves and 15 percent on plantations with at least 20. Clearly, small plantations were the rule in Hyde County during the eighteenth century. The predominance of small plantations could well have had an effect on the slaves' speech because individual slaves would have had more contact with whites.

Records documenting the origins of Hyde County's slaves are unknown. However, Kay and Cary (1995) argue that most slaves in colonial North Carolina, except in the Cape Fear valley to the south, were brought from Virginia and Maryland. They estimate that over 70 percent of the slaves brought into North Carolina were transported overland and the remainder, who were mostly from the West Indies, by sea. Many of the slaves brought overland were castoffs from other colonies. Because North Carolina lacked good ports that slave ships could enter, very few slaves came directly from Africa (Kay and Cary, 1995:21). Farming became more diversified in North Carolina than in Virginia (Kay and Cary, 1995:15), and this trend must have been especially true of Hyde County, where the mucky soils were unsuited to tobacco.[3] This fact certainly had an impact on slavery in the county.

4.3 Hyde County from the Revolutionary War to the Civil War

To a large extent, Hyde County history from the Revolutionary War to the Civil War has to be inferred from census records, though some other information is available to complement these records. Among the important

Table 4.1 Total population and African American percentage of Hyde County from 1755 through 2000, based on colonial censuses and US Census records

Year	Total population	% African American
1755	1412	19.8
1767	2341	22.8
1790	4120	26.3
1800	4829	30.0
1810	6029	32.2
1820	4967	34.7
1830	6184	34.0
1840	6458	37.9
1850	7636	37.7
1860	7732	39.4
1870	6445	36.9
1880	7765	43.0
1890	8903	44.3
1900	9278	43.3
1910	8840	41.9
1920	8386	38.9
1930	8550	40.9
1940	7860	41.2
1950	6479	42.2
1960	5765	42.2
1970	5571	41.3
1980	5873	35.6
1990	5411	32.9
2000	5826	35.1

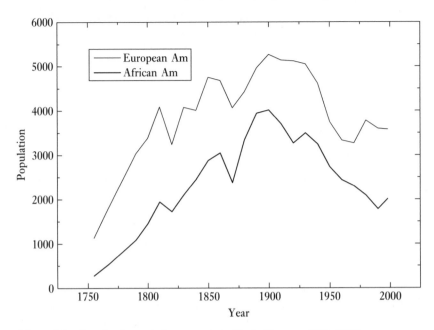

Figure 4.2   Graph of population growth in Hyde County, 1755–2000

developments in Hyde County during this period are the establishment of several of the most important villages and the founding of the first churches in the county (Selby et al., 1976). In-migration, at least among European Americans, does not seem to have been significant. Most of the prominent family names (Gibbs, Spencer, Mann, Credle, Swindell, Cahoon, Midyett, etc.) found in the county today first appeared there before the Revolutionary War, not after it. There was some out-migration, notably to White County, Tennessee (Hyde County Webpage, http://www.rootsweb.com/~nchyde/hyde.htm). Total population in Hyde County and the African American percentage from 1755 to 2000 are shown in table 4.1. Population records from colonial censuses reported in Kay and Cary (1995) and from the US Census from 1790 through 2000 are shown graphically in figure 4.2.

These data reveal a steadily growing population between the Revolutionary and Civil Wars. The decrease between 1810 and 1820 is due to the transfer of the section west of the Pungo River to Beaufort County in 1819, and the decrease between 1860 and 1870 is due to transfer of a section to Dare County in 1870.

The type of infrastructure present in Hyde County probably explains the relative stability of the population. Selby et al. (1976:3.13, 5.28) note that transportation out of the county was almost exclusively by boat before 1920. Travel geographer Bill Sharpe observes:

For a long time, Hyde was as isolated from the rest of the state as Ocracoke is now. The hemming marshes and bogs forbade even travel by horseback, and all traffic was by boat. This insularity kept Hyde from development, but it also helped preserve some of its assets – its fine hunting, its neighborliness and independence of its people, its rural ways, and the distinctive speech which is known as "Hoide" talk. (Sharpe, 1958:894)

This dependence on water travel reflects the lack of roads connecting Hyde County with other areas. There were, however, many local roads, which new residents began laying out as soon as they inhabited the county. A detailed analysis of archival road records in Mann et al. (1986) shows that as early as 1737 commissioners were appointed for the upkeep of roads east of the Pungo River. By 1790, a network of local roads covered much of the southern part of the county, and by 1815 a road ran around the north shore of Lake Mattamuskeet, connecting Fairfield with the settlement that later became Engelhard. Nevertheless, there was only one road leading out of present-day Hyde County. Maps shown in Waynick (1952) indicate that a post road was constructed from Washington to western Hyde County between 1796 and 1804 and was extended to southeastern Hyde County by 1844. This road became the main thoroughfare in the county, as indicated in Mann et al. (1986). All of these roads, however, were merely one-lane dirt tracks that were virtually impassable during wet weather, with bridges that were sometimes washed out during storms. Maintenance was conducted by local citizens. Difficulty entering the county over land undoubtedly deterred in-migration from inland areas and fostered the isolation of the region from inland parts of North Carolina.

Residents who lived away from the Pamlico Sound soon turned to canals for transportation, and canals became important links not only to the out-side, but for travel within the county (Simmons, 1907; Selby et al., 1976:3.13). Canals were also utilized to drain swampland for farming (Selby et al., 1976:1.6). The building of canals was thus of major importance to residents. A 1773 proposal to build a canal from Lake Mattamuskeet to the Pamlico Sound at Wysocking Creek was approved by the state legislature but re-jected by the governor on the grounds that it would cut across private property (Saunders, 1886–90). In 1789, when the governor no longer held veto power, a bill to construct a canal from Lake Mattamuskeet to the Pamlico Sound at Juniper Bay was approved by the legislature (Clark, 1895–1906; see also Fortescue, 1923). A canal connecting Fairfield with the Alligator River (and thereby with the Albemarle Sound) was built starting in 1839 (Fortescue, 1923; Selby et al., 1976:2.18). The New Lake Canal northwest of Fairfield was also begun in 1839 (Welch, 1886:6, 41). Numer-ous other canals had apparently also been dug by the time of the Civil War.

Slave labor was used for canal building before the Civil War, convict labor afterward (Selby et al., 1976:1.6). As a result of the dependence on water transportation, Hyde County's strongest ties were with North Carolina ports such as New Bern, Washington, and Elizabeth City, and with Norfolk, Virginia.

It is fairly clear that there were wide economic disparities within the European American population as well as cross-ethnically. One native, Z. T. Fortescue, stated that Hyde County whites in colonial times were divided into "the educated class, usually the land owners" and "[t]he freemen, who were usually hard laborers" (Fortescue, 1923:3–4). This division undoubtedly persisted long after the Revolutionary War. A number of antebellum plantation houses built by wealthier residents still survive in the Lake Landing Historical District (see Selby et al., 1976:3.72–82). Until 1872, the only schools in the county were private (Selby et al., 1976:3.48).

The economy of Hyde County reflected its coastal location and wet, peaty soils. Fishing and oystering were important. Agriculture dominated the local economy, however. Records from the 1840 census (*Compendium of the Enumeration of the Inhabitants and Statistics of the United States*, 1841) show that the biggest crop then, by far, was corn (maize). Other important crops included sweet potatoes, wheat, oats, and cotton. Because of the predominance of grain crops over a long period of time, Hyde County was called "the granary of the South" in the nineteenth century (Welch, 1886:24). Significantly, no tobacco was produced in the county, which set it off from the interior regions of the state. Poultry and cattle, especially dairy cattle, were the leading livestock. Lumber was an important product, but manufacturing was essentially nonexistent.

Another important aspect of the economy in Hyde County during this period, of course, was slavery. Unlike in many parts of the North Carolina coastal plain and Piedmont, though, small plantations continued to predominate in the county as they had in colonial times. This fact is apparent in a comparison of data from the 1790 and 1850 Censuses. In 1790, in the entire county (including the Outer Banks part and the sector of the mainland later annexed to Beaufort County), the largest plantation comprised only 36 slaves. Of the 1,048 slaves recorded for the county, 15 percent were in slaveholdings of 20–36 slaves, 22 percent in holdings of 10–19, 35 percent in holdings of five to nine, and the remainder in holdings of fewer than five (Clark, 1895–1906). In 1850, for the mainland part of the county, the largest holding – that of an absentee landlord, Judge John R. Donnell – comprised 220 slaves, but the next largest had only 45. Of the 2,440 slaves recorded in the mainland section in 1850, 9 percent lived on the Donnell plantation, 28 percent on holdings of 20–45, 27 percent on holdings of 10–19, 23 percent on holdings of five to nine, and the remainder in holdings of fewer than five. Although the slaveholdings increased somewhat in size from 1790 to 1850, the average slave in 1850 still lived in a holding of only 15 slaves. Nonetheless, these holdings were large enough to produce black communities. Census data reported in Spencer (2000) show that the Donnell plantation had the largest holding from its inception in the 1840s through the Civil War, and that the only other holdings ever to surpass 100 slaves were two – of 153 and 131 slaves, respectively – reported in 1840. One of the latter holdings may have been bought by Donnell to form his holding. Holdings of 50–99 slaves were rare, too; one was reported in 1820, three in 1830, and three in 1860. In addition to slaves, small numbers of free African Americans lived in the county throughout this period.

There is little evidence as to whether most of the slaves in Hyde County during this period were natives of the county, but some were probably brought in from various other port cities. Spencer (1984) includes slave records from six Hyde County families listing the births of 142 slaves, the earliest dating from 1763. All or nearly all of these slaves were apparently born in Hyde County. Carawan (2000) speculates that many slaves on the Donnell plantation were brought from New Bern, where Donnell had previously lived and owned a plantation, but she also presents evidence that at least some were born in Hyde County. The Donnell plantation, however, was certainly not typical in Hyde County, not only because of its size, but also because most other slaveowners lived in the county and thus may have been less likely to bring in slaves. Cecelski (1994b:177) notes that runaway slaves from Hyde County often fled to Washington, where they could find ships heading to the North.

Mainland Hyde County played a modest role in the Civil War. According to Harris (1995:125–38), although Hyde County contributed soldiers both to the regular Confederate army and to local brigades, local sentiments were divided and many men refused to enlist. Letters from John Donnell's overseer, Henry Jones, indicate that Union sympathizers were quite numerous (Spencer, 1982a), as does a letter from a Fairfield planter to the governor (Selby et al., 1976:2.74). Harris (1995) notes that Hyde County grain was important to the Confederate army as long as it could be shipped out, which became difficult because the Union army gained control of the Outer Banks in 1861 and of New Bern and Washington in 1862. A few minor skirmishes between Union raiding parties and local brigades occurred in 1863 and 1864. Local tradition holds that the Confederate soldier who accidentally shot General Stonewall Jackson was from Hyde County. The proximity of the Union army caused many slaves to anticipate imminent emancipation throughout much of the war, and thus many slaves escaped from their plantations well before the war ended (Spencer, 1982a)

4.4 Reconstruction to the Great Depression

A comparison of census data from 1860 and 1870 (*Statistics of the Population of the United States*, 1872) suggests that most former Hyde County slaves remained in the county after emancipation. Comparison of these data is complicated by the fact that part of Hyde County was partitioned off to form Dare County in 1870 (Corbitt, 1950:126) and the 1870 data reflect the new boundary. However, comparing the drop in African American population between 1860 and 1870 with that of the European American population provides some idea of the extent of migration. The African American population of Hyde County decreased by 22 percent, while the European American population decreased by 13 percent. These figures indicate that a few African Americans left, but the majority stayed. Much of the drop not caused by the formation of Dare County may be due to the fact that freed slaves vacated Ocracoke, which was occupied by Union forces for nearly the entire Civil War. According to Cloud (1995), Ocracoke had as many as 150 slaves before the war. It seems likely that many of the Ocracoke slaves tried to emigrate to the North, as runaway slaves had before the war. Thus the African American population of mainland Hyde County was probably fairly stable.

Most of the freed slaves probably continued to work as agricultural laborers, taking whatever other jobs they could find as well. A description by Cecelski (1994a:21) of later African American dwellings suggests that freed slaves were compelled to settle in shanties, many of them along mosquito-filled creeks and canals – often, perhaps, in former slave quarters. Patterns of residential segregation developed that still persist today. For example, the village of Swan Quarter has traditionally been nearly all European American, while the nearby neighborhood of Job's Corner has always been African American (Welch, 1886:57; Cecelski, 1994a:23). African Americans founded their own churches, which were separate from European American churches, soon after the Civil War.

Hyde County received an influx of Northern investors after the Civil War. As in most parts of the South, these Northerners were not welcomed by all residents, partly because they disrupted the existing social order in which wealthy planters held most of the power. A notable example is an incident on the former Donnell plantation. The Donnell plantation was bought in 1893 by a New Yorker, Stephen B. Ayres, who began a venture in market produce. The previous owners engaged in a long dispute with Ayres and then paid some African Americans to fire shots into Ayres' house in 1895, barely missing him and his wife (Spencer, 1982b). Nevertheless, such incidents did not prevent other changes that the new immigrants brought.

The greatest impact of Northern investors in Hyde County during the late nineteenth and early twentieth centuries was the timber boom. Soon after the Civil War, a number of Northern entrepreneurs established lumber mills in Hyde County and began cutting the county's virgin timber (Harris, 1995:139 ff.). Most valuable was Atlantic white-cedar, locally known as "juniper" (hence Juniper Bay, east of Swan Quarter), but baldcypress and oak were also prized. Railroads were constructed for the logging industry during this period (Selby et al., 1976:1.14). Communities such as Mak(e)leyville grew up around mills, and African American and European American residents were typically segregated in these communities. Both European Americans and African Americans worked for the timber companies, though it is not clear whether they worked side by side. Hyde County reached its largest recorded population, 9,278, in 1900, at the peak of the timber boom (see table 4.1). After 1900, the virgin timber began to run out and, even though a few new mills appeared, the industry declined. With it, the population declined, too, and the mill communities disappeared. The railroads were abandoned and ultimately taken out. The final blow to the large mills of Hyde County was the deflation of lumber prices during the Great Depression (Harris, 1995). Much of the county was left denuded of trees, and although second-growth forests soon sprang up, the great stands of Atlantic white-cedar never returned.

Other developments spearheaded by Northern investors were less successful. Had they succeeded, they would have changed Hyde County dramatically. One scheme was to create three cities in the pocosins of northwestern Hyde County, drawing settlers from Northern states. In 1870, about 25 families moved to one of the proposed cities, Hyde Park City, but most soon left after experiencing the difficulties of life in a swamp. By 1920, the settlement had vanished (Selby et al., 1976:1.36–37; Harris, 1995:155 ff.). Another scheme was to drain Lake Mattamuskeet and farm its bed. An attempt to drain the lake in the 1840s had failed (Lefler and Newsome, 1973:366–67). However, as described by Forrest (1989) and Harris (1995:185 ff.), between 1909 and 1932, a renewed effort was made and the lake actually was drained and farmed for a few years. A succession of Northern-owned companies poured money into the project, with one planning a village called New Holland and another building a railroad. Financial losses, water-pumping problems, and wet weather ultimately doomed the enterprise. In 1934, the lake was sold to the US government and became the Mattamuskeet National Wildlife Refuge. Harris (1995:201 ff.) describes how young men from the Civilian Conservation Corps (CCC) helped to prepare both the Mattamuskeet refuge and the Swanquarter National Wildlife Refuge near Swan Quarter (established in 1932). The CCC was segregated, and the camps that were set up in Hyde County – which included many Hyde County natives – were all white; African American CCC enrollees from Hyde County were sent elsewhere.

The period between the Civil War and the Great Depression brought other major changes to Hyde County. After the state legislature made the Board of County Commissioners into a Board of Education in 1872 (Selby et al., 1976:3.48), the commissioners divided the county into school districts and public schools appeared in the county for the first time. Fortescue (1923:7) states that there were 30 public schools in the county for whites and 29 for African Americans by 1880. All of these were primary schools. Welch (1886:46) states that numerous college preparatory private schools continued to exist, and for several years the only high schools in the county were private. Early on, the public schools met for only four months each year. As years passed, schools were gradually consolidated, the school term was lengthened, and public high schools were established.

Although tenant farming replaced slavery, the crops grown in Hyde County underwent only minor changes after the Civil War. Figures given in Welch (1886:30) indicate that rice overtook corn as the principal crop. The large amounts of rice, corn, oats, and wheat produced reflected the ongoing dominance of grains, and the virtual absence of tobacco continued to set the county apart from other regions of the state. Sweet potatoes and cotton were also important crops, as in many parts of the South. Large amounts of all these crops were shipped out by water to North Carolina ports, as well as to Norfolk and Charleston. Starting during World War I, Hyde County began to follow the nationwide trend of growing soybeans extensively (Selby et al., 1976:3.11). The advent of soybeans was permitted by another nation-wide trend that Hyde County followed, the increasing mechanization of agriculture. Mechanization certainly affected labor within the county and may have contributed to the steady drop in population throughout the twentieth century.

Other changes included the establishment of telephone service, improvements in roads, the construction of the Intracoastal Waterway, and the advent of electricity. Telephone service was begun in 1903 in Swan Quarter and later extended to the rest of the county. During the 1920s, as part of Governor Cameron Morrison's road-improvement program, Hyde County saw its first paved road. Maps included in Brown (1931) show that the road from Washington to Swan Quarter had been paved by 1930, though the section from Swan Quarter to Engelhard was still graded dirt. This road, now US Route 264, gave Hyde County its first reliable overland link with the rest of North Carolina and fundamentally changed its transportation patterns: no longer was water the primary means of travel into and out of the county. With the improved roads, Hyde County's first car dealership opened in Swan Quarter in the early 1920s (Selby et al., 1976:5.11). The Intracoastal Waterway was constructed through northern Hyde County beginning in 1924 (Harris, 1995:168–69). Designed for long-distance travel, it seems to have had only a minor effect on Hyde County commerce.

Finally, electricity reached the county with the establishment of the Pamlico Power and Light Co., Inc., in 1935. The company began in Engelhard and gradually extended lines to other parts of the county (Selby et al., 1976:3.66–67; Harris (1995:245–47). Cecelski (1994a:22) states that improved roads and utilities tended to be routed away from African American neighborhoods, but the inability of many impoverished African Americans to pay for utilities may have played a role in the location of lines.

4.5 Hyde County since 1940

The shift toward land transportation that began in the 1920s presaged other changes that happened after World War II. Road improvement accelerated during the administration of Governor Kerr Scott (1949–53), when many of the back roads and even some of the main highways in Hyde County were paved for the first time. R. S. Spencer, Jr. (personal communication) says that the road from Engelhard to Dare County was laid out in the late 1920s and early 1930s, but was not paved until the late 1940s. The road from Fairfield north to Columbia had been built sometime previously, but it likewise was not paved until later. These two roads provided additional thoroughfares out of the county. Once land transportation had become the preferred means for people to travel, more people began working outside the county, attending college (that is, European Americans, who largely attended East Carolina and North Carolina State Universities), and marrying outside the county.

Perhaps the most explosive change in the county was the desegregation of the schools. The process is described in detail by Cecelski (1994a), and his account is summarized here. The school board in Hyde County, responding to pressure from African American leaders, spent large sums of money from 1953 to 1964 improving the two remaining African American schools in the county, the Davis School near Engelhard and the O. A. Peay School at Job's Corner. Nevertheless, the county's schools remained segregated in defiance of the US Supreme Court's ruling in the 1954 *Brown vs. Board of Education of Topeka, Kansas*, case. In 1965, the Department of Housing, Education, and Welfare (HEW) ordered the school board to comply. Students were allowed to choose their school, but only a few African American students attended the previously all-white Mattamuskeet School and no European American students attended either African American school. As a result, HEW ordered full desegregation. The school board's answer was a plan to convert the Davis School to a community college and the Peay School to office space, and then to send all students to the already overcrowded Mattamuskeet School. African Americans, who had invested a great deal of their own efforts in the Davis and Peay Schools over the years, were incensed and began a massive protest in 1968. African American students boycotted the schools for the 1968–9 school year and occupied the superintendent's office in an incident that attracted national attention. African Americans staged daily marches on the county courthouse in Swan Quarter and two marches to Raleigh. There was even a shoot-out between African Americans and the Ku Klux Klan in Middletown in 1969. Later in 1969, a new superintendent who was willing to compromise with the African American community was installed. The compromise was that the Davis and Peay Schools became integrated elementary schools, while the Mattamuskeet School became the high school.

The economy of Hyde County since 1940, as in many agricultural areas in the United States, has been sluggish. Economic disparities persist within the county. As Cecelski (1994a:21) notes, by the 1950s a few large-scale farmers and seafood cannery owners had become wealthy, and there were others such as merchants and fishing families who were prosperous, but much of the population – African American and European American – remained mired in poverty. Today, poverty levels are still among the highest in the state. In 1989, Hyde County had the fourth lowest median family income among North Carolina counties. It was also tied for ninth in the percentage of persons below the poverty level, at 24.0 percent (1990 Census of Population. Social and Economic Characteristics, 1993). As always, poverty continues to be worse among African Americans, and many of them now live in mobile homes, which have proliferated in the county, or in a government housing project near Job's Corner. A shortage of jobs, as well as the seasonal and low-paying nature of many available jobs, are the main reasons for the poverty. Some subjects interviewed for the NCLLP described having to work at a variety of jobs in order to subsist. One elderly African American man, for example, reported that he had, at different times in his adult life, worked as a farm laborer, in house construction, as a janitor, and in lawn care. Similarly, one elderly European American man reported that he had farmed, trapped game, and worked as a store clerk, as a hunting guide, and on fishing boats in addition to hunting to provide food for his family.

Seafood packing plants have become some of the most important employers, boosting the local economy after World War II (Harris, 1995:255 ff.). Although oystering has declined precipitously, the seafood business shifted, first to shrimp and, more recently, to crabs (Selby et al., 1976:3.12–13). Agriculture has become highly mechanized, but the crops produced remain mostly the same except that rice production has virtually ceased and truck farming is becoming more prominent. Teams of Mexican migrant workers now provide much of the seasonal agricultural labor, as well as some of the labor in the seafood packing plants. Considerable logging of second-growth forests for ground sawmills and for chip mills – especially for the Weyer-haeuser mill in nearby Plymouth – has occurred since World War II (Harris, 1995:146–50). Such logging has led to the conversion of a great deal of land from forest to cropland. Tourism has been a small source of income for Hyde County for the entire twentieth century. Hunters have long visited the county for its waterfowl, deer, and bears. There is some sportfishing, and the Mattamuskeet refuge is a popular destination for birders. In order to increase tourism, a driving tour for viewing nineteenth-century buildings was developed and two annual festivals, Swan Days in December and the Engelhard Seafood Festival in May, were initiated. A new state prison built in Hyde County in 1997 brought promises of new jobs (Allegood, 1997).

In spite of these efforts, the slow economic conditions have prompted many residents to leave the county. Although the population decreased slightly as the timber industry waned from 1900 until 1930, it plummeted from 1930 to 1960, as shown in table 2.1 and figure 2.1. This decrease was due to out-migration as young people moved elsewhere in order to find work. It is greatest between 1940 and 1950, when many GIs were exposed to job opportunities in other parts of the country. Since 1960, the decrease in European American population has leveled off somewhat, but the African American population continued to decline until it rebounded moderately after 1990. Based on information gathered in NCLLP interviews, it appears that European Americans who leave the county tend to move inland, most frequently to the urban centers of North Carolina, such as Raleigh, but often to neighboring states. African Americans tend to be drawn toward coastal cities. Some have moved to Washington, North Carolina, but many have moved to large cities, especially Norfolk and New York City. In-migration is minimal and results in large part from marriage and from former residents returning for their retirement. However, a group of Mennonites from other states settled in northwestern Hyde County during the 1960s (Selby et al., 1976:48–50) and the recent influx of Mexican migrant workers has included some who are settling in the county. It appears that agribusiness and seafood will continue to dominate life in mainland Hyde County during the early twenty-first century.

4.6 Sociohistorical Effects on Language

The sociohistorical profile presented here provides an important background for understanding and explaining the sociolinguistic patterns we describe in the following chapters. Several historical and current conditions estab-lish Hyde County as a unique sociolinguistic site for examining language change and variation in general and in AAVE in particular. First, we have documented the early habitation of both European Americans and African Americans in the region, which was typified by small slaveholdings, thus establishing that Hyde County represents a distinctive, long-standing biracial situation. We have also established the continuity of the residents of the county, with many of the families dating back to the earliest European American and African American inhabitants. This continuity is of particular relevance as we examine the founder effect for both the black and white communities. We have also set forth the physical and social conditions that justify our designation of the area as "historically isolated." The dependence on water travel, and the fact that there was only a single muddy road leading into the county until the twentieth century, rank high among these conditions. In this context, we have discussed the demographic and contact ecology between European American and African Americans that will help explain the patterns of dialect congruence and dissimilarity that emerge from our sociolinguistic analysis. Finally, we have described the more recent development of the county as it emerges from its long-standing insularity. At various points in our description, all of these factors are essential to understanding how and why language has developed as it has in Hyde County. These factors also help justify our assertion that this situation can offer an exceptional perspective on the earlier and contemporary development of the speech of African Americans, not only in Hyde County, but elsewhere as well.

Notes

1 Breen and Innes (1980:60) state that most indentured servants came to Virginia voluntarily, though they were regularly lured by false advertising.

2 Fischer has been criticized as overemphasizing Royalism and downplaying economic motivations among the Virginia elite (see the discussion in the *William and Mary Quarterly*, volume 48 [1991]). Our concern here, however, is with determining where immigrants came from and when they came.

3 Breen and Innes (1980:39) note that the eastern shore of Virginia, an important source of Hyde County settlers, had switched from tobacco to grain crops by 1700.

5

Morphosyntactic Alignment in Hyde County English

Several morphosyntactic variables have been pivotal in the controversy over the historical development and current status of AAVE. Questions include: (1) how these structures emerged among African American speakers to begin with; (2) how they developed in earlier African American speech; and (3) how they are structured within contemporary AAVE. Structures such as copula absence (e.g., *She nice* or *You nice*) and inflectional -*s* absence (e.g., for 3rd sg. as *The dog bark_*, possessive as in *the boy_ foot*, and plurals as in *two cup_*), for example, continue to figure prominently in the debate over earlier AAVE (e.g., Bailey, 1965; Wolfram, 1974a; Baugh, 1983; Rickford, 1997; 1998; Poplack, 1999; Winford, 1997; 1998; Walker, 1999) after four decades of close sociolinguistic scrutiny.

At the same time, dialect descriptions of Pamlico Sound English have identified some distinctive morphosyntactic traits that set it apart from other regional and social dialects of American English, including AAVE (Schilling-Estes and Wolfram, 1994; Hazen, 1996, 2000b; Wolfram, Hazen, and Schilling-Estes, 1999). For example, leveling to *were(n't)* in past tense (e.g., *She weren't there*) and verbal -*s* marking with 3rd pl. subjects (e.g., *The dogs barks*) are distinctive dialect markers of the region. Although some aspects of these traits are shared with other regional varieties (Wolfram and Christian, 1976; Montgomery, 1989, forthcoming; Hazen, 1996, 2000b), there are some aspects that now seem distinctive to the coastal dialect area that encompasses Hyde County.

Given the unique sociolinguistic status of Hyde County detailed in chapter 4, the examination of a sample of both traditional AAVE structures and distinctive Pamlico Sound features should be quite indicative of the influence of regionalized speech on the past and current development of the African American English. On the one hand, accommodation to distinct Pamlico Sound morphosyntactic features by African Americans would show that they were sensitive to regionalized dialect norms. On the other hand, the persistence of dialect features associated exclusively with the African American speech community would give us insight into the maintenance of long-term ethnolinguistic distinctiveness.

By comparing patterns of variation and change for AAVE-exclusive structures and distinctive Pamlico Sound morphosyntactic structures across different generations of African American and European American speakers, we hope to ascertain the ways in which the vernaculars were aligned at an earlier period in their history and how this alignment is changing. The representative variables selected for comparative analysis here include two morphosyntactic patterns typically associated with the Pamlico Sound regional variety, past tense leveling to *weren't* and 3rd plural -*s* marking, and two features commonly associated with the core morphosyntactic structures of AAVE, copula/auxiliary absence and 3rd sg. -*s* absence. Our focus is on past and present patterns of alignment as compared with the detailed systematic linguistic constraints on variability amply documented in studies of these structures in other settings (e.g., Labov, 1969; Baugh, 1983; Rickford, 1997; Poplack and Tagliamonte, 1989; Tagliamonte, 1991, Poplack, 1999), though there are points in the comparison where linguistic constraints on variability figure significantly in the alignment pattern.

5.1 Issues in Attribution

Several issues must be confronted in sorting out the development of dialect patterning in Hyde County. First, there is the *donor issue*. Where did speakers in the European American and African American communities in Hyde County acquire the structural features that unite them and set them apart? While we might rely on a version of the founder principle (Mufwene 1996a, 1999) as set forth in chapter 2, the application of this principle assumes that we know the structural traits of the original dialects brought to the region, and that we can discern such putative influence from other developments, such as later dialect diffusion, influence from language contact, and parallel, independent linguistic change. It assumes further that we have a clear understanding of dialect lineage over an extended period of time, including knowledge of dialect traits found in the original, transplanted dialects from the British Isles, as well as those developed within colonial America and subsequently diffused to Hyde County. For an enclave community whose dialect history goes back almost three centuries, identifying original donor sources can be quite elusive and highly speculative.

Another consideration is the *diffusion issue*. How did dialect diffusion take place in this region after settlement by European Americans and African

Americans? In what ways has it been similar and different for the respective ethnic speech communities? What is the current pattern of dialect transmission and how is it affecting the different ethnic communities? In chapter 4 we documented the early patterns of migration to Hyde County through the coastal waterways as a basis for understanding Hyde County's participation in a seaboard dialect region that extends from coastal areas of North Carolina up through the coastal and island communities of Chesapeake Bay. We need to posit viable diffusion patterns for specific dialect structures that spread throughout this region over several centuries.

We must also consider the *contact issue*. Although our historical description of Hyde County revealed a region geographically and socially isolated throughout a large portion of its history, no community is a linguistic island, standing continually apart from all contact with other groups. In this case, however, we need to consider both intraregional and interregional contact patterns. Contact dynamics between African American and European Americans within Hyde County and external contact patterns for these respective groups have to be sorted out in determining patterns of convergence and divergence.

Finally, we must acknowledge the possibility of *independent, parallel development*. While dialectologists and historical linguists certainly recognize the potential for change from within in enclave dialect situations, the role of internal language change and innovation in such situations tends to be slighted in favor of other explanations (Andersen, 1988). As noted in chapter 3, there seems to be an assumption that dialect forms in enclave varieties will be quite conservative with respect to innovation and that relic forms will remain relatively intact in their linguistic composition. Empirical evidence from other enclave dialect situations (Andersen, 1988; Schilling-Estes, 1997, 2000b; Schilling-Estes and Wolfram, 1999; Wolfram and Schilling-Estes, forthcoming), however, suggests that we cannot ignore the possibility of independent parallel development in explaining some of the morphosyntactic structures we consider here, including some fairly extensive cases of language change.

An authentic account of change in Hyde County must include the full range of explanatory possibilities set forth here. At the same time, we must admit that the validity of our reconstruction does not rest on a single morphosyntactic pattern. While single-structure studies may reveal significant insight into a particular linguistic process and/or dimensions of an ethnolinguistic boundary, they sometimes obscure or even distort our understanding of the overall relationship of African American and European American speech. A valid account of earlier African American and European American speech can emerge only if a wide array of dialect structures is considered in a comparison, including the kinds of morphosyntactic variables we consider in this chapter as well as the dialect traits considered in the following chapters.

5.2 Past Tense *be* Regularization

Recent studies of coastal dialects of American English extending from the Outer Banks of North Carolina (Schilling-Estes and Wolfram, 1994, 1997; Wolfram et al., 1999) to the islands of the Chesapeake Bay (Schilling-Estes, 1997, 2000b; Shores, 2000) have shown a distinctive pattern of past tense *be* regularization in which leveling to *was* may take place in affirmative constructions (e.g., *The dogs was down there* or *We was down there*) and leveling to *weren't* takes place in negative constructions (e.g., *I weren't there; It weren't nice*). This pattern contrasts with the standard English norm of concord based on plurality as well as the widespread vernacular pattern of leveling to *was* in which subject–verb concord for past *be* is eliminated (e.g., *I/you/ (s)he/we/they was/n't there*). The Mid-Atlantic coastal pattern represents a significant morphological restructuring, or *remorphologization*, of the two past *be* stems, as the *was*-stem is now used as a marker of affirmative rather than singular, and the *were*-stem is now used as a marker of negativity rather than plurality. The leveling pattern based on polarity rather than plurality has been noted in some dialect areas in England (Cheshire, 1982; Trudgill, 1990; Britain, forthcoming), along with a more generalized leveling pattern in which *were* serves as the pivot form without remorphologization; that is, *were* is used as the pivot form regardless of polarity (e.g., *I were there/I weren't there; she were there/she weren't there*) (Orton et al., 1962–71; Trudgill, 1990).

The *weren't* leveling pattern is clearly a minority pattern compared with the predominant vernacular pattern of leveling in which *was* serves as a single pivot form. In fact, the remorphologized alternative has often been overlooked in surveys of vernacular structures of US English, although Atwood (1953:32) noted that *weren't* is found "in several communities in coastal N.C., and there are a few scattered occurrences elsewhere." However, Wolfram (1991) did not mention it in a summary of major vernacular dialect structures within the USA compiled just a decade ago.

The historical distribution of *weren't* leveling in Atwood (1953: fig. 24) includes representation on the Eastern Shore of Maryland and Virginia, as well as some locations in the Appalachian Mountain range in West Virginia, North Carolina, and Virginia. In the USA, productive use of the remorphologized pattern, however, now seems to be confined to a primary dialect region along the Mid-Atlantic coastal area that extends from the Eastern Shore of Maryland and Virginia, including Tangier Island (Shores, 2000) and Smith Island (Schilling-Estes, 1997, 2000b) in the Chesapeake Bay area, to the Outer Banks barrier islands and the adjacent coastal region of mainland North Carolina (Schilling-Estes and Wolfram, 1994; Wolfram et al., 1999). The regional delimitation for *weren't* leveling based on current dialect information is given in figure 5.1.

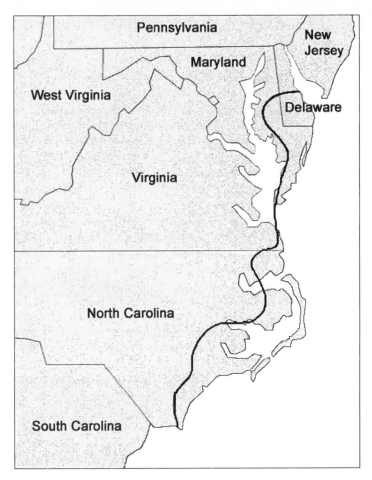

Figure 5.1   The contemporary regional distribution of leveling to *weren't*

Apart from the Mid-Atlantic coastal region of the USA and some areas in
England (e.g., Trudgill, 1990; Cheshire, 1991), there is no documentation
of leveling to *weren't* among English language varieties around the world.
Furthermore, descriptions of English-based creoles (Holm, 1988, 1989) also
fail to note this structure as a characteristic, and descriptions of concord and
negation in AAVE (Labov et al., 1968; Weldon, 1994; Rickford, 1999) do
not mention *weren't* leveling as characteristic of AAVE; neither do descriptions of African American English in enclave, transplant situations (e.g.,
Tagliamonte and Smith, 1999). It thus seems reasonable to assume that the
pattern of leveling to *weren't* described here is a distinct, regionally restricted
pattern within the USA; as such, it is an ideal variable for examining the

extent to which African Americans in Hyde County have been impacted by local morphosyntactic norms.

5.2.1 The historical development of leveling to weren't

Documenting the current regional distribution of leveling to *weren't* is a lot easier than reconstructing its historical development in the USA. LAMSAS records from one of the two Hyde County speakers interviewed in their survey, a European American born in 1858 from near Engelhard, however, include a citation of *weren't* use (*No, it weren't me*) as well as an example of leveling to *were* in a positive construction (*I were talking*). An examination of over 20 letters written by a plantation overseer in Hyde County to a slaveholder in Raleigh during the Civil War (The Donnell Family's Hyde County Civil War Letters, Perkins Library, Special Collections) did not reveal any instances of leveling to *weren't*, but such evidence is inconclusive since there were very few occasions for using past *be* with negatives in the letters. Schilling-Estes and Wolfram (1994) cite some written documentation of *weren't* in the second half of the nineteenth century on the Outer Banks, but documentation before that period is scant. Our reconstruction is therefore guided by examining the regional parameters of its past and present distribution and by considering the sociohistorical circumstances that framed the development of this region over the past few centuries.

Although we cannot be certain, it does not seem likely that leveling to *weren't* in the coastal Mid-Atlantic resulted from simple, direct transmission by a group of English speakers from the British Isles who exclusively used past tense leveling to *weren't*. The feature may have been present in several of the English varieties brought to regions of the Eastern Seaboard of America, including settlers who originally came from the Southwest and Southeast of England (Orton et al., 1962–71), but from that point, it probably developed into a regional feature in the USA. Dialect studies of the Highland South documented scattered cases of *weren't* and *were* leveling in isolated regions in the Appalachian mountain range (Atwood, 1953, fig. 24; Brandes and Brewer, 1977), but apparently it did not develop into a productive form and sustain itself there as it did along the Mid-Atlantic coast. For example, while Atwood (1953, fig. 24) documented some examples of *weren't* leveling among speakers from Southeastern West Virginia born in the mid-1800s, Wolfram and Christian's (1976) sampling of almost 150 speakers in that region in the mid 1970s did not document it.

While other dialect forms represented in the speech of the original English inhabitants in the Mid-Atlantic coastal region were lost or became part of an American English koiné, past tense leveling to *weren't* appears to have developed into a regional dialect feature within the USA. Most likely, *weren't* and *were* leveling were available from a donor dialect in England in an "embryonic" state (Trudgill, 1999) at the earliest stage of English language use in Virginia, and later developed into a full-blown dialect feature in the Mid-Atlantic coastal region. We cannot completely rule out independent innovation as a basis for the emergence of *weren't* leveling, but the prevalence of leveling to *was* among vernacular varieties of English around the world militates against this explanation. Chambers (1995:243), in fact, argues that "invariant *was*" is so dominant that it is one of the few primitives of global vernacular English that can be attributed to independent development.

It is a matter of speculation as to when the distinct dialect area of the Mid-Atlantic coast developed. One possibility is that the formative period took place as early as the first half of the 1700s, as residents of the Tidewater Virginia region moved to various coastal sites, including islands in the Chesapeake, the Eastern Shore of Maryland and Virginia, and south to coastal North Carolina, including the Outer Banks. This is the position implied in our discussion in chapter 4. Shores (2000: 305), however, disputes the early transmission hypothesis. Instead, he takes the position that "the formative stages of these dialects [i.e., island and coastal dialect communities in the Chesapeake], that is, the period at which they took on the characteristics that they have today, would have been between 1800 and 1850, give or take a decade or two." If the emergence of this coastal Mid-Atlantic dialect took place in the early 1800s, then we must sort through several levels of dialect development and diffusion in reconstructing the historical emergence of *weren't* leveling in coastal North Carolina. Given the marine-based economy shared by those along the coast, and primary route of travel through the waterways until the twentieth century, dialect diffusion in the region could have taken place well after the original resettlement of residents from Tidewater Virginia and Maryland into these outlying areas. However, most water travel during the 1800s linked Hyde County with cities such as Norfolk and New Bern, North Carolina, rather than the Eastern Shore and Chesapeake Island islands.

Even if we could determine a precise time period for the emergence of *weren't* leveling as a dialect feature in the Mid-Atlantic region, we would have to admit the possibility that the dialect changed at various points over the course of a couple of centuries. We cannot, for example, rule out the likelihood that there has been a kind of ebb and flow in the dialectal prominence of leveling to *weren't* in this area. For example, Schilling-Estes and Wolfram (1994) show that there has been somewhat of a revitalization in the use of leveling to *weren't* in Ocracoke: older speakers favor its use, middle-aged speakers show a recession, and younger speakers exhibit a mild renewal as they use more leveling to *weren't* than their middle-aged counterparts. *Weren't* leveling on Ocracoke is, in fact, one of the few features of the traditional Outer Banks dialect that has not shown a significant recession over three generations in apparent time. At the same time, Schilling-Estes (2000b) shows that the use of *weren't* leveling is clearly intensifying for the younger speakers on Smith Island in the Chesapeake, and our analysis of Hyde County European American vernacular speech here shows its intensification by younger speakers. Furthermore, older speakers in Ocracoke and in mainland Hyde County show vestiges of *were* leveling as well as *weren't* leveling, suggesting that its remorphologization is intensifying as well. Similar cycles of robustness and recession may well have typified the use of *weren't* leveling in past generations of speakers.

5.2.2 Was/weren't *leveling in Hyde County*

As noted above, leveling to *weren't* is a minority structural pattern for past tense *be* leveling. Vernaculars around the world (Chambers, 1995:243; Tagliamonte and Smith, 1999), including AAVE (Labov et al., 1968, Weldon, 1994), show a strong preference for leveling to *was* regardless of polarity. Accordingly, the patterning of past tense *be* leveling among African American speakers in Hyde County should be quite indicative of earlier and/or present-day alignment in terms of a regional variety of past *be* leveling.

In figure 5.2, we chart the incidence of leveling to *weren't* for past *be* in negative constructions and leveling to *was* in affirmative constructions. Our tabulation is based on 49 speakers, 35 African American speakers divided into four age groups of speakers (12 young, aged 14–23; six middle-aged, aged 32–43; six senior, aged 55–70; and 11 elderly, aged 77–102) and 14 European American speakers divided into an elderly (six elderly, aged 77–92) and a young (eight young, aged 15–27) group. The 14 European American speakers were classified as primary speakers of a vernacular version of Pamlico Sound English, based on independent linguistic criteria and background sociodemographic data, in order to match the African American vernacular-speaking group.[1] The occurrence of past tense *be* leveling was tabulated in relation to possible cases for leveling to *was* (e.g., *We was here* for *We were here*) and for leveling to *weren't* (e.g., *I weren't there* for *I wasn't there*) in the sociolinguistic interviews of each speaker within each age group to arrive at the raw figures and percentages presented in the tables accompanying figure 5.2. Preliminary analysis indicated that leveling to *were* in affirmative constructions (e.g., *I were there* for *I was there*) was so low (below 3%) that it was not considered a viable alternative for the consideration of variation in this analysis (cf. Schilling-Estes and Wolfram, 1994).[2] The graph in figure 5.2 is based on the percentage of leveling for each age-group aggregate for the four age groups of African Americans and for the two age groups of European American speakers. Also included are several types of VARBRUL analyses. First, a run was done each for *was* and *weren't* leveling

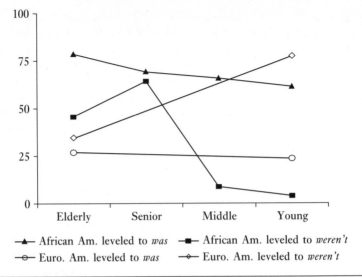

Figure legend:
—▲— African Am. leveled to *was*   —■— African Am. leveled to *weren't*
—⊖— Euro. Am. leveled to *was*   —◇— Euro. Am. leveled to *weren't*

Ethnicity and Generation	Leveled to was		Leveled to weren't	
	No./Tot.	% Leveled	No./Tot.	% Leveled
European American				
Elderly (77–94)	25/93	26.9	9/26	34.6
Young (15–27)	16/68	23.5	17/22	77.3
African American				
Elderly (77–102)	98/124	78.4	37/81	45.7
Senior (55–70)	50/72	69.4	9/14	64.3
Middle (32–43)	23/35	65.7	2/23	8.7
Young (14–23)	68/111	61.3	2/53	3.8

VARBRUL Results: Ethnicity and generation

	Leveled to was	Leveled to weren't
	Input probability = .57	Input probability = .27
European American		
Elderly	.22	.59
Young	.19	.90
African American		
Elderly	.75	.70
Senior	.64	.83
Middle	.60	.21
Young	.55	.10

Figure 5.2   Incidence of *was* and *weren't* leveling in Hyde County

VARBRUL Results: Ethnicity and subject type

Leveling to was		*Leveling to* weren't	
Subject type		Subject type*	
Existential	.78	Existential	.60
3rd pl. NP	.62	3rd sg. NP	.50
1st pl.	.50	3rd sg. Pro	.49
2nd pl.	.39	1st sg.	.38
3rd pl. Pro	.35		
Ethnicity		Ethnicity	
African Am.	.60	African Am.	.68
European Am.	.19	European Am.	.46
Chi square per cell	.791	Chi square per cell	.388

* Subject type thrown out in step-down procedure

Figure 5.2   Continued

by ethnic group and generation. Another run considered the factor groups of subject type and ethnicity.[3] Previous studies have shown both *was* and *weren't* leveling to be sensitive to a type of subject constraint (Schilling-Estes and Wolfram, 1994, Hazen, 1996, Tagliamonte and Smith, 1999; Wolfram and Sellers, 1999). For example, leveling to *was* is typically favored when the subject is a noun phrase (e.g., *The dogs was*) versus pronoun (e.g., *They was*), and strongly favored with existential subjects (e.g., *There was dogs at home*). Studies of variable constraints on *weren't* leveling show more varied patterning, as some varieties (Schilling-Estes and Wolfram, 1994) show a favoring effect for existentials (e.g., *There weren't a dog*) and other varieties (Wolfram and Sellers, 1999) exhibit a favoring effect with first person subjects (e.g., *I weren't there*). In the VARBRUL analysis for subject type and ethnicity, the different age groups were conflated since the focus was on independent linguistic constraints. However, only the three oldest groups of speakers were included for *weren't* leveling among African American speakers, since the youngest group of speakers has virtually eliminated this option.

The figures for *was* and *weren't* leveling show that elderly African Americans in Hyde County align with the *weren't* leveling pattern characteristic of the local European American vernacular pattern, whereas young African Americans have abandoned this pattern in favor of a more generalized version of *was* regularization that applies to both negatives and positives – the common pattern for AAVE elsewhere (Weldon, 1994). The results for elderly African Americans reveal high levels of both *was* and *weren't* leveling, thereby indicating a fairly remorphologized version of the rule in which *was* leveling is applied to positive constructions and *weren't* leveling to negative constructions. The surrender of *weren't* leveling by the younger speakers is a significant departure from the older, localized vernacular norm. By the same token, leveling to *was* remains robust across the different generations of African American speakers. We attribute the slight reduction of *was* leveling among younger African Americans as compared with their elderly cohorts to the effects of more extensive exposure to mainstream standard dialects.

The young group of European Americans maintain a slightly reduced level of *was* leveling compared to their older cohorts, and have significantly less *was* leveling than their young African American cohorts. At the same time, however, they show a major difference in leveling to *weren't* when compared with their young African American cohorts. Whereas younger African Americans relinquish the use of leveling to *weren't*, younger European Americans show the heightened incidence of *weren't* leveling. In this respect, they parallel the maintenance pattern found for Ocracoke (Schilling-Estes and Wolfram, 1994), but Hyde County shows a more dramatic intensification. Older African Americans and Europeans were aligned in their use of *weren't* leveling – in fact, elderly African Americans used it more frequently than their European American cohorts – but younger generations of speakers change in quite different directions: African Americans shift entirely to *was* leveling while European American vernacular speakers intensify the use of *weren't* leveling while maintaining modest levels of *was* leveling. In an important sense, both groups participate actively in an expanding ethnolinguistic divide that characterizes the current generation of vernacular speakers. The two speech communities were once aligned in their use of *weren't* leveling, but now have gone their separate ways, with the European American vernacular speech community now intensifying a local dialect feature which the African American community has moved away from.

The VARBRUL analysis of subject type and ethnicity shows the unity of the two speech communities for the effect of subject type on *was* leveling, with existential subjects strongly favoring *was* leveling, and third plural noun phrases favoring leveling over pronouns. This pattern replicates the widely documented constraint patterning summarized in Tagliamonte and Smith (1999). However, there is an important ethnic difference in terms of the overall incidence of *was* leveling, as it is much more common among African Americans. The data on subject constraints on *weren't* leveling are not quite as clear; *weren't* is favored for existentials (e.g., *There weren't a person there*) and disfavored for 1st sg. subjects (e.g., *I weren't there*), as was found by Schilling-Estes and Wolfram (1994), for Ocracoke, but subject type was eliminated as a constraint in the VARBRUL step-down procedure. Further investigation may indicate that there is an interactive effect between ethnicity and subject type for *weren't* leveling. For example, it appears that European Americans favor leveling of *weren't* with pronoun subjects whereas African Americans do not. For European Americans 60.6 percent (20 of 33) of past *be* with third sg. pronouns are leveled to *weren't* whereas only 28.7 percent (27 of 94) are for African Americans. However, this difference needs to be investigated further before it is concluded that different subject constraints on *weren't* leveling exist for the two ethnic groups.

5.3 Copula/Auxiliary *Is* and *Are* Absence

The absence of copula and auxiliary for contractible forms of *is* and *are* (e.g., *She nice* for *She's nice* or *They acting silly* for *They're acting silly*) is one of the most highlighted structures of AAVE (e.g., Labov, 1969; Wolfram, 1969; Fasold, 1972; Fasold and Nakano, 1996; Baugh, 1980, 1983; Rickford, 1997, 1998, 1999; Walker, 1999). Nonetheless, its synchronic and diachronic status remains controversial. In fact, Walker (1999:35) asserts that "the copula is probably the most studied but least understood variable in socio-linguistics." Descriptive issues involve the structural status of "null copula" (Martin, 1992), the relationship of copula contraction to deletion (Labov, 1969; McElhinney, 1993; Fasold and Nakano, 1996), and the explanation of structural linguistic constraints on the variability of deletion (Labov, 1969; Rickford et al., 1991; Walker, 1999). The ethnolinguistic status of copula absence in AAVE vis-à-vis its status in cohort rural Southern European American vernacular varieties is also an issue. For example, Wolfram (1974a) and Feagin (1979) note that AAVE shares copula absence with some South-ern white rural vernacular varieties of English, but that there are also some essential qualitative and quantitative differences in these respective vari-eties. Its use in European American varieties in the American South has generally been attributed to linguistic accommodation to African American speech rather than to donor dialects in the British Isles or independent development (Wolfram, 1974a).

Diachronically, copula absence has figured prominently in the debate over the origin of AAVE (Winford, 1998:109), as it has sometimes been con-sidered the most conspicuous example of creole influence in AAVE, given the prominence of null copula in English-based creoles in the African diaspora (Bailey, 1965; Holm, 1984; Rickford, 1996, 1997, 1998). Alternative analyses, however, attribute copula and auxiliary absence to a natural, independent development feeding off the phonological process of contraction.

Despite intense scrutiny over the past three decades, the origin and development of copula and auxiliary absence remains in considerable dis-pute. While our analysis of copula absence in Hyde County may not resolve this dispute, past and present alignment patterns do, in fact, have implications for understanding the distribution and development of this process over time and place. As with other morphosyntactic structures, our discussion focuses on the past and present ethnolinguistic alignment of copula absence in Hyde County as a basis for gaining insight into the more general development of AAVE.

5.3.1 The historical development of copula absence

Most sociolinguists agree that copula and auxiliary absence has been a prominent trait of African American English for centuries now, and that this pattern contrasts with that found for earlier varieties of English in the British Isles. Until Martin and Tagliamonte (1999) observed it in Northern England, most dialectologists and sociolinguists had agreed that copula absence was not a prominent feature of English varieties spoken in the British Isles (Wolfram, 1974a). At the same time, most linguists agree that copula absence is a widespread trait of English-based creole and pidgin languages spoken in the African diaspora. These observations have led a number of linguists, particularly creolists (Bailey, 1965; Stewart, 1968; Holm, 1984; Singler, 1991; Rickford, 1996, 1998; Rickford and Blake, 1990; Winford, 1992), to the conclusion that copula absence in AAVE is derived from a creole predecessor. At the same time, there are a number of structural incongruities between the operation of copula absence in AAVE and its operation in English-based creoles, leading some variationists to question the assumed line of creole ancestry (Poplack and Tagliamonte, 1991; Meechan, 1996; Walker, 1999). For example, copula deletion appears to feed off contraction (Labov, 1969), unlike its null copula status in creoles and pidgins. Furthermore, copula absence in AAVE does not apply to the 1st sg. copula form *am*, again unlike its operation in creoles. And variable constraints related to subject type (viz. Pronoun > NP) and to verbal complementation (viz. *gonna* > V-*ing* > adjective (ADJ)/locative (LOC) > NP) do not parallel the structure of null copula in English-based creoles spoken in the African diaspora. Such discrepancies have led some researchers to offer alternative explanations for the development of copula absence in AAVE. For example, Walker (1999) explains copula and auxiliary variability on the basis of the interaction of syntactic, semantic, and prosodic factors that led to an independent development within English. Such a position is, of course, in sharp contrast to the creolist position that attributes donorship to a creole substrate with subsequent decreolization leading to its present state in AAVE.

Although it is beyond this study to consider each point and counterpoint in alternative reconstructions of copula absence, several observations can be made. It should be noted that the attribution of copula absence to creole influence does not necessarily entail the position that AAVE *per se* developed from a widespread plantation creole language in the antebellum South (Winford, 1998). In other words, it is quite possible to maintain that contact with speakers of English-based creoles influenced a developing variety of English without assuming that a widespread pidgin or creole language existed. As sociohistorical and demographic evidence accumulates (Mufwene, 1996b, 1999; Winford, 1997, 1998) in opposition to recognition of a widespread plantation creole in the antebellum South, the likelihood that copula absence developed through a direct creole lineage has lessened. But this hardly rules out any role for creoles in the development of copula absence in AAVE. It is well documented (e.g., Winford, 1997; Rickford, 1997), for example, that many of the earlier slaves were brought from the Caribbean Islands speaking some form of creole. It may well be the case that influence from a creole converged with generalized interlanguage strategies and African substrate language transfer to account for the development of copula absence in AAVE. It is not necessary to reduce the explanation for copula absence to a single, unitary source. As Winford (1998) notes:

> the copula pattern of AAVE is best explained as the result of imperfect second language learning, with transfer from creolized or restructured varieties playing a significant role. In other words, multiple causation was at work here. (Winford, 1998:111)

There may well have been multiple sources leading to the development of copula absence, including fossilized transfer from African languages with null copula, borrowing from Caribbean creole languages, interlanguage strategies, and independent language development.

Another relevant observation about the development of copula absence in AAVE concerns its ethnolinguistic distribution in the USA. For the most part, copula absence is limited to African Americans and to restricted groups of European Americans in Southern rural lowland areas characterized by heavier concentrations of African Americans (Wimberly and Morris, 1997). It is not, for example, found among European Americans in Highland areas of the South with more limited populations of African Americans; similarly, it is not found in the speech of European Americans in coastal dialect regions such as Hyde County and the Outer Banks (Wolfram, Hazen, and Tamburro, 1997). Furthermore, copula absence among European Americans tends to be restricted to *are*, and to be found only in regions that are largely nonrhotic (Wolfram, 1974a; Feagin, 1979; Bailey and Maynor, 1985b). In these regions, there is no apparent lineage for copula absence from donor dialects in the British Isles, supporting the contention (Wolfram, 1974a) that copula absence among European Americans in the rural southern USA is due to dialect accommodation to the AAVE pattern rather than independent development or a founder effect from dialects in the British Isles.

Finally, it must be kept in mind that it is quite possible for transferred forms to undergo extensive restructuring as they are integrated into a new variety. Thus, Fasold (1976; Fasold and Nakano, 1996) posits the origin of copula absence as a transferred syntactic phenomenon, which was restructured into a phonological process feeding off contraction in contemporary AAVE. Such a restructuring might help explain the kinds of interactive constraints and the prominent role of prosody in copula and auxiliary absence as posited in Walker's (1999) analysis.

While identifying the ultimate donor source of copula absence in AAVE is surely more complicated than originally posited (Bailey, 1965; Dillard, 1972), it seems apparent that it developed exclusively as an earlier trait of African American English and that it was diffused primarily among African Americans in the USA. We assume that the African American population brought this trait to Hyde County from Virginia and Maryland and that it has been maintained as a distinctive ethnolinguistic marker over the centuries. In this respect, we will see that it is quite unlike the case of past tense *be* leveling discussed in the previous section.

5.3.2 Copula absence in Hyde County

Figure 5.3 summarizes the incidence for the overall absence of *is* and *are* for the same group of 35 African American and 14 European American speakers considered in the analysis of past tense *be* leveling. Although there are different tabulation procedures used for calculating the absence of *is* and *are* (Rickford et al., 1991), we have followed the general procedure in which the percentage of absence is calculated out of the total number of contracted (e.g., *She's nice*), full (e.g., *She is nice*), and null (e.g., *She nice*) forms. The raw figures for *is* and *are* absence are given in the table that accompanies figure 5.3, along with two different VARBRUL analyses. One VARBRUL run includes the ethnic/generational grouping of speakers and the form of the copula: *is* and *are* absence.[4] A different VARBRUL analysis focuses only on independent linguistic effects for the African American speakers in the sample to determine if these constraints replicate those found in other studies (e.g., Labov, 1969; Wolfram, 1969; Fasold, 1972; Baugh, 1980, 1983; Rickford, 1997, 1999; Rickford et al., 1991). Following the tradition of these studies, we consider factor groups related to the surface form of the copula form (*is* vs. *are*), subject type (NP vs. pronoun) and predicate complement type (predicate nominative as in *She the woman*, predicate adjective as in *She nice*, predicate locative as in *She in the house*, verb *-ing* as in *She running*, and *gonna* as in *She gonna go*).

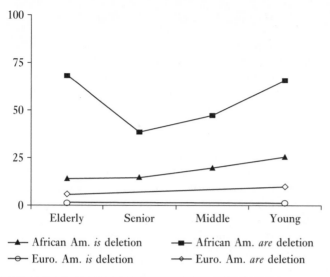

		African Am. *is* deletion		African Am. *are* deletion
		Euro. Am. *is* deletion		Euro. Am. *are* deletion

Ethnicity and generation	Is *copula absence*		Are *copula absence*	
	No./Tot.	% Leveled	No./Tot.	% Leveled
European American				
Elderly (77–94)	1/100	1.0	4/93	4.3
Young (15–27)	1/137	0.7	14/131	10.7
African American				
Elderly (77–102)	17/119	14.3	41/60	68.3
Senior (55–70)	12/82	14.6	7/18	38.9
Middle (32–43)	11/55	20.0	10/21	47.6
Young (14–23)	79/309	25.6	96/145	66.2

VARBRUL Results: Ethnicity/generation and copula type
Input probability = .15
Ethnicity/Generation
  European American
    Elderly = .08; Young = .16
  African American
    Elderly = .73; Senior = .63; Middle = .70; Young = .79
Are/Is:
  Is = .33
  Are = .76

Chi square per cell = .555

VARBRUL Results:Grammatical factors for African American English
Input probability   = .28
  is/are: *is* = .44; *are* = .69
  Subject: NP = .43; pro = .56
  Pred. comp.: nom = .34; adj = .54; loc = .45; V-*ing* = .65; *gonna* = .76

Chi square per cell = 1.285

Figure 5.3 Incidence of copula/auxiliary absence in Hyde County English

The comparison in figure 5.3 suggests that copula absence has been, and remains, a distinctly African American trait in Hyde County. Although some rural Southern European American vernacular varieties share copula absence to a limited degree (Wolfram, 1974a, Feagin, 1979; Bailey and Maynor, 1985b), Pamlico Sound English is not one of them (Wolfram, Hazen, and Schilling-Estes, 1999). Thus, we see a significant discontinuity in both earlier and current versions of African American and European American speech in Hyde County with respect to copula absence. At the same time, there are a couple of patterns that deserve comment.

Copula absence has been fairly stable among African Americans over the four generations of speakers in this sample, with some intensification of the pattern among younger speakers, particularly for *is*. By comparison, elderly European Americans do not have copula absence to any degree. In this respect, the European American community in Hyde County seems more like Highland rhotic areas of the South (Wolfram and Christian, 1976) than some of the lowland nonrhotic plains areas (Wolfram, 1974a). We do, however, acknowledge that some younger European American speakers seem to have incipient *are* copula absence. This minor trend may indicate some AAVE influence on younger European American speakers from the African American community, though other structures, such as leveling to *weren't* discussed in the previous section, show divergence in linguistic structures among younger European and African American speakers.

The VARBRUL run for independent linguistic constraints on copula absence in Hyde County AAVE shows close parallels with constraints found in other studies (Labov, 1969; Rickford, 1998): *are* favors absence over *is*, preceding pronouns favor absence over NPs, and the complements *gonna* and verb -*ing* favor absence over predicate nominatives and predicate adjectives. In this respect, Hyde County AAVE seems no different from other varieties of AAVE in the USA (Labov, 1969; Wolfram, 1969; Fasold, 1972; Baugh, 1980, 1983; Rickford, 1999; Rickford et al., 1991).

The evidence clearly indicates that copula absence has been, and continues to be, a distinguishing trait of AAVE in Hyde County. There is no evidence of earlier copula absence among European Americans but there is evidence of persistent copula absence for African Americans. In this respect, it is quite different from past tense *be* leveling, which showed apparent accommodation to the local regional dialect form by African Americans. It seems obvious that African Americans did not acquire this feature from their cohort Hyde County European Americans. Given the long-standing isolation of both European American and African American populations in Hyde County, it seems most reasonable to assume that copula absence was present in earlier Hyde County African American speech. We can only speculate as to why it should persist while other features of the local dialect were accommodated, but it seems evident that its ethnolinguistic marking is historically and currently secure. It also demonstrates that select-ive ethnolinguistic distinctiveness can indeed endure in the face of wide-spread dialect accommodation.

5.4 Third Person -*s* Marking

With respect to dialect alignment in Hyde County, there are two dimen-sions of third person -*s* attachment that are noteworthy.[5] First, there is a dialect pattern that marks verbal -*s* on a verb occurring with a third person plural subject (e.g., *The dogs barks at the ducks*). This is now a widely documented pattern of concord found in varieties of English influenced by Scots Irish historically as well as other British English varieties (Christian et al., 1989; Montgomery, 1989, 1994, 1997; Godfrey and Tagliamonte, 1998), including Pamlico Sound English (Hazen, 1996, 2000; Wolfram, Hazen, and Schilling-Estes, 1999). One of the noteworthy dimensions of this con-cord pattern is the influence of the type of subject; plural -*s* is favored with noun phrase subjects such as *The dogs barks at the ducks* as opposed to pronominal subjects such as *They barks at the ducks*. Another important constraint is adjacency: -*s* attachment with 3rd plural subjects is favored when the verb is nonadjacent to the subject (e.g., *The dogs that barks all the time* > *The dogs barks all the time*).

The other dimension of subject–verb concord relevant to our examina-tion involves 3rd sg. -*s* absence. It is well established (e.g., Labov et al., 1968; Wolfram, 1969; Fasold, 1972; Winford, 1998) that present-day AAVE has optional attachment of -*s* to verbs with 3rd sg. subject forms, as in *The dog live_ in the swamp* or *She like_ to run*. In fact, some studies (Labov et al., 1968; Fasold, 1972) suggest that basilectal AAVE does not have subject–verb concord. The absence of 3rd sg. -*s* is also a trait found in some vernacular varieties of English in the British Isles, particularly East Anglia (Trudgill, 1990, 1998), and some have suggested that the donor source for AAVE might have a British-dialect origin (Poplack and Tagliamonte, 1989).

5.4.1 The historical development of verbal -s marking

The marking of verbal -*s* with 3rd pl. subjects is well established in the history of English in the British Isles and in colonial English in the USA (Murray, 1873; Ihalainen, 1994; Montgomery, 1994, 1997, forthcoming). Montgomery (forthcoming) traces the pattern to fourteenth-century Scot-land, with substratum influence ultimately from Gaelic. The concord pattern was transferred from Scotland to Ulster, Ireland, and distributed throughout much of Northern England, with its Southern limits the English Northern Midlands (McIntosh, 1983); in fact, it is sometimes referred to as the *Northern Present-Tense Rule*. Early Scots-Irish immigrants and residents of Northern and Midlands England throughout the midland area of colonial America and beyond no doubt transmitted this concord pattern. It was established as a fairly pervasive dialect feature in regions that range from Highland Appalachia to the coast of the Mid-Atlantic South (Atwood, 1953:29), and may have been a general Southern feature. We also find documentation of its use in The Donnell Family's Hyde County Civil War Letters. Hazen (2000a:39) further documents its use on the Outer Banks as a persistent feature for almost three centuries now, and both speakers in the LAMSAS sample from Hyde County, born in 1858 and 1897 respectively, were recorded to have *-s* with third plural subjects, at least with the collective noun *people* (e.g., *people thinks*). There is little doubt that it was a general dialect feature of earlier coastal North Carolina speech that has persisted in varying degrees over the centuries (Hazen, 2000b).

The historical development of *-s* 3rd sg. absence is a quite different matter. The lack of concord marking can be dated to Middle English (Bailey et al., 1989; Wright, 1999), and has been well documented in Southern English varieties, particularly East Anglia (Trudgill, 1990, 1998) but also Southwest England (Wakelin, 1986:36; Godfrey and Tagliamonte, 1998) and even in the West Midlands of England (*Linguistic Atlas of England*, map 34). While its status in earlier dialects of England is fairly secure, its transmission to and diffusion within colonial American English is much less certain. It is indisputably a part of contemporary AAVE, and the data we consider in this analysis suggest that it was a part of earlier African American speech in Hyde County as well. On the other hand, evidence of *-s* 3rd sg. absence in earlier and present-day European American varieties in the region is negligible. Atwood (1953:29) finds some attestation for constructions such as *She do* from coastal Virginia to Georgia, but Schneider and Montgomery (1999) find the lack of concord in only 4 percent of cases in early European American English in the USA. Wolfram, Hazen, and Schilling-Estes (1999) observe that the Outer Banks is an area that has been, and continues to be, an *-s* 3rd sg. marking region, a conclusion confirmed in our examination of older European American speakers in Hyde County. While there may be regions of colonial America and contemporary European American English that can be characterized by 3rd sg *-s* absence, there is simply no indication that this pattern extended to Hyde County. It is possible that the lack of 3rd sg. marking may have typified European American speakers in the region only to be lost among subsequent generations of speakers, but this seems unlikely given the persistence of other earlier dialect patterns. For example, we would have to explain why such earlier features as 3rd plural -*s* marking and leveling to *weren't* were maintained while 3rd sg. nonconcord was lost if we posited that 3rd sg. -*s* was a feature of earlier Hyde County American English. It is thus implausible to suggest that the absence of 3rd sg. -*s* among African Americans was learned from their European American cohorts at an earlier point in their history when there is no evidence of it in earlier European American English in the Pamlico Sound. It seems more likely that African Americans brought this dialect feature with them when they came to the area or acquired it later from other African Americans.

5.4.2 Verbal -s marking in Hyde County

Figure 5.4 summarizes the incidence of plural verbal -*s* for the two generational groups of European Americans and for the four generational groups of African Americans. The figures are broken down according to noun phrase subjects versus pronoun subjects. They are not, however, divided on the basis of adjacency due to the relative infrequency of nonadjacent subjects in the corpus. Results of a VARBRUL analysis in terms of an ethnicity/generation factor group and NP versus pronoun subject accompany the figure.

Figure 5.4 reveals a socially convergent but structurally disjunctive pattern for Hyde County European Americans and African Americans. Elderly European Americans and African Americans are quite alike in their attachment of verbal -*s* with plural noun phrase subjects but differ with respect to the subject constraint; European Americans restrict the attachment of -*s* exclusively to noun phrase subjects, whereas African Americans generalize the rule to verbs regardless of the type of subject. In other words, European American speakers never use verbal -*s* with the subject *they* but African Americans routinely do, thus indicating a subtle but significant difference in the concord pattern. At the same time, subject type is a constraint for African Americans in Hyde County; plural -*s* is favored with NP subjects across different generations. Most studies of verbal plural -*s* show subject type to be an essential constraint, including Montgomery et al.'s (1993) study of some written documents of earlier African-American speech, although Godfrey and Tagliamonte (1998) have documented plural -*s* attachment pattern with no subject type constraint in some British varieties. In this regard, both European American and African Americans follow the general constraint pattern, but in differing degrees; for European American Hyde Countians, it is a categorical constraint, while for African Americans it is variable.

The data also reveal that plural verbal -*s* is a rapidly receding dialect trait in both African American and European American speech communities. In

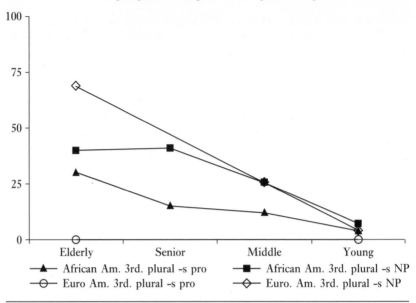

Ethnicity and generation	3rd plural -s pro subjects		3rd plural -s NP subject	
	No./Tot.	% Leveled	No./Tot.	% Leveled
European American				
Elderly (77–94)	0/29	0.0	18/26	69.2
Young (15–27)	0/93	0.0	3/74	4.1
African American				
Elderly (77–102)	22/73	30.1	12/30	40.0
Senior (55–70)	4/27	14.8	9/22	40.9
Middle (32–43)	5/42	11.9	5/33	25.2
Young (14–23)	4/108	3.7	4/55	7.3

VARBRUL Results: Ethnicity/generation and subject type
Input probability = .08
Ethnicity/Generation
  European American
    Elderly = .83; Young = .15
  African American
    Elderly = .87; Senior = .79; Middle = .61; Young = .36
Subject Type:
  Noun Phrase = .68
  Pronoun = .33

Chi square per cell = 1.642

Figure 5.4   Incidence of verbal -*s* with 3rd pl. subject

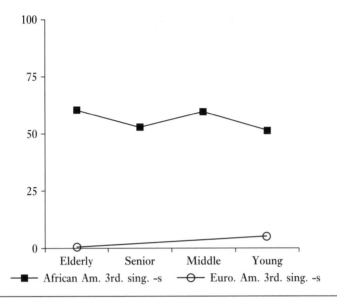

Ethnic and age group	3rd Sg. -s absence	
	No./Tot.	% Absent
European American		
Elderly (77–94)	1/104	1.0
Young (15–27)	6/165	3.6
African American		
Elderly (77–102)	85/140	60.1
Senior (55–70)	39/74	52.7
Middle (32–43)	38/64	59.4
Young (14–23)	120/235	51.1

VARBRUL Results: Generation and ethnicity
Input probability = .24
Ethnicity/Generation
  European American
    Elderly = .03; Young = .11
  African American
    Elderly = .83; Senior = .78; Middle = .83; Young = .77

Chi square per cell = .000

Figure 5.5 Incidence of 3rd sg. -*s* absence in Hyde County

fact, younger Hyde County residents, regardless of ethnicity, rarely use this trait.

Figure 5.5 summarizes the incidence of 3rd sg. -*s* absence. Although a number of structural linguistic constraints, including some environmental

Table 5.1   Summary of Hyde County earlier and contemporary verbal -*s* marking varieties

	Earlier variety		Contemporary variety	
Structural Trait	European American	African American	European American	African American
3rd sg. -*s* absence (e.g., *The dog bark_*)	–	+/–	–	+/–
3rd pl. -*s* marking NP subject (e.g., *The dogs barks*)	+/–	+/–	–	–
3rd pl. -*s* marking Pro subject (e.g., *They barks*)	–	+/–	–	–

phonetic constraints, have been identified in various studies (Poplack and Tagliamonte, 1989, 1991, 1994), we are concerned here with the overall pattern of -*s* marking rather than minor constraints on its variability.

Figure 5.5 demonstrates that 3rd sg -*s* absence differs sharply for European Americans and African Americans in Hyde County and that this difference has apparently persisted for generations. Hyde County African Americans participate in a pattern of optional third singular -*s* absence; in fact, every African American speaker with five or more potential examples of -*s* 3rd sg. in our sample exhibits some 3rd sg. -*s* absence. By contrast, elderly European Americans obligatorily mark 3rd sg. -*s* and younger European American speakers rarely have 3rd -*s* absence. We thus see a significant difference between the communities in this respect.

The pattern of verbal -*s* attachment described in the previous paragraphs obviously shows some alignment, but it also reveals significant differences between the groups. The elderly group of African Americans aligns with elderly European Americans for plural -*s* attachment, but relaxes the noun phrase subject constraint. At the same time, African Americans have maintained and continue to maintain optional -*s* marking for 3rd sg. whereas European American have obligatory -*s* marking. The summary of the similarities and differences for earlier and contemporary Hyde County speech varieties is presented in table 5.1, where + indicates -*s* marking, – indicates no marking, and +/– indicates optional marking.

Table 5.1 indicates that that the pattern of -*s* marking alignment is not straightforward and isomorphic. Earlier African American English in Hyde County apparently had a generalized version of -*s* attachment in which third person forms were marked regardless of number and subject type, while current younger African Americans only had optional -*s* marking for 3rd sg.

The earlier African American variety apparently was constructed by mixing a modified local dialect pattern with a distinct ethnolinguistic pattern apparently brought to the region by the African Americans. The contemporary version of the third person marking remains distinct from European American speakers, but it is reconfigured in that the more generalized version of the optional -*s* marking rule is now restricted to 3rd sg. forms. Both the earlier and the current versions of -*s* attachment for African Americans are distinct from their European American cohorts, but in different ways.

5.5 Conclusion

The morphosyntactic variables examined in this chapter show a selective kind of alignment. The pattern of past tense *weren't* leveling shows African American participation in distinctive Pamlico Sound dialect traits, as does the pattern of verbal -*s* marking with plural verbs. However, the alignment is not isomorphic; the AAVE version of verbal -*s* marking relaxes the noun phrase subject constraint as it restructures subject–verb concord into a generalized optional rule for 3rd person -*s* marking regardless of person. Such a pattern of rule extension is hardly unusual in language contact situations; in fact, it might well be expected as a manifestation of regularization and overgeneralization (Weinreich, 1953; Thomason and Kaufman, 1988; Thomason, forthcoming; Winford, forthcoming).

At the same time, there are a couple of features of AAVE in Hyde County that appear quite disconnected from the earlier and the contemporary version of Pamlico Sound English variety, namely, the optional marking of verbal -*s* on 3rd sg. forms and copula absence. The elderly groups of African Americans and European Americans are clearly distinguished on the basis of these structures, thus supporting Clarke's (1997:253) contention that "Early AAVE, then, appears by no means to simply reflect present-tense concord patterns in the nonstandard white varieties with which they came into contact."

To a large extent, the exclusive dialect features in earlier Hyde County African American speech in Hyde County seem to be additive rather than replacive. Elderly African Americans participated in primary local dialect patterns but they also showed additional structural dialect traits alongside them. This is true not only for the features examined here but for other features as well. For example, elderly African Americans participate in other dialect traits found in Hyde County, such as the absence of plural marking with quantified measure nouns (e.g., *five pound*) and vernacular patterns of irregular verb structure such as bare root (e.g., *Yesterday she give the ducks some food*) and regularized (e.g., *She knowed it*) past tense forms.

But they also show more plural -*s* absence for non-measure nouns (e.g., *two mule_*) and possessive -*s* absence (e.g., *the mule_neck*) along with these patterns, thus remaining ethnolinguistically distinct. To some extent, such a pattern continues to the present, as younger African Americans in Hyde County add newer features of AAVE. Thus, Addy (2000) shows that older African American Hyde County residents rarely use "habitual be" in *be* verb-*ing* constructions while younger African American speakers are acquiring the generalized AAVE habitual use of invariant *be*.

How might we explain the pattern of mixed alignment in which many features of the local variety were congruent while, at the same time, some structures were distinctively maintained? There are several possible explanations. One possibility is that the differences found in AAVE and Pamlico Sound English simply reflect a time lag in language change, and that the dialects of Hyde County African Americans and European Americans actually were identical at an earlier time period. It must be remembered that the time depth for our data only extends to the turn of the twentieth century though the community has existed for almost three centuries. So it is possible that structures such as copula absence and 3rd sg. -*s* absence – distinctive traits among African Americans by the turn of the century – may have been shared at one time by both communities, and that the European American community has now moved away from this pattern while the African American community has been more conservative. This explanation is, however, highly unlikely for an item like copula absence. There is no evidence of copula absence in the donor dialects of English from the British Isles that might be responsible for such a distinctive trait. Furthermore, there is no apparent-time indication that copula absence is a more recent acquisition, as is the case for habitual *be* (Addy, 2000). Instead, it seems most reasonable to conclude that copula absence, like other features found among elderly African Americans in Hyde County, is a long-standing, distinctive structure of African American community.

It also seems unlikely that the communities once shared 3rd sg. -*s* absence and that European Americans acquired 3rd sg. -*s* marking while African Americans resisted this change. Such an explanation is consistent with neither the sociohistorical nor the sociolinguistic context of the European American community in Hyde County. There is simply no evidence that earlier European American English varieties in the area were characterized by 3rd sg. -*s* absence. The fact that Pamlico Sound English retains other relic verbal concord patterns such as 3rd pl. verbal -*s* and *weren't* leveling would lead us to expect vestiges of 3rd sg. -*s* absence as well if, in fact, it had been an integral part of the earlier dialect pattern of European Americans in the area.

Another possibility is that Africans Americans and European Americans shared a common dialect at an earlier stage and that African Americans independently developed structures that set them apart from their European American cohorts over time. Certainly, structures such as the 3rd sg. -*s* and copula absence are vulnerable to independent language change based on natural principles of language change, but these explanations ignore the obvious affinity found between Hyde County African American speech and these AAVE structures found in a host of other communities throughout the United States. It would indeed be highly coincidental for these structures to result from parallel, independent development in Hyde County when they are so widespread in AAVE as it is commonly spoken throughout the USA.

It might also be argued that the distinctive African American structures found in Hyde County African Americans came from the later transmission of external AAVE models. For example, we know that some African Americans from outside the area came there to log timber around the turn of the twentieth century, and that this infusion may have brought distinctive AAVE structures from outside the area. But the wholesale persistence of the traditional Pamlico Sound features alongside the unique AAVE structures does not support this conclusion. If our elderly speakers were modeling their speech on the basis of AAVE norms from outside the area, then why would the local Pamlico Sound features be maintained so robustly by the elderly speakers in our corpus?

The most reasonable conclusion is that the distinctive AAVE features have been present for an extended period of time in Hyde County African American speech, probably the vestige of ethnolinguistic features brought to the area. It is impossible to determine if features such as copula absence and 3rd sg -*s* absence were present at the time that African Americans were first brought to Hyde County from Virginia and Maryland, but the widespread use of these features in the English spoken by blacks in the African diaspora, along with long-term, isolated coexistence with European Americans that resulted in extensive convergence in other dialect traits, suggests that these selected structures may have already been present in the speech of African Americans when they came to Hyde County. Once in Hyde County, contact with European Americans obviously impacted the subsequent development of African Americans' speech, particularly with respect to local phonology (see chapters 6 and 7) but also with respect to some salient morphosyntactic features such as *weren't* leveling. Meanwhile, some deep-seated features not directly in conflict with salient regional dialect features continued to coexist with local dialect norms.

Studies of other isolated situations confirm the conclusion that ethnolinguistic differences can be perpetuated long-term, even when the minority population is overwhelmed by the majority. For example, Wolfram, Hazen, and Tamburro's (1997) study of a single African American family who lived in Ocracoke for over a century shows the persistence of some distinct AAVE morphosyntactic patterns. The resistance of some morphosyntactic features to dialect assimilation is well documented (Rickford, 1985; Wolfram, 1974a; Wolfram et al., 1997; Ash and Myhill, 1986); in this context, the selective perpetuation of a few morphosyntactic features given an overwhelming pattern of local dialect accommodation is especially noteworthy. Ethnolinguistic distinctiveness is obviously sensitive to more than mere demographic statistics.

Although African Americans were a minority population in Hyde County, blacks and whites have maintained concentrated, segregated social communities from the days of slavery to the present (Cecelski, 1994a). Hyde County thus provided a context for maintaining differentiated ethnolinguistic features even in the face of long-term isolation within a larger group characterized by distinctive, localized dialect. We are impressed with the extent of Pamlico Sound regional dialect influence on the historic Hyde County African American community, but we are struck even more by the persistence of some morphosyntactic features that may have marked ethnicity for several centuries in the remote environs of Hyde County.

The other phenomenon that warrants explanation is the current direction of change in Hyde County. Although there are still some vestiges of the localized Pamlico Sound vernacular in the speech of some younger African Americans, particularly with respect to phonology (see chapter 6), the recession of the traditional Pamlico Sound dialect has been rather dramatic among younger speakers. The pattern of overall recession for the traditional dialect is not unlike the decline found in the speech of Pamlico Sound European European Americans (Wolfram, Hazen, and Schilling-Estes, 1999), with a couple of noteworthy exceptions. First of all, African Americans are clearly supplanting the vernacular Pamlico Sound English with core AAVE features whereas European Americans are replacing it with a combination of Southern and Midland vernacular structures (Wolfram and Schilling-Estes, 1997). However, in the case of past tense leveling to *weren't*, younger European American vernacular speakers are actually intensifying the local dialect structure even as younger African Americans relinquish it. So there is also apparent dialect focusing among younger European Americans and that does not include African Americans.

In part, the explanation for the current divergence from the localized variety by African Americans may be attributed to the expanded contact of Hyde County residents with other African American communities, as set forth in chapter 4. The increasing movement of Hyde County African American towards the widespread AAVE norm certainly is due in part to the expanded contacts and increased mobility of Hyde County African Americans with other AAVE-speaking communities. Along with a contact-based explanation, however, we need to consider the role of cultural identity in accounting for the movement toward core AAVE features and away from local norms. Over the past half century, there has been a growing sense of ethnic identity associated with AAVE. This identity is supported through a variety of informal and formal social mechanisms that range from community-based social network norms to stereotypical media projections of African American speech (Lippi-Green, 1997). Although there are varying definitions of the essential linguistic ingredients of this variety (Smitherman, 1994, 1998; Mufwene, 2001), there is growing recognition of this ethnic variety – by European Americans and African Americans alike – that includes a general core of vernacular linguistic structures.

The definition of African American speech, however, is not only found in the adoption of features associated with AAVE; it is also maintained by disassociation with features that are coupled with "white speech" (Ash and Myhill, 1986; Graff et al., 1986). As it has developed in the latter half of the twentieth century, AAVE has become much more of an urban than a rural phenomenon (Bailey and Maynor, 1985a, 1987). In this developing ethnolinguistic milieu, the traditional Pamlico Sound dialect carries strong associations of white, rural speech. For example, younger African American subjects in this study describe the speech of older Hyde County African Americans as "sounding country" and "more white" than the speech of younger African Americans. The strong association of the traditional Pamlico Sound dialect with rural, white speech thus militates against the growing ethnic identity associated with AAVE. Younger speakers who identify strongly with African American culture contra "white culture" would therefore be inclined to change their speech away from the localized regional norm and towards a more generalized and urban version of AAVE. In this change, traditional local morphosyntactic dialect features are lost for the African American population.

Notes

1 Judgments of vernacularity were made on the basis of independent linguistic variables and sociodemographic background information. Speakers in the sample who used negative concord and/or vernacular irregular verb patterns such as participial past tense forms (*I seen it*) or bare root past irregular forms (*Yesterday they come there*) were considered to be vernacular for the composition of this sample.

2 Although the present-day incidence of *were* leveling is extremely low, the generational distribution seems to be significant. As found in Ocracoke and mainland Hyde County, only older speakers show leveling to *were*. As noted above, this pattern suggests that the restructuring of *weren't* on the basis of polarity is intensifying as well as increasing in overall incidence.

3 For African Americans, the youngest group of speakers was excluded from this VARBRUL analysis since they tend to show categorical absence of leveling to *weren't*.

4   Green (1998) rightly notes that distinguishing cases of *is* and *are* for copula absence is confounded by the fact that there is often fairly extensive leveling to *is* in AAVE (e.g., *They is here*). Accordingly, she devised an adjustment formula based on the incidence of *is* leveling in cases where the copula is present. Since we have not considered present tense *is* leveling in this analysis, however, we cannot follow this procedure. Nonetheless, it should be recognized that the levels for *is* absence are probably higher than indicated here due to the incidence of present tense *is* leveling in Hyde County.

5   A third dimension of *-s* marking might be generalized *-s* marking throughout the verbal paradigm. However, in our data, *-s* marking on forms other than third person is so low (less than 5%) that it is not considered in this account.

6

Vocalic Alignment in Hyde County English

Vowels are the aspect of Hyde County English, and of Pamlico Sound English in general, that stands out most prominently in the minds of casual observers. The local pronunciations of /ai/, as in *high tide*, and /au/, as in *about* and *down*, have lent themselves to stereotypes for decades. Popular articles as early as Chater (1926) depicted the "hoi toide" and "abaoht" pronunciations of the Outer Banks. Various scholarly discussions of the speech of Pamlico Sound mention those two sounds and others (Howren, 1962; Jaffe, 1973; Labov, 1991, 1994; Labov et al., 1972; Morgan, 1960; Wolfram, Cheek, and Hammond, 1996; Wolfram, Hazen, and Schilling-Estes, 1999; Wolfram, Hazen, and Tamburro, 1997; Wolfram and Schilling-Estes, 1995, 1996; Wolfram, Schilling-Estes, Hazen, and Craig, 1997; Wolfram, Thomas, and Green 2000; see also Kretzschmar et al., 1994:348–50). Mainland Hyde County shares these forms; some residents interviewed for the NCLLP were well aware of the "hoi toide" stereotype, and Sharpe (1958:894) wrote of the "'Hoide' talk" spoken there. What makes mainland Hyde County especially interesting, however, is that the Pamlico Sound vowel variants cross ethnic boundaries. They typify not only older European Americans in Hyde County, but older African Americans as well. Furthermore, even though the majority of the traditional vowel variants have disappeared among younger speakers, they are subsiding in similar patterns among both European Americans and African Americans. Other studies based on disparate types of data have shown that African American vowels usually differ dramatically from European American vowels within a given community (Bailey and Thomas, 1998; Bernstein, 1993; Dorrill, 1986; Graff et al., 1986; Hall, 1976; Labov and Harris, 1986; Thomas, 1989; Thomas and Bailey, 1998). Accommodation by African Americans to European American vowel variants has been found only a few times (Thomas, [1989] 1993; Anderson, 2002; but see also McDavid, 1958).

6.1 An Overview of Hyde County Vowels

The vowel sounds /ai/ and /au/ are certainly not the only vowels with distinctive variants in Hyde County and the rest of the Pamlico Sound region. Variants of /ɔ/, as in *caught*, and the /er/ sequence, as in *fair*, are also quite salient. Variants of various other vowels have also been cited as being different in the region. Of these vowels, /o/ is of greatest interest for this study. The use of vowel formant plots for illustrating vowel variants has now become commonplace in sociolinguistics, so we present a number of such plots here. All of these plots are based on measurements of vowels in conversational speech except for that in figure 6.4b, for which reading passage speech was used.

Production of these vowel plots involved several steps. Signals were fed into a Kay Computerized Speech Laboratory (CSL), model 4300B, Software Version 5.X, and were digitized at a sampling rate of 10 kHz with 16-bit resolution and Blackman window weighting. They were lowpass filtered at 4 kHz. Pre-emphasis of 6 dB/oct at a factor of 0.85 was applied. Spectrographic displays of the vowels and diphthongs were then created by means of a Fast Fourier Transform, using a frame length of 100 points. From these displays it was determined where to take readings. For monophthongs, a reading was taken for a 20 ms window in the center of the vocoid. For diphthongs, two 20 ms windows were taken: one for the region 25 to 45 ms from the beginning of the diphthong, and the other 45 to 25 ms from the end. The 25 ms buffer was intended to eliminate most of the consonantal transition. For triphthongs, readings were taken as for diphthongs, but a third reading was taken between the other two where the trajectory of the formants changed. The median of linear predictive coding (LPC) values was taken for each 20 ms window. Usually, 12 LPC coefficients were used, but anywhere from 8 to 20 were used if 12 failed to produce a satisfactory reading. The points shown on the plots represent mean values of seven to ten tokens of each vowel. Arrows indicate the gliding of diphthongs. No more than two instances of a single lexical item were used in order to ensure that the phonetic contexts are not badly skewed. Certain phonetic contexts, such as pre-/g/, prenasal, pre-/l/, and pre-/r/ (except where they are shown separately) were avoided because their effects on formant values are particularly strong.

Figures 6.1a–c show vowel plots of three older African Americans, while figures 6.2a–b show vowel plots of two elderly European Americans, all of whom are lifelong residents of mainland Hyde County. In general, their vowel configurations are fairly similar, though each shows individual deviations, especially the speaker whose vowels are depicted in figure 6.1c. In interpreting these plots, it is best not to focus on the exact placement

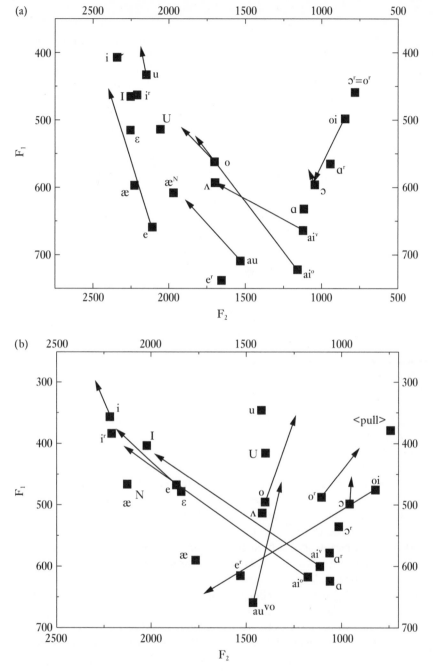

Figure 6.1   Vowel formant plots of three elderly African Americans from Hyde County: (a) a woman born in 1906; (b) a man born in 1910; (c) a woman born in 1909

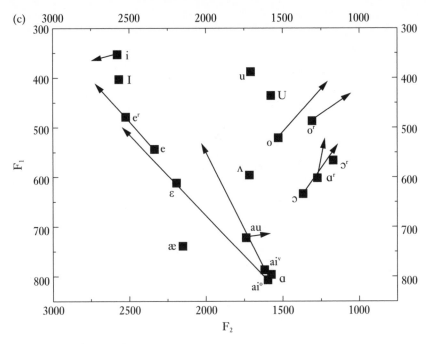

Figure 6.1   Continued

of a vowel, as the mean value can be affected by the phonetic contexts of the words that were measured. Instead, one should focus on the general position of a vowel relative to the rest of the vowel system.

The sound whose local variants are most often noted by outsiders is /ai/. The "hoi toide" stereotype reflects the fact that the traditional local variants show strong glides, instead of the weakening of glides that occurs farther inland, and show nuclei that are backed, often moderately rounded, and perhaps slightly raised. The result is variants such as [ɑe~ɒe~ɑˆe]. All five speakers featured here show strong /ai/ glides. The fact that the glides reach only to [e~ɛ] may make it appear that they are weakened. However, such glides are normally perceived by listeners as full, and Northerners typically show /ai/ glides in that range. For Southerners who show weakening of the glide of /ai/, the glide reaches only as far as [æ]. The nucleus of /ai/ appears to be back of center for all seven speakers, though less so for the speaker in figure 6.1c.[1] Speakers from other parts of the country, both Northerners and Southerners, tend to have this nucleus close to the midline or slightly back of center. For Hyde Countians, the /ai/ nucleus is very close to the nucleus of /ɑ/, as in *cot*. The speaker in figure 6.2a tends toward triphthongization and often produces /ai/ as [ɐɑɛ].

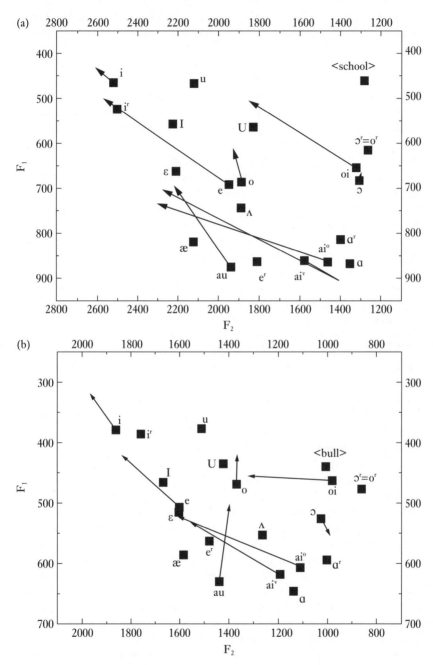

Figure 6.2   Vowel formant plots of two elderly European Americans from Hyde County: (a) a woman born in 1902; (b) a man born in 1910

For /au/, the nucleus is not as fronted as in inland regions. However, it is the glide of /au/ that shows well-marked local variants. In fact, it exhibits some internal variation among older Hyde Countians that seems to represent a diachronic progression. The most distinctive aspect of /au/ is that its glide is fronted; it is the degree of fronting that varies. Some natives, such as the one featured in figure 6.1b, show central glides, as indicated by the rightward tilt of the glide movement of /au/ in this plot. The resulting pronunciation is something like [aɵ~aɢ]. Other speakers, such as the one featured in figure 6.2b, show front, rounded glides, indicated by gliding movement that appears to go nearly straight upward on that plot. This pronunciation is something like [aø~aœ]. Yet other speakers, such as those featured in figures 6.1a and 6.2a, show front, unrounded glides, yielding forms like [ae~aɛ]. Of these variants, [aɵ~aɢ] is surely the oldest and [ae~aɛ] the youngest, though all three occur simultaneously among Hyde Countians born in the early twentieth century. Among all these speakers, /au/ may be realized as monopthongal [a] when its duration is short. The reason is that /au/ typically shows a long onset steady state but no offset steady state, and since shortening of duration leads to truncation of the diphthong, the glide – unprotected by a steady state – is the part that is lost. The speaker featured in figure 6.1c is anomalous. She shows a backward-gliding /au/ that is more typical of inland regions.

The traditional variant of /ɔ/ found around Pamlico Sound is raised and monophthongal, approaching [o], somewhat like the form found in standard British English. It differs noticeably from the upgliding [ɒɔ~ɔo] forms found in inland parts of North Carolina. The speakers featured in figures 6.1a–b and 6.2 show this variant; the formant movement that they show is negligible. The speaker whose vowels are shown in figure 6.1c stands out as the only one with a clearly upgliding form of /ɔ/.

The vowel sound /er/ is strongly lowered for most of these speakers. It is usually realized as [aɹ~æɹ], but it remains quite distinct from /ar/, as in *far*, which is backed and rounded to [ɒɹ]. As usual, the speaker featured in figure 6.1c differs; she shows a nonlowered form, more like [eə].

The vowel sound /o/ is typically fronted in Hyde County. The nucleus is generally shifted to a central position and may be slightly lowered. A central nucleus appears for the speakers whose vowels are plotted in figures 6.1a–b and 6.2. As with /au/, the glide varies. For some speakers, such as the one featured in figures 6.1b, the glide moves backward, resulting in a form approaching [ɜu]. For others, such as those featured in figures 6.1a and 6.2a, the glide moves frontward, so that the diphthong is produced as [ɜü]. Many speakers show intermediate forms.

Among the other vowels, /e/ (as in *bay*), /i/ (as in *bee*), /I/ (as in *bid*), /ɛ/ (as in *bed*), /æ/ (as in *cat*), and /ʌ/ (as in *cut*) are sometimes depicted as showing shifted forms around Pamlico Sound. Kurath and McDavid (1961) found that /e/ showed some lowering of the nucleus, and the speakers shown here do tend to have the nucleus of /e/ very close to that of /ɛ/. Labov (1991, 1994) and Labov et al. (1972) state that the nucleus of /i/ is centralized and the nuclei of /I/ and /ɛ/ are fronted ("peripheralized"). Centralization of /i/ is not apparent for any of the speakers shown here, but some fronting of /I/ and /ɛ/ appears. Lowering of /æ/ toward [a] and fronting of /ʌ/ to a position described as [ɜ] are reported by Howren (1962) and in some of Guy Lowman's informant biographies published in Kretzschmar et al. (1994). The lowered variant of /æ/ does not appear in any of the plots shown here, but slight fronting of /ʌ/ seems to occur in figures 6.1a and 6.2a (though it could be an artifact of the phonetic contexts of the words measured). Lowman's biographical sketches note another aspect of /æ/ that sets the Pamlico Sound region off from inland regions. Inland areas formerly showed an [æɛ] diphthong in such words as *bath, half, pass,* and *calm,* distinct from the [æ] in *bat, bad, hand,* etc. This [æɛ] diphthong is absent in the Pamlico Sound area. Lowman suggested that there is no difference at all between the vowels in *bath* and *bat* around Pamlico Sound, though it is possible that the simple length difference that must have been present at one time (with *bath* longer) may have persisted. All seven of the speakers featured here lack an [æɛ] diphthong in words like *bath.*

For comparison, figures 6.3a and 6.3b show formant plots of two rather typical older natives of inland localities in eastern North Carolina, an African American from Robeson County and a European American from Raleigh.[2] The speaker in figure 6.3a shows a vocalic pattern that is widespread in AAVE. Her /ai/ shows strong glides before voiceless obstruents (marked as *ai⁰* on the plot) but is monophthongal before voiced obstruents (marked as *aiᵛ*), as well as before sonorants and word-finally. Her /au/ glides backward, thus being realized as [aʊ]. Her /ɔ/ shows a strong upglide. Her /o/, as well as her /u/, is back of center. The European American featured in figure 6.3b is similar in showing back-gliding /au/, upgliding /ɔ/, and back-of-center /o/ (though her /au/ is triphthongal). She differs from the speaker in figure 6.3a in that her /au/ and /u/ nuclei are fronted; fronting of these nuclei sets European Americans off from most African Americans in most parts of the South (see Thomas and Bailey, 1998). She also shows an upgliding diphthong in words such as *bath,* denoted by *æ:* on the plot. Her /ai/ shows a clear glide before voiced obstruents, though monophthongal forms are common among inland European Americans.

The vowels of Hyde County English have changed dramatically among the youngest generations. Figures 6.4a and 6.4b are format plots of the vowels of two young natives, the first African American and the second European American. Both have lost several features that typified traditional Hyde County English. The older forms of /ai/ have subsided. The African

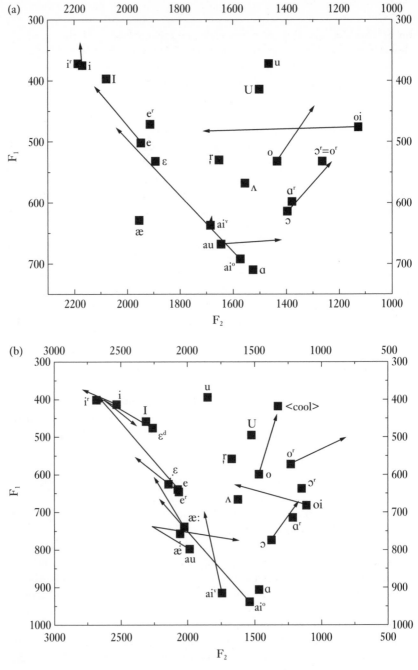

Figure 6.3 Vowel formant plots of representative inland speakers: (a) an African American woman from Robeson County; (b) a European American woman from Raleigh

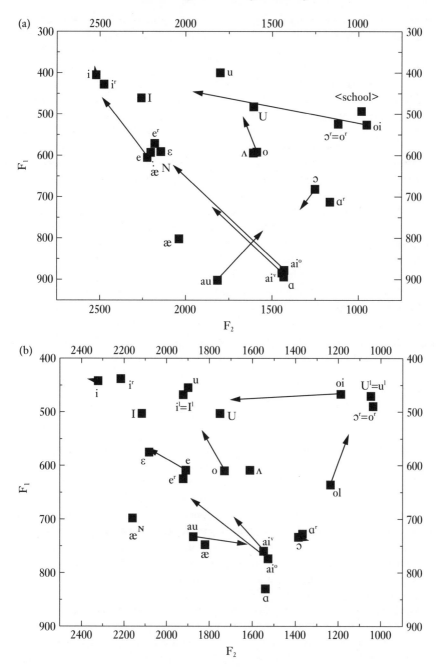

Figure 6.4 Vowel formant plots of young Hyde County natives: (a) an African American woman born in 1981; (b) a European American woman born in 1979

American speaker in figure 6.4a shows a noticeable difference between the glides of /aiᵛ/ and /aiᵒ/, indicating that the glide of /ai/ before voiced obstruents is weakened. The European American speaker shows weakening of the glide before voiceless obstruents, too, and even more weakening before voiced obstruents. She also shows a more fronted nucleus than the older speakers showed. Both speakers have backward-gliding forms of /au/. The shift in /au/ is especially clear for the European American, who produces a form like [æɑ~æɒ]. Neither shows the lowering of /er/ that typifies older speech. The European American does not have /ɔ/ as raised as the older speakers had. Neither young speaker shows upgliding forms of /ɔ/, however, so it appears that /ɔ/ is losing its Pamlico Sound quality only in part.

Certain vowels have not lost their traditional quality. /o/ remains central for the African American in figure 6.4a and has actually become even more fronted for the European American in figure 6.4b. /o/ glides forward – toward [ü] – for both speakers, too. /I/ and /ɛ/ also remain near the periphery. These variants have probably persisted because they have become widespread in inland regions and thus escape notice as anything unusual. However, the retention of central /o/ among young African Americans is noteworthy because nonback variants of /o/ are rare among African Americans in most parts of the United States (Graff et al., 1986; Hall, 1976; Thomas, 1989, 2001a; though see Thomas, [1989] 1993).

6.2 The Historical Background of Hyde County Vowels

The dialect of the Pamlico Sound region is often regarded as a relic area – hence the frequent popular references to "Elizabethan English" spoken in the area. Some of the vocalic features of the dialect, such as /ai/ with strong glides, are obvious cases of relic forms. In other cases, though, it seems clear that internal changes have affected the dialect; the progression of /au/ from [aɵ~aɞ] to [aɵ~aœ] to [ae~aɛ] is one example, and the most extreme form of /ai/, that is, [ɒe], is probably an innovation as well. Attempting to sort out the evidence might allow us to project back to what Hyde County vowels were like in earlier time periods. A picture of earlier Hyde County vowels, in turn, could be compared with what is known about the vowels of earlier forms of AAVE in order to allow reconstruction of the contact situation that led to present-day Hyde County AAVE vowels.

The most extensive evidence on earlier Hyde County English vowels, as well as earlier AAVE vowels, comes from the Linguistic Atlas of the Middle and South Atlantic States (LAMSAS; see Kretzschmar et al., 1994). LAMSAS covered most of the counties of North Carolina, including Hyde

County. The normal practice was to interview two people in each county, one elderly and the other middle-aged, and this protocol was followed in Hyde County. The older informant was a man from near Engelhard who was 82 when interviewed in 1936, with his birthdate thus in 1853 or 1854. The younger informant was a woman from Tiny Oak, just east of Swan Quarter, who was 39 at the time of her interview in 1936, placing her birthdate in 1896 or 1897; she was the same age as the oldest NCLLP speakers and, for that reason, can be compared with them. The data from the older informant represents the only direct information available on Hyde County speech of the mid-nineteenth century. Both of these informants were European American. Seven African Americans from other parts of eastern North Carolina, however, were interviewed for LAMSAS. They, together with African American informants from Virginia and Maryland (from where most North Carolina slaves were initially brought), provide some clues about what the speech of the first slaves in Hyde County may have been like. European American informants from the rest of eastern North Carolina also provide indirect information about earlier European American speech in Hyde County.

Linguistic atlases such as LAMSAS have certain weaknesses, of course. Interpretation of the phonetic transcriptions is often problematic, particularly when different transcribers were involved. This problem is minimized by the fact that all the North Carolina interviews were conducted and transcribed by one person, Guy S. Lowman, Jr. LAMSAS interviews followed a question-and-answer format, and Lowman was especially rigid about avoiding digression into conversation. Consequently, the interviews represent basically citation-form speech, a more formal style than sociolinguists usually prefer. In addition, as numerous critics have pointed out, two speakers cannot possibly provide a full picture of the speech of a community. Nevertheless, when used judiciously and in conjunction with other evidence (such as the NCLLP interviews), LAMSAS data represent a valuable tool in reconstructing the dialectal history of an area.

Because the analysis in the next section concentrates on /ai/, /au/, and /o/, the analysis of LAMSAS evidence presented here focuses on those three sounds as well. Copies of the field records of the two interviews from Hyde County were obtained from the LAMSAS office in Athens, Georgia. Copies of a number of list manuscripts of particular items were also obtained; some of them are now available from the LAMSAS website (http://hyde.park.uga.edu).

The two Hyde County informants differ little from each other in the variants of /ai/ that Lowman recorded. For both, the most common forms were [ɑɪ] and [ɑˑɪ]. Lowman often marked a back shift on the nucleus, yielding [ɑˑɪ] and [ɑˑˑɪ]. Lowman denoted full glides with [ɪ]. This symbol by far appears most often in the Hyde County interviews. Weakened glides,

● 5–6 words
○ 3–4 words
Δ 1–2 words
× no words
(a)

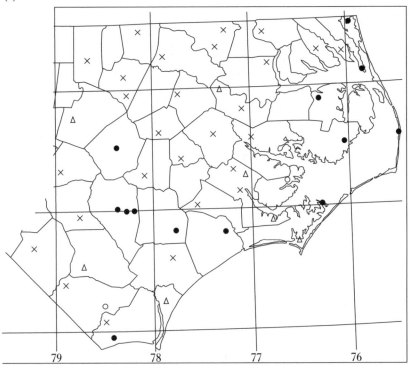

Figure 6.5   Incidence of [ɑɨ~ɑɨ~ɒɨ] in *five, nine, died, died off with, library*, and *Carolina* among eastern North Carolina LAMSAS informants who were born (a) before 1875; (b) 1875 or later

indicated by [ɛ˔] (often in superscript), appear occasionally, and more so for the younger informant. Lowman's usual transcriptions of /ai/ before voiced consonants in inland parts of the South were [a˔ᵋ] and [a˔ᵊ]. His usual depiction of /ai/ in the North was [aɨ]. The Hyde County forms are distinctive, then, in showing both backing of the nucleus and strong glides. These forms also show up in Lowman's records for other Pamlico Sound counties. However, they have a wider distribution in the LAMSAS records. Figures 6.5a and 6.5b show the incidence of [ɑɨ] (disregarding shift and length marks) in six words for eastern North Carolina informants born before 1875 and 1875 or later, respectively. [ɑɨ] is widespread among informants born before 1875, but it is limited almost exclusively

(b)

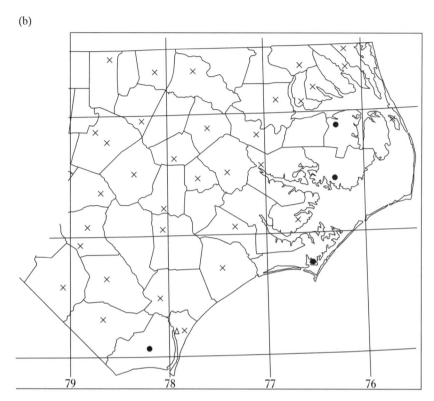

Figure 6.5   Continued

to the Pamlico Sound area among the younger informants. This evidence suggests that the [ɑɪ] form now associated with Pamlico Sound predominated throughout eastern North Carolina at one time. Applying a three-generation S-curve model of linguistic change to the LAMSAS data, one might project that time to be the beginning of the nineteenth century. It should be noted that similar variants still occur among older Lumbees in Robeson County, on the South Carolina border (Schilling-Estes, 2000a). The newer forms with weak glides appear to have been spreading south from Virginia.

In contrast to /ai/, the two Hyde County informants diverge markedly from each other in their production of /au/. Their /au/ nuclei do not differ much: Lowman usually marked both with [æ~æ⁼~æ˅~aˆ]. It is their glides that show the discrepancy. Lowman always marked the older informant's /au/ glides as back [u], usually with an up-shift mark ([uˆ]). For the younger informant, he usually marked the glide as central [ʉ] or occasionally front [ʏ⁼], seldom with an up-shift mark. These transcriptions seem to

● [ʊ^~ɐ^]
× glide with no up-shift mark

Figrure 6.6   The glide of /au/ in *proud (flesh)* among North Carolina LAMSAS
informants, as transcribed by Guy S. Lowman, Jr.

reflect the frontward progression noted earlier. The up-shift mark in the
older informant's records probably indicates moderate fronting, not raising.
The reason is that /u/ tends to have higher F_2 values than /ʊ/ or /o/ in
nearly every dialect, and so a moderately fronted glide would sound more
[u]-like, hence Lowman's notation.[3] At present, fronting of the /au/ glide is
largely restricted to the Pamlico Sound region, though it occurs among the
Lumbees as well; it also occurs before voiceless consonants in areas where
the nucleus is raised in that context, such as eastern Virginia. LAMSAS
records suggest that it was once more widespread. Figure 6.6 shows the
incidence of raised [ʊ^~ɐ^] for the glide of /au/ in *proud* in North
Carolina. Two facts about its distribution are obvious. First, it was essentially restricted to the Coastal Plain. Second, it was found much more widely
in the Coastal Plain than it is today. As with /ai/, then, the Pamlico Sound
region preserves a form of /au/ that probably predominated at one time in
eastern North Carolina.

   The situation for /o/ differs from that of /ai/ and /au/ because the
traditional Pamlico Sound variant spread during the twentieth century instead of receding. In addition, there is reason to suspect that the central
variants that marked the Pamlico Sound dialect are an innovation, not a
retention. The two Hyde County LAMSAS informants provide some clues
here. An analysis of the variants of /o/ (excluding pre-/r/ tokens) in
the two records shows that Lowman marked the nucleus as central [ɵ~ə]
for 44 percent of the older informant's tokens but for 93 percent of the
younger informant's tokens.[4] He marked the nucleus as [ɔ] for 44 percent
of the older informant's tokens but never for the younger informant's.
Two speakers cannot demonstrate that there was a trend, but LAMSAS

provides other evidence. Older informants in nearby Dare, Carteret, and Craven Counties often show [ɔu], while only one younger informant in the area (from Carteret County) does so. In addition, on the Eastern Shore of Chesapeake Bay, which often shows affinities with Pamlico Sound (e.g., in variants of /ai/ and /au/ and in being *r*-ful), central variants of /o/ were absent but [ɔu] did occur (Kurath and McDavid, 1961: maps 20–21).[5] It thus appears that central variants of /o/ supplanted an earlier [ɔu] form with a lowered but unfronted nucleus. With regard to the glide of /o/, the two Hyde County informants suggest another possible trend. Lowman always marked the older informant's /o/ glides as [u] (often with an up-shift mark, suggesting possible fronting), but he frequently marked the younger informant's glides as central [ʉ]. A fronting trend for the glide matches the patterns found in NCLLP data.

LAMSAS data for other vowels also provides some evidence on earlier Hyde County speech. Lowman usually marked /ɔ/ as [ɔˇ] for both Hyde County informants, but he wrote [ɔ] without a shift mark more often for the younger informant, suggesting a possible trend. Both of these variants probably differ little from the forms found in NCLLP recordings, though, and Lowman's indication of the height may have been conservative. Nevertheless, they still indicate raising because Lowman's notation for the unshifted form of /ɔ/ found in other parts of the USA was [ɒ]. Lowman usually marked /e/ as [ɛɨ] and occasionally as [æɨ], indicating that lowering of /e/ is not new. He marked /er/ as [æɚ] or occasionally as [aɚ] for both speakers; Kurath and McDavid (1961) show that this variant was once widespread in the South.

From this historical evidence, we can reconstruct what the vowels of Hyde County European Americans were like around 1800. The distinctiveness of the Pamlico Sound dialect in the twentieth century is due mostly to retentions of older features, with a few internal developments added. In 1800, the speech of most other parts of eastern North Carolina was probably indistinguishable from it. The retentions include /ai/ with a moderately backed nucleus and a strong glide ([ɑe]), /au/ with a moderately fronted glide ([aə] or perhaps [æə]), lowered nuclei of /er/, monophthongal /ɔ/, and monophthongal but probably lengthened [æː] in *bath*, *half*, and so forth. Fronting of /o/ had probably not occurred yet, but moderate lowering of the nuclei of /o/ and /e/ may have. To this configuration may be added some nonvocalic retentions, particularly *r*-fulness and *weren't* leveling. During the nineteenth century, a wave of innovations, such as weakening of /ai/ glides, diphthongization of /ɔ/ and [æː], and *r*-lessness, seem to have swept through North Carolina from Virginia, establishing themselves earliest (probably before 1800; see Stephenson, 1977, on *r*-lessness) along the Virginia border and then percolating southward. Virginia was regarded at the time as a seat of prestige and culture, while North Carolina was viewed as a backwater. Powell (1977:4) notes the saying that "North Carolina is a vale of humility between two mountains of conceit [i.e., Virginia and South Carolina]." Although North Carolinians resented Virginians, they emulated them anyway. However, the innovations did not reach the Pamlico Sound region, which was protected by its isolation.

The available evidence, then, yields a reasonable picture of what the contact dialect for AAVE in Hyde County was like. However, what was earlier Hyde County AAVE itself like? This question is harder to answer because Lowman did not interview any African Americans in Hyde County. LAMSAS records from other counties yield some clues about the earlier AAVE of eastern North Carolina in general, though. Dorrill (1986) analyzed the records of the African American LAMSAS informants from North Carolina (seven informants), Virginia (seven), and Maryland (two), comparing each with a European American from the same vicinity. He examined Lowman's transcriptions of all the vowels in several phonetic contexts. For /ai/, he found few ethnic differences; he noted that African Americans in North Carolina seemed more likely to show [ɐɪ] before voiceless consonants, as was typical of Virginia speech, but this tendency appeared in only three communities. For /au/, African Americans were much less likely than European Americans to show [æʊ] forms with a fronted nucleus, but Dorrill found no apparent trends for the glide. For /o/, and for /e/, /i/, and /u/ as well (but not for /ɔ/), Dorrill found a clear tendency for African Americans to show monophthongs and for European Americans to show diphthongs. Dialectologists (e.g., Kurath and McDavid, 1961) assumed that monophthongal forms of /o/ and /e/ in the South were derived from early Modern English forms. However, Thomas and Bailey (1998) argue that they were due to interference from African languages, noting that the monophthongs occur in European American speech only where there were large slave populations.

In the older AAVE of eastern North Carolina, then, it would appear that the following tendencies were present: /ai/ probably differed little from its realization in European American speech; /au/ had a central or even back nucleus in African American speech. Because the nucleus of /au/ was not fronted, it does not seem likely that the glide was fronted, either. The reconstructed form of /au/ is thus [ao~ɑo], perhaps varying to [ʌu] near Virginia. /o/ was realized as monophthongal [o:], and /e/ similarly as monophthongal [e:]. /ɔ/ probably differed little from its realization in European American speech, which would have been monophthongal. The quality of the nucleus of /er/ is uncertain, but /er/ was most likely *r*-less in African American speech. The slaves who were first brought to Hyde County probably exhibited these variants. By the beginning of the twentieth century, they had largely accommodated to the local European American system, though there were a few holdouts such as the speaker featured in figure

6.1c. As will be shown in the next section for the /o/ glide, more general ethnic differences were possible, too.

6.3 Quantitative Analysis of Hyde County Vowels

The speakers featured in figures 6.1, 6.2, and 6.4 represented some of the vocalic traits that are common in the speech of mainland Hyde County. Not all of the developments can be discerned in the speech of just seven people, however. For this reason, we conducted a more intensive analysis of the vowels of 49 Hyde Countians – 27 African Americans and 22 European Americans – from the NCLLP collection. We limited this analysis to three diphthongs, /ai/, /au/, and /o/, because adequate numbers of tokens could be obtained for them. For each nucleus and glide, a speaker was included only if at least five tokens had been measured. This restriction reduced the impact of phonetic context on the mean values. Mean values for a speaker, not individual tokens, were used for the analyses. The analyses confirmed some expected trends, revealed other subtler trends that were not otherwise apparent, and contradicted a few expectations. We also limited the analysis to two social variables, the ethnicity of the speaker and the year of birth of the speaker. Other factors, such as socioeconomic status, sex/gender, and speaking style, are beyond the scope of our aims.

Acoustic measurements were taken as described earlier for 43 of the 49 speakers. For the other six, the readings were taken with a newer version of CSL, CSL for Windows, Version 2.3. This version does not permit the technique of taking the median value for a window of time, so we took formant readings 35 ms from the beginning and end of each diphthong. The effects of this difference on our analysis are insignificant.

To conduct the quantitative analysis, we had to add one step to the acoustic measurement process: normalization of the vowels. Normalization is necessary because different speakers have different vocal tract sizes and as a result have different formant values for the "same" vowel. Human speech perception normalizes these differences effectively. Numerous mathematical normalization procedures have been developed, but all have different strengths and weaknesses. We required one that would fulfill the following goals: to reduce interspeaker differences, to be unaffected by dialectal differences, and to be simple to use (not requiring measurement of the entire vowel system). One that does so is described by Syrdal and Gopal (1986) and is based on Bark unit differences between formants. The Bark scale is based on human discriminatory abilities, which are better for lower-frequency sounds than for those at higher frequencies (see Zwicker and Terhardt, 1980). Syrdal and Gopal (1986) asserted that listeners base their normalizations on such differences and suggested that they could be used for mathematical normalization as well. They named two scales, the F_1-F_0 and F_3-F_2 Bark differences, as the preferred ones. We found that the F_3-F_2 scale normalized the front/back dimension effectively, but the F_1-F_0 distance was problematic because of variation in F_0. Aging and prosody affect F_0; our sample of speakers covered a wide range of ages, and the tokens were taken from conversational speech, for which prosody could not be controlled. Because of these problems with F_0, we substituted the F_3-F_1 distance for the F_1-F_0 distance. F_3 is relatively stable, so this scale served us well in normalization of the height dimension.[6] The main instability with F_3 is caused by *r*-coloring, but to counteract this factor we excluded post-/*r*/ tokens (such as *right* and *road*) from our calculations for the nuclei.

The analysis of the nucleus of /ai/ produced some of the most surprising results. Figures 6.7a and 6.7b plot the normalized values of the F_3-F_1 and F_3-F_2 dimensions, respectively, for the /ai/ nucleus. Interpretation of the numbers as phonetic transcriptions is complicated. In figure 6.7a, values below about 8.75 indicate low, unrounded nuclei, that is, [ɑ~a], while higher values indicate rounding (to [ɒ]) and/or raising. In figure 6.7b, values below about 4.0 indicate [a], those in the range of about 4.0 to 5.5 indicate a more backed [ɑ~ʌ], and those above about 5.5 indicate a rounded [ɒ]. Linear regression was performed for each ethnicity on each graph. In figure 6.7a the regression line is virtually flat for the European Americans but slopes downward for African Americans. In figure 6.7b, both regression lines are nearly flat. Statistics for independent t-tests on the slopes of these lines and those in subsequent graphs are given in table 6.1. The results show that only the slope for African Americans in figure 6.7a is significant at the $p < .05$ level. Thus younger African Americans are unrounding or lowering the nucleus of /ai/, while younger European Americans are not changing its quality at all. This conclusion seems odd, considering that the general impression among both the populace and scholars is that the nucleus is undergoing fronting. There are various possible explanations, however. First, the "hoi toide" stereotype may have been based on the most extreme [ɒe] forms, which were used by only a minority of older speakers. Second, older generations may have exhibited more prolongation of the nuclear steady state than younger speakers, which would have drawn more attention to the nucleus (though we have not investigated this possibility rigorously). Third, the quality of the nucleus may not have differed much after all between "average" Pamlico Sound pronunciations and inland forms with glide weakening; in fact, Lowman often transcribed inland forms as [ɑˑᵊ], with a backed nucleus. Fourth, listeners may have confused more salient changes in the glide with changes in the nucleus.

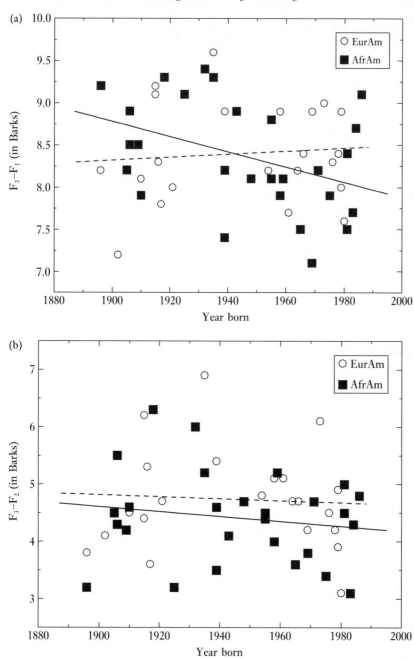

Figure 6.7 Normalized values for the /ai/ nucleus: (a) F_3–F_1 (in Barks);
(b) F_3–F_2 (in Barks)

Table 6.1　Linear regression statistics for figures 6.7–6.13

	Slope	Error	y-int.	Error	R	SD	n	p<
6.7a (Afr.Am.)	−0.0090	0.0041	25.91	8.06	−0.399	0.606	27	0.0393
6.7a (Eur.Am.)	0.0018	0.0045	4.92	8.83	0.088	0.606	22	0.698
6.7b (Afr.Am.)	−0.0043	0.0056	12.78	10.89	−0.152	0.819	27	0.450
6.7b (Eur.Am.)	−0.0018	0.0068	8.20	13.20	−0.059	0.906	22	0.796
6.8a (Afr.Am.)	−0.0176	0.0043	43.46	8.34	−0.657	0.590	24	0.0005
6.8a (Eur.Am.)	−0.0104	0.0048	29.74	9.29	−0.439	0.638	22	0.0409
6.8b (Afr.Am.)	0.0073	0.0044	−11.31	8.60	0.332	0.608	24	0.113
6.8b (Eur.Am.)	0.0148	0.0053	−25.81	10.26	0.530	0.705	22	0.0112
6.9a (Afr.Am.)	−0.0182	0.0077	45.26	14.97	−0.550	0.848	15	0.0339
6.9a (Eur.Am.)	−0.0025	0.0059	14.48	11.41	−0.096	0.724	21	0.680
6.9b (Afr.Am.)	0.0026	0.0064	−2.47	12.52	0.111	0.709	15	0.694
6.9b (Eur.Am.)	0.0081	0.0058	−13.36	11.23	0.307	0.713	21	0.177
6.10a (Afr.Am.)	−0.0016	0.0038	11.10	7.44	−0.092	0.469	22	0.684
6.10a (Eur.Am.)	0.0074	0.0034	−6.06	6.60	0.440	0.453	22	0.0405
6.10b (Afr.Am.)	−0.0025	0.0040	8.10	7.71	−0.139	0.486	22	0.536
6.10b (Eur.Am.)	−0.0024	0.0053	8.01	10.28	−0.102	0.706	22	0.651
6.11a (Afr.Am.)	−0.0110	0.0044	30.44	8.50	−0.490	0.535	22	0.0206
6.11a (Eur.Am.)	−0.0089	0.0042	26.62	8.23	−0.428	0.565	22	0.0472
6.11b (Afr.Am.)	0.0016	0.0056	0.14	10.90	0.064	0.686	22	0.777
6.11b (Eur.Am.)	0.0232	0.0067	−41.57	13.04	0.612	0.895	22	0.0025
6.12a (Afr.Am.)	−0.0085	0.0046	26.25	8.84	−0.414	0.556	19	0.0777
6.12a (Eur.Am.)	−0.0003	0.0042	10.08	8.27	−0.016	0.568	22	0.943
6.12b (Afr.Am.)	−0.0074	0.0058	18.11	11.32	−0.294	0.712	19	0.221
6.12b (Eur.Am.)	0.0015	0.0044	0.55	8.47	0.078	0.581	22	0.729
6.13a (Afr.Am.)	−0.0061	0.0045	22.24	8.72	−0.290	0.575	22	0.190
6.13a (Eur.Am.)	−0.0006	0.0044	11.50	8.51	−0.032	0.584	22	0.889
6.13b (Afr.Am.)	−0.0108	0.0075	24.97	14.48	−0.307	0.954	22	0.165
6.13b (Eur.Am.)	−0.0070	0.0051	16.78	9.93	−0.295	0.682	22	0.183

Such changes in the glide have been rather dramatic in Hyde County. Figures 6.8a and 6.8b show F_3–F_1 and F_3–F_2 plots, respectively, for the glide of /ai/ before voiced obstruents. Figures 6.9a and 6.9b do the same for the glide of /ai/ before voiceless obstruents. These contexts are shown separately because they behave differently in many dialects of English.[7] Both ethnicities show a falling slope in figure 6.8a and a moderately rising slope in figure 6.8b, indicating that the quality of the glide before voiced obstruents is shifting from [e~ɛ] for older speakers to [ɛ~æ~a] for younger speakers. As seen in table 6.1, both slopes in figure 6.8a are significant at the p < .05 level and the slope for European Americans in figure 6.8b is significant, too. Young African Americans and young European Americans are both producing weaker /ai/ glides than their elders, though not necessarily for the

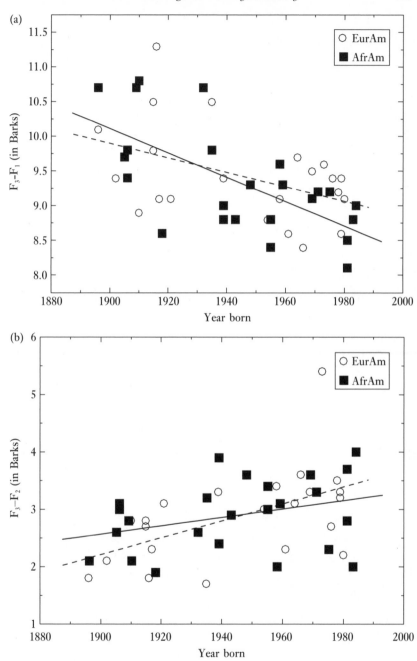

Figure 6.8 Normalized values for the glide of /ai/ before voiced obstruents: (a) F_3–F_1 (in Barks); (b) F_3–F_2 (in Barks)

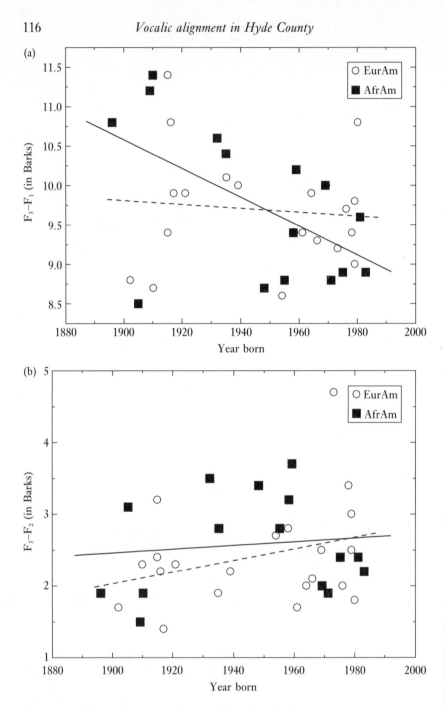

Figure 6.9 Normalized values for the glide of /ai/ before voiceless obstruents: (a) F_3–F_1 (in Barks); (b) F_3–F_2 (in Barks)

same reason. African Americans may be moving closer to the nationwide AAVE norm, for which /ai/ is weak-gliding or monophthongal before voiced obstruents, while European Americans may be moving toward the general Southern norm, which is the same as the AAVE norm.

The results for the glide of /ai/ before voiceless obstruents, shown in figures 6.9a and 6.9b, are puzzling. Only one of the slopes is significantly different from zero: that of F_3–F_1 for African Americans. All of the other regression lines on these two figures are relatively flat, with slopes that are not statistically significant. Thus, while European Americans are maintaining values in the [e~ɛ] range, African Americans seem to be lowering the glide. This trend would appear to contradict the nationwide pattern in which African Americans produce strong /ai/ glides before voiceless obstruents. However, our sample of African Americans for this variable was depleted because we were unable to obtain adequate numbers of tokens of /ai/ in this context from many of the recordings. A larger sample might have yielded different results.

F_3–F_1 and F_3–F_2 plots for the nucleus of /au/ are shown in figures 6.10a and 6.10b. We did not expect to find much change here, except possibly for a shift from [a] to [æ] among European Americans. As it turned out, the only statistically significant trend was among European Americans, but it was in the F_3–F_1 dimension, as seen in figure 6.10a and table 6.1. Younger European Americans are raising the nucleus, with many approaching mid qualities (indicated by values over about 8.75). In figure 6.10b, both ethnicities show a slight fronting trend, indicated by the falling regression lines, but the slopes were not statistically significant. Only a few speakers usually show nuclei with the quality of [æ], with F_3–F_2 values under about 2.75. In figure 6.10a, there appears to be an overall difference in F_3–F_1 values between African Americans and European Americans. An independent t-test confirmed the significance of this difference (t = −2.63, p < 0.012, df = 42). African Americans tend to produce /au/ nuclei in the range of [a], while European Americans – especially younger ones – tend to produce nuclei closer in quality to [ɐ]. The [ɐ] could result from truncation of a form with a target value of [æ]; younger speakers produce glides in the range of [ɒ~ɔ] and [ɐɒ] would be the expected result of truncation of [æɔ].

The glide of /au/ has undergone major changes. As noted in section 6.1, the older fronted realizations of the glide, such as [ɵ~ø~e], are disappearing. Figures 6.11a and 6.11b show F_3–F_1 and F_3–F_2 plots for the /au/ glide for the larger sample of speakers. Both regression lines in figure 6.11a slope downward and the slopes are significant at p < .05, indicating that the glide is being lowered. In figure 6.11b, the regression line for European Americans slopes upward, and the slope is highly significant (see table 6.1), indicative of the backing and rounding of the glide by young European Americans. In fact, there is a stark division between European Americans born before

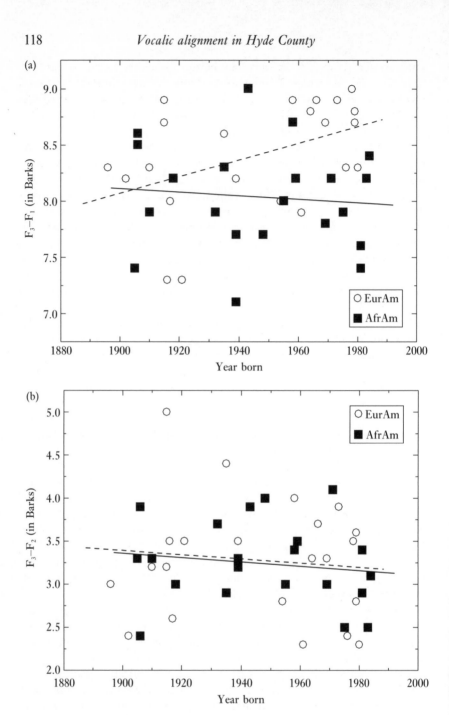

Figure 6.10 Normalized values for the /au/ nucleus: (a) F_3–F_1 (in Barks);
(b) F_3–F_2 (in Barks)

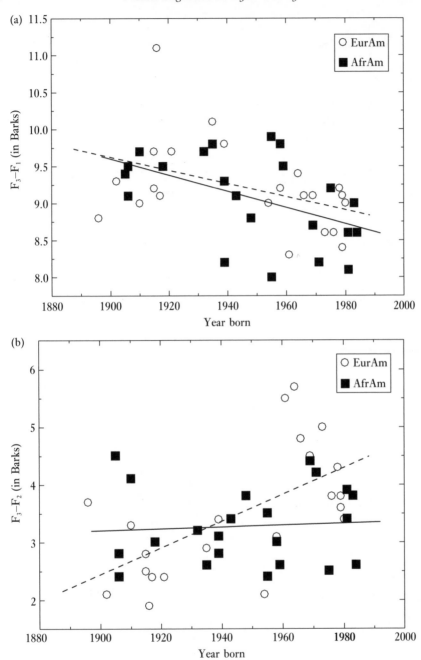

Figure 6.11   Normalized values for the /au/ glide: (a) F_3–F_1 (in Barks); (b) F_3–F_2 (in Barks)

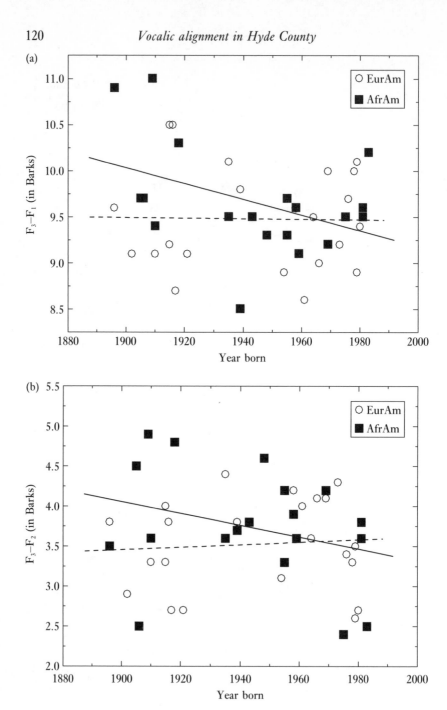

Figure 6.12 Normalized values for the /o/ nucleus: (a) F_3–F_1 (in Barks);
(b) F_3–F_2 (in Barks)

1960, who exhibit fronted /au/ glides, and those born after 1960, who exhibit backed glides. Young European Americans produce /au/ glides in the range of [ɔ~ɒ]. Although the glide of /au/ in American English is usually depicted as [ʊ] or [w], its quality in most dialects, including those of inland parts of North Carolina, actually seems to be closer to [ɔ~ɒ] (see Thomas, 2001). Thus European Americans in Hyde County are simply moving toward inland norms. Among African Americans, conversely, the regression line in figure 6.11b is flat and its slope is not significant. Thus African Americans are lowering the glide but not backing it. Young African Americans produce forms that are monophthongal, that is, [aː], or nearly so, that is, [aɐ].

In contrast to /ai/ and /au/, /o/ is relatively stable in Hyde County speech. Figures 6.12a and 6.12b show F_3–F_1 and F_3–F_2 plots for the /o/ nucleus. In both figures, the regression line for African Americans slopes downward, suggesting that lowering and fronting trends are present, but the slopes are not significant at $p < .05$. Two elderly African Americans who show unusually high nuclei and three speakers who show backed forms seem to be skewing the regression lines. The European Americans show relatively flat lines with nonsignificant slopes in both figures. Both ethnic groups, then, are maintaining a quality of [ɜ~ɤ] for the nucleus. As noted in section 6.1, any form of /o/ that is not backed is highly unusual for African Americans in the United States as a whole. It is unclear why Hyde County African Americans are not moving toward the nationwide AAVE norm for the /o/ nucleus.

Similarly, neither ethnic group is shifting the glide of /o/ significantly. Figures 6.13a and 6.13b show F_3–F_1 and F_3–F_2 plots for the /o/ glide. Three of the four regression lines on these plots slope downward, suggesting lowering of the glide for African Americans and fronting for both groups, but none was statistically significant at $p < .05$. However, another trend is apparent in figure 6.13b: African Americans as a group have greater F_3–F_2 values for the /o/ glide than European Americans. This difference indicates that their glides are more backed than those of European Americans. That is, /o/ tends to glide toward [u] for African Americans but toward [ʉ~ü] for European Americans. An independent t-test showed that the difference was statistically significant ($t = 3.89$, $p < 0.0004$, $df = 42$).

6.4 Conclusions

Table 6.2 summarizes the trends in quality of each of the three diphthongs considered in section 6.3 for each ethnicity. During the twentieth century, European Americans were clearly influenced by inland Southern norms for

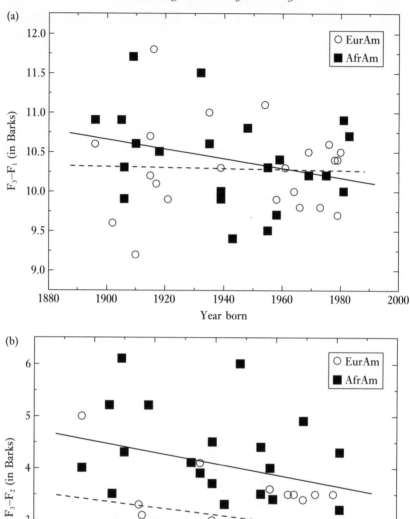

Figure 6.13 Normalized values for the /o/ glide: (a) F_3–F_1 (in Barks);
(b) F_3–F_2 (in Barks)

Table 6.2   General trends in the quality of /ai/, /au/, and /o/

	/ai^v/	/ai^n/	/au/	/o/
African Americans, ca. 1800 (or earlier?)	[ɑe~ɑɛ]	[ɑe~ɑɛ]	[ao~ɑo]	[oː]
European Americans, ca. 1800	[ɑe~ɑɛ]	[ɑe~ɑɛ]	[aɵ~aɢ] (~[æɵ])	[ɔu~ɔʊ]
Older African Americans	[ɑe~ɑɛ] (~[ɒe~ɒɛ])	[ɑe~ɑɛ] (~[ɒe~ɒɛ])	[aɵ~aɢ~aɵ~aœ~ ae~aɛ]	[ɜu]
Older European Americans	[ɑe~ɑɛ] (~[ɒe~ɒɛ])	[ɑe~ɑɛ] (~[ɒe~ɒɛ])	[aɵ~aɢ~aɵ~aœ~ ae~aɛ]	[ɜʊ~ɜü]
Younger African Americans	[ɑɛ~ɑæ~ɑɑ]	[ɑɛ~ɑæ~ɑɑ]	[aː~aɐ]	[ɜu]
Younger European Americans	[ɑɛ~ɑæ~ɑɑ]	[ɑe~ɑɛ]	* [ɐɒ] (~[æɔ])	[ɜʊ~ɜü]

each diphthong. They were losing the distinctive Pamlico Sound variants for /ai/ and /au/ but were retaining fronted /o/, which has spread widely in the South. Nevertheless, it appears that they are returning to a state of conformity with inland areas that they lost during the nineteenth century. Innovations that spread into eastern North Carolina from Virginia did not penetrate the speech of the isolated Pamlico Sound region, which evolved in its own direction for many years. Now that Hyde County is connected to the rest of the state by reliable overland roads, European Americans are returning to the fold.

African Americans show a more chaotic pattern. For /ai/ before voiced obstruents and probably for /au/, they are moving toward nationwide AAVE norms, but they are not doing so for /o/ and they may even be moving away for /ai/ before voiceless obstruents. We lack a principled explanation for this pattern. Perhaps contact with European Americans has helped to maintain fronted /o/ nuclei; the trends for /ai/ and /au/ among African Americans largely mirror those among local European Americans. It is also possible that the nucleus of /o/ simply has not become a marker of African American identity in Hyde County. If detailed analysis of other vowels, such as /ɔ/ and /er/, had been possible, the picture might be clearer.

Other questions remain with regard to African American vowels. Two of the more important questions are when the accommodation of African Americans to European American vowels occurred in the first place and why it happened in Hyde County but not elsewhere. The first question is more difficult to answer. The speakers in the NCLLP survey provide a few clues. The presence of holdout speakers like the one featured in figure 6.1c, as well as the persistence of the difference in /o/ glides, suggest that the accommodation process was in its final stages at the beginning of the twentieth century. The patterns for morphosyntactic variables discussed in chapter 5 and for consonants in chapter 7 indicate the same scenario. The accommodation may have been going on for several generations before that, however. There is no clear evidence for when it started. The second question, which is why the accommodation process happened in Hyde County, has two obvious potential answers. One is that the slaveholdings in Hyde County were, on average, smaller than in more inland areas, as shown in chapter 4. Smaller slaveholdings would have led to more contact between slaves and European Americans. The second possible answer is the lack of in-migration into Hyde County throughout most of its history. This factor would have cut Hyde County African Americans off from African Americans elsewhere, especially after the Civil War, when slave importation ceased.

Notes

1 On the plots, /aiᵛ/ denotes /ai/ before voiceless obstruents, as in *tide* and *five*, while /aiº/ denotes /ai/ before voiceless obstruents, as in *tight* and *knife*. This practice follows Labov et al. (1972) except that they also included word-final and prenasal tokens (as in *tie* and *time*, respectively) under the /aiᵛ/ designation and we have omitted them.

2 The recording of the speaker from Raleigh was provided to us by the Dictionary of American Regional English (DARE). She was DARE informant NC 007.

3 Lowman also used [ʊ] for the /au/ glide in western North Carolina, where it probably indicated an [ə]- or [ɑ]-like value. East Tennessee records from the Linguistic Atlas of the Gulf States often have /au/ as [æə]. Moreover, Lowman's [ʊ] transcriptions from western North Carolina are often accompanied by a down-shift mark, and he apparently did not mark [ʏ] in that part of the state.

4 Lowman used [ɒ] to denote a lower-mid, *central*, rounded vowel, which is more conventionally denoted with [ɔ].

5 Greet (1933) reported that fronted /o/ predominated in the Delmarva Peninsula but his statement is based on the speech of college students born after 1900. The LAMSAS informants were nearly all born before 1900.

6 The use of the names "height" and "front/back" for these dimensions is for convenience. The height and advancement of the ridge of the tongue are certainly not the only factors that affect formant values. Lip rounding and other factors such as pharyngeal expansion do, too.

7 Not only the glide but the nucleus of /ai/ also may differ in its quality depending on the voicing of the following consonant, as is well known. We did not distinguish the two contexts for the nucleus because there do not seem to be any contextual quality differences for the nucleus in Hyde County.

7

Consonantal Alignment in Hyde County English

To most observers of Hyde County speech, the vowel traits discussed in chapter 6 are the salient characteristics that distinguish it from other varieties of English. The iconic status of vowels, however, particularly the diphthongs /ai/ and /au/, hardly means that there are no significant dialect distinctions in consonants or that consonants are not implicated in the ethnolinguistic configuration of Hyde County speech. In this chapter, we consider some of the consonant patterns of Pamlico Sound English, including their historical and current alignment among African Americans and European Americans. Based on the records of interviews with lifetime residents of Hyde County by LAMSAS fieldworker Guy Lowman in 1936 and our own interviews with elderly speakers, we attempt to reconstruct some of the consonant features of earlier Pamlico Sound English. We also attempt to show how some of these features have been changing in the twentieth century. In the first part of the chapter, we summarize the primary diagnostic consonant structures and, where possible, suggest the extent to which European American and African American communities within Hyde County have shared these features. In this profile, we restrict ourselves to qualitative observations for the most part. In the second part of the chapter, we examine a couple of features in quantitative detail, namely, consonant cluster reduction and postvocalic *r* vocalization, to show the more precise patterning of past and present ethnolinguistic alignment. In this way, we will see how Hyde County European American and African American varieties have been maintaining and/or changing their alignment patterns.

7.1 Earlier Hyde County Consonants

Although we may assume that the earlier consonant system of Hyde County was, for the most part, much like that used by Hyde County speakers today, there is evidence that a couple of features have changed from earlier forms or are currently undergoing change. In some cases, there are still vestiges of the earlier traits, but there is also one case, the /w/-/v/ merger, for which there is little or no evidence about its earlier existence based on present-day Hyde County English.

Like many other enclave dialects of American English, Hyde County English retained syllable-onset /h/ in the pronoun *hit* [hIt] for *it* and the negative *hain't* [heInt] for *ain't*. In the history of English, of course, there were a number of pronouns and auxiliaries that originally had syllable-onset /h/. Through a general process starting with the *h* of unstressed forms, however, many of these items eventually deleted *h*. Jespersen (1933) notes:

> *H* tends to disappear in weak forms of pronouns and auxiliary verbs, not only in cases like *it* for *hit*, where the *h* form has totally disappeared, *'em* for old *hem* (not developed from *them*), *I've* for *I have*, *you'd* for *you had*, etc., which are frequently written, but also in the colloquial pronunciations like *if (h)e took (h)is hat; you must (h)ave seen (h)im; we see (h)er every day.* (Jespersen, 1933:57)

Although initial *h* is deleted in unstressed syllables in casual speech styles for most varieties of American English, the *h* is typically still retained when the auxiliary or pronoun is stressed. Thus, *h* must occur in *You may think it's me, but it's really hím*, or *It's hér, not me*. At the same time, other varieties of English have completely lost the *h* in the pronoun *hit* and the auxiliary *hain't*. Earlier Pamlico Sound English, like more insular varieties throughout the United States, including Appalachian English (Wolfram and Christian, 1976), Ozark English (Christian et al., 1989), and Outer Banks English (Wolfram, Hazen, and Schilling-Estes, 1999), still shows remnants of this pattern for *h*. Both older African American and European American speakers in Hyde County do so, although it appears to be more prominent for older African American speakers in our corpus than for corresponding European Americans. Its patterning in Hyde County seems to follow the principle offered in Wolfram and Christian (1976:59), in which "the greater the degree of stress on the pronoun or auxiliary verb form, the greater likelihood that *h* will be retained." Younger speakers of both ethnic groups in Hyde County have abandoned this pattern completely.

One of the noteworthy patterns found in earlier Pamlico Sound English is the merger of /v/ and /w/ in items like *vine* and *wine*. Although this merger has been documented in a number of colonial varieties of English in the North Atlantic (e.g., Bahamas, Bermuda) and elsewhere (Trudgill et al., forthcoming), it is usually not associated with American English dialects. Trudgill et al. (forthcoming) observe that it is not a trait of contemporary British dialects and major varieties of English such as American, Canadian, Australian, New Zealand, and South African English. However, the LAMSAS interview conducted with the Hyde County speaker born in 1858 contains a number of instances in which the voiced labiodental approximant [ʋ] is transcribed for either /v/ or /w/. LAMSAS field records indicate that the Hyde County speaker born in 1858 has [ʋ] for /v/ in initial position (e.g., *victuals, vase, vegetables*), syllable-coda position (e.g., *five, twelve, have*), and intervocalic position (*shivering, clever*); there is also one case in which /v/ is realized as the labiovelar glide [w]. At the same time, /w/ is also realized as [ʋ] in syllable-onset position (e.g., *waistcoat, wound, midwife, woman*) and in intervocalic position (*January, February*). The extent of the merger in terms of phonetic environment and lexical items suggests that it probably was quite robust in this region at one time.

The documentation of /w/-/v/ merger in Coastal North Carolina is corroborated by other LAMSAS observations. LAMSAS fieldworker Guy Lowman noted occasional uses such as *wery* for *very* and *salwage* for *salvage* in two island communities in neighboring Carteret County (Harkers Island and Cedar Island), and also reported that residents from one coastal area (Atlantic) use *w* for *v* "all the time" (Kretzschmar et al., 1994:354). LAMSAS records for the item *wife* show [ʋ] or [β] in several nearby counties: Currituck, Gates, Pasquotank, Martin, Tyrrell, Dare, and Craven. A recently published dialect dictionary compiled by a group of women from Harkers Islanders (Harkers Island United Methodist Women, 1991:300, 306) indicates the /w/-/v/ merger by spelling dialect words such as *aggravated* as *aggawaited* and *voyage* as *wige*. Several older people in our study of Harkers Island (Wolfram, Hazen, and Schilling-Estes, 1999) reported that the merger was used among older speakers when they were growing up.

While there is sufficient documentation to conclude that the /w/-/v/ merger was once characteristic of some coastal regions of North Carolina, we have found little evidence of its preservation. The LAMSAS Hyde County speaker born in 1897 only used the bilabial approximant a few times, limited to syllable-coda position (e.g., *have, give*). In our present Hyde County speech sample, we have only noted a couple of instances for one older African American. Younger African American speakers may have approximant-like [ʋ] in syllable-coda position in items like *five* or *move*, but these cases may be due to a more generalized weakening process restricted to syllable-coda voiced fricatives such as /v/ and [ð] rather than a more expansive *v-w* merger; no cases of merger were found among these speakers in syllable-onset position.

The reversal of the merger that once may have existed in Hyde County is also corroborated in other coastal locales in the Pamlico Sound English area. Thus, our study of contemporary Harkers Island speech (Wolfram et al., 1999) did not indicate that the /w/-/v/ merger was currently in use, and Jaffe (1973) makes no mention of it in her study of Carteret County. We therefore conclude that although /w/-/v/ merger once may have been a prominent dialect trait of Pamlico Sound English, it has reversed. In this respect, it appears to be similar to the situation described for British English by Trudgill et al. (forthcoming), who note that the /w/-/v/ merger was documented earlier in a number of varieties of English, including East Anglia, vernacular London English, Cockney, and dialect regions in the Southwest. However, according to Trudgill et al. (forthcoming), this merger has now subsided to the point that "there are now no native speakers of English anywhere in the British Isles who have this feature." We would speculate that the original merger in Pamlico Sound English may be attributed to the founder dialect of English in the area, and that it has retreated within the last century due to contact influence from outside dialects, including the standard varieties of English used in education.

Another dimension of /w/ is worthy of mention in connection with the past and present development of Pamlico Sound English, namely, the deletion of syllable-onset /w/ in unstressed syllables. In most dialects of English, there are syntactically constrained phonetic conditions under which the initial /w/ of some items can be deleted. Most commonly, this process affects modals such as *will* and *would* as part of contraction process. In Pamlico Sound English, as in some other rural Southern and remnant varieties of English (Wolfram and Christian, 1976; Feagin, 1979), the rule is expanded so that it is possible to get [w] loss with the past tense form *was* in both auxiliary (e.g., *She "uz goin" down there*) and copula functions (e.g., *She 'uz down there*) and with the pronoun *one* in an unstressed syllable (e.g., *young 'un*). It is further possible for the reduced vowel to be deleted completely, so that contracted forms of present tense *is* and past form *was* are homophonous. That is, one might get *She [z] down there* for both *She is down there* and *She was down there*. Similarly, the reduction of *one* may lead to a syllabic nasal as an alternate to the unreduced vowel following voiceless stops ([fɜˑstn̩] "first one"). This process has even become lexicalized in some cases, as in the case of *young 'un* for "child". In Pamlico Sound English, one would not say *young one* to refer to a child, only *young 'un*. The more generalized process of initial /w/ reduction in Pamlico Sound English does not appear to be any different from that described for other rural dialects of Southern American English, and we have not noted any qualitative differences in its ethnolinguistic differentiation. At this point, however, we have not subjected it to quantitative analysis that might reveal some variable differences.

Scanty evidence exists for two very old consonantal variables in Hyde County English. Williams (1989:107) reproduces an eighteenth century will in which *daughter* is spelled *dafter*, reflecting the old [f]/Ø alternation derived from Middle English /x/ after back vowels. Some elderly Hyde County residents reported hearing *sink* pronounced as *zink*, which might represent a survival of the southwestern England voicing of initial voiceless fricatives. A third variable that is more current is the epenthetic [k] after *thing, everything, nothing*, and so forth; it appears for both LAMSAS informants and in the speech of some older and younger speakers in the corpus collected by the NCLLP.

A consonantal variable that has remained diagnostic in American English is postvocalic *r*. Previous studies have shown postvocalic *r*-vocalization to be strongly associated with regional (Kurath and McDavid, 1961; Kretzschmar et al., 1994), social (McDavid, 1948; Labov, 1966; Levine and Crockett, 1966; Wolfram, 1969; Anshen, 1970), and ethnic differentiation (Myhill, 1988; Wolfram, 1994a; Feagin, 1997; Bailey and Thomas, 1998). Although the precise origin of *r*-vocalization in American English is disputed (e.g., Downes, 1998), its regional distribution in the USA was fairly well established by the early 1800s.

The distribution of *r*-lessness is of particular interest in Hyde County, and one of the variables we examine in quantitative detail later in this chapter. At this point, we simply set forth its status in the earlier history of Hyde County. In doing so, we will see why it is of particular interest in terms of the examination of ethnic alignment between European and African Americans over time. In the first place, we should note that virtually all descriptions of AAVE phonology, regardless of region and rural or urban context, describe it as a primarily *r*-less variety (Labov et al., 1968, Wolfram, 1969, Myhill, 1988, Bailey and Thomas, 1998). Even in Northern contexts such as Detroit, Michigan, where a rhotic European American population surrounds the African American community, AAVE remains *r*-less (Wolfram, 1969). Furthermore, this essential *r*-lessness seems to have been a long-standing trait of African American speech in the USA (Feagin, 1990; Bailey and Thomas, 1998).

At the same time, earlier European American English in Hyde County and the Outer Banks was essentially rhotic. Thus, Howren (1962), Jaffe (1973), and Wolfram et al. (1999) note that Outer Banks speech maintained the postvocalic *r* production while adjacent mainland regions such as the Coastal Plain participated in postvocalic *r* vocalization that has typified many regions of the South in the nineteenth and twentieth century (cf. Kurath and McDavid, 1961, map 156; Stephenson, 1977). Records from Kretzschmar et al. (1994) for the two European American informants from Hyde County indicate that they were rhotic "in all positions except finally after [ð]," as in *together* and *mother* (when it is not followed by a vowel)

(Kretzschmar et al. 1994:349). The transcription records for the LAMSAS Hyde County speaker born in 1858 indicate that all 79 cases of words with the canonical shape (C) V(C)-[ð] Cɚ(C) are rhotic, whereas four out of nine cases after [ð] and not followed by a vowel are *r*-less. Transcriptions for the younger LAMSAS speaker (born 1897) show 60 cases following non-[ð] as rhotic, three with "weak" *r*, and one as *r*-less, whereas 7 out of 12 cases after [ð] are *r*-less. LAMSAS fieldworker Guy Lowman, who conducted over 800 interviews for this survey, noted that this peculiar pattern of restricted *r*-lessness after [ð] was "not encountered elsewhere." The patterning of rhoticity and *r*-lessness in Hyde County will be taken up in more detail in our quantitative analysis. At this point, it is sufficient to note that earlier European American Hyde County speech was, for the most part, rhotic, with a restricted, distinctive pattern of *r*-lessness after [ð].

Not only is Hyde County essentially rhotic, but it is also among those rural Southern dialects (Wolfram and Christian, 1976) in which unstressed syllables ending in /o/ (phonetically [oʊ] or [ə]) may be retroflexed as [ɚ], as in *feller* and *yeller* for *fellow* and *yellow*. In fact, the name of one of the towns in the area, *Pantego*, was assumed by a couple of NCLLP fieldworkers to be spelled with a final -*er*, *Panteger*, because it was so commonly pronounced with a final [ɚ] by the Hyde County speakers.

As in many American English dialects, Hyde County has participated in a process in which voiced fricatives before nasals are stopped. The most general version of this process may affect [v], [ð], and [z] across a range of items. LAMSAS records indicate that it was once prevalent in [b] for [v]; for example, all five cases of prenasal [v] in the items *seven*, *seventy*, and *eleven* are realized as [b] for the LAMSAS speaker born in 1858. At the same time, the realization of [d] for [z] in *hasn*'t, *wasn*'t, or *isn*'t was not indicated for this speaker. In contemporary Hyde County speech, stopping for prenasal *z* seems fairly widespread in items such as *wasn*'t, *isn*'t, and *doesn*'t, whereas the prenasal stopping of [v] to a bilabial or labiodental stop appears to be receding. It may well be that the stopping process started with [v] and then generalized to other voiced fricatives. The prenasal stopping of [z] in contracted forms is now a fairly widespread phenomenon in dialects through the United States and is not particularly socially stigmatized. On the other hand, stopping for [v] in *seven* and *eleven* and for [ð] in *heathen* and *breathin*' has become socially marked and stigmatized. The differential social significance of [z] stopping in contracted negative forms as compared with in [v] and [ð] stopping in lexical items such as *seven* and *heathen* may have been responsible for the more recent changes in the pattern.

In syllable-onset position and coda position, Hyde County appears to be much like other rural areas with respect to interdental fricatives. Matarese and Downs (2001) found stopping of /ð/ to [d], as in *dat* for *that*, to be common among African Americans, especially males, of all ages. It was infrequent among older European Americans but common among younger European Americans. Assimilation of /ð/ to a preceding consonant, as in *up pere* for *up there*, occurred sporadically among all age groups and both ethnicities. Stopping of /θ/ to [t], as in *tink* for *think*, was relatively rare and found only among young speakers (of both ethnicities). Substitution of [f] for /θ/, as in *mouf* for *mouth* or *teef* for *teeth*, occurred occasionally, but only among African Americans.

Several phonotactic patterns in Hyde County speech are noteworthy, both in terms of their regional distribution and their ethnic distribution. One trait common to the coastal region for some time now is the use of an alveolar sibilant rather than the palatal production of the sibilant in *shr* clusters, as in *shrimp*, *shrink*, or *shrill*, that is, [sr] instead of [ʃr]. No differentiation in terms of European American and African American speakers has been noted in relation to this pattern. Several other patterns, however, seem to follow an ethnic boundary. The realization of *str* clusters in items such as *street*, *straight*, and *stream* as [skr] – *skreet*, *skraight*, and *skream* respectively – is a quite salient dialect trait with wide distribution among African Americans. Some speakers in our corpus mentioned that this feature was a prime target for "correction" when they attended school and that they were sent to special speech classes (referred to as the "S-K-R Club") to eradicate it. Whereas Wolfram and Fasold (1974:144) report that *skr* correspondences for *str* are found in the speech of younger children and are "given up automatically as the children grow older," this is certainly not the case in Hyde County. It is used by vernacular African American speakers of all ages and apparently has been used for some time now. At the same time, there is no evidence that this production was ever used to any extent by European Americans in Hyde County. In fact, it seems to be one of the features that European Americans in the area use to caricature ethnic differences in the County. Along with this feature is the well-known AAVE pronunciation of *ask* as *aks*, which is also used throughout the AAVE-speaking community. Again, there is no indication that this variant was a part of the past or current speech of European American community, although it has been pointed out that it might be derived from the retention of [ks] as an earlier variant, Old English *acsian*, rather than a more recent metathesis of *sk*.

Finally, we should note some differences in syllable-coda consonant clusters in which the final member of the cluster is a stop that shares voicing with the preceding member of the cluster. That is, a cluster such as *wind*, *west*, or *cold* may be reduced whereas a cluster such as *jump*, *colt*, or *rank* may not be reduced. The patterned production of *wes'* for *west*, *fin'* for *find*, or *col'* for *cold* has been scrutinized in a number of different social and ethnic situations (e.g., Labov et al., 1968; Wolfram, 1969, 1974b, 1980; Fasold, 1972, Guy, 1980; Wolfram et al., 1986; Galindo, 1987; Santa Ana, 1991; Bayley, 1994; Wolfram, Childs, and Torbert, 2000; Torbert, forthcoming).

Whereas all dialects of English reduce clusters to some extent when followed by a consonant (e.g., *bes' pear* for *best pear*), reduction in prevocalic position (e.g., *bes' apple* for *best apple*) is particularly diagnostic of dialect variation and contact history (Wolfram, Childs, and Torbert, 2000). Because of its diagnostic role in ethnolinguistic alignment and its sensitivity to a variety of system-internal and external social factors, we will examine the detailed quantitative distribution of this feature in the next section. At this point, we simply anticipate our discussion by noting that there is evidence that African American speakers in Hyde County have participated in long-term prevocalic consonant cluster reduction that persists today. In contrast, there is no evidence that Hyde County European American speakers have ever participated in a comparable pattern of prevocalic consonant cluster reduction, nor is there any indication that their variety is evolving in this direction. The empirical basis for this assertion will be considered below.

7.2 The Case of Consonant Cluster Reduction

In many respects, the reduction of syllable-coda consonant clusters (CCR) in vernacular English dialects has been the paradigm case of systematic variability in social dialectology. In the earliest formulations of language variation analysis (Labov et al., 1968; Wolfram, 1969; Fasold, 1972), CCR was a critical test case for the examination of ordered structural and nonstructural effects on language variation. Furthermore, the results of the earliest studies have been replicated with remarkable confirmation in a number of different sociolinguistic contexts (e.g., Guy, 1980; Wolfram, 1974b, 1980; Wolfram, Christian, and Hatfield, 1986; Galindo, 1987; Santa Ana, 1991; Bayley, 1994). Although there are still unresolved issues about the phonetic nature of CCR (Browman and Goldstein, 1991; Surprenant and Goldstein, 1998), about some of the minor descriptive details of CCR (Fasold, 1972; Guy, 1980), and about the most adequate explanatory account of the process in which a syllable-coda stop preceded by another consonant with alpha voicing (e.g., *fact*, *cold*, and *find* are licensed for reduction, but not *count* or *colt*) may be variably deleted (Guy, 1991, 1992, 1997; Guy and Boberg, 1997; Santa Ana, 1996), there is widespread agreement on the types of clusters that may be affected by this process. Thus, most analysts agree that syllable-coda *t*, *d*, *k*, or *p* in clusters such as those listed in table 7.1 may be deleted.

As shown in table 7.1, CCR may operate whether the cluster comprises a unitary morpheme, a *monomorphemic* cluster (e.g., *guest*, *mist*), or is created through suffixation and thus represents a *bimorphemic* cluster (e.g., *guessed*, *missed*).

Table 7.1 Inventory of English clusters subject to syllable-coda cluster reduction

Phonetic Cluster	Monomorphemic	Bimorphemic
[st]	*test, post*	*missed, guessed*
[sp]	*wasp, clasp*	
[sk]	*desk, risk*	
[ʃt]		*finished, cashed*
[zd]		*raised, amazed*
[ʒd]		*judged, charged*
[ðd]		*bathed, smoothed*
[ft]	*craft, cleft*	*laughed, stuffed*
[vd]		*loved, paved*
[nd]	*mind, find*	*rained, fanned*
[md]		*named, rammed*
[ld]	*cold, old*	*called, smelled*
[pt]	*apt, adapt*	*rapped, stopped*
[kt]	*act, contact*	*looked, cracked*

Detailed studies of variation in the application of CCR have shown that certain kinds of structural phonetic factors and functional grammatical factors systematically affect the relative incidence of reduction. For example, virtually all studies indicate that CCR is more frequent in monomorphemic than in bimorphemic clusters, and that it is more frequent when the following segment is a consonant rather than a vowel. In the former case, the absence of isolated meaning in one member of the cluster (monomorphemic) favors reduction over clusters in which members of the cluster represent different morphemes (bimorphemic) – a functional explanation; in the latter case, the less natural canonical sequence of a preconsonantal phonetic environment (e.g., *west side* or *find time*) favors CCR over the more natural sequence preceding a vowel (e.g., *west end* or *find out*) – a structural explanation. In addition to the structural and functional linguistic explanations, an array of social variables have been shown to correlate with the relative frequency of CCR in a systematic way. A summary of the various systematic constraints found in representative studies of CCR such as Labov et al. (1968), Labov (1972a), Fasold (1972), Wolfram (1969, 1974b, 1980, 1984), Wolfram et al. (1986), Guy (1980), Galindo (1987), Bayley (1994), and Santa Ana (1996) is given in table 7.2.

Table 7.2 shows that the canonical form of the following segment, the phonetic composition of the cluster in terms of a sonorancy hierarchy, the prosodic status of the syllable, and the grammatical function of the final stop in the cluster may all constrain the relative rate of CCR, as well as independent social variables such as status, ethnicity, style, and language

Table 7.2   Summary of variable effects on cluster reduction

Following context
preobstruent > presonorant > prevocalic
e.g. [bɛs kɪd] 'bes' kid' > [bɛs nem] 'bes' name' > [bɛs æt] 'best at'

Preceding context
nasal > lateral > sibilant > stop
e.g. [wɪn] *win'* > [waɫl] *wil'* > [wɛs] *wes'* > [æk] *ac'*

Stress
[−stress] > [+stress]
e.g. [kántræk] *cóntrac'* > [kəntræk] *contrák'*

Morphological marking
monomorphemic > redundant bimorphemic > bimorphemic
[gɛs] *gues'* > [slɛp] *slep'* > [gɛs] *guess'*

Social factors
lower social status > higher social status
casual style > formal style
AAVE > Anglo vernacular varieties
Hispanicized Vernacular English > Anglo vernacular varieties
Vietnamese English > Anglo vernacular varieties

background. Perhaps most noteworthy is the fact that there has been such impressive replication of the various systematic effects on the relative incidence of CCR, leaving little dispute about the kinds of systematic effects on its variability.

One of the obvious influences on the relative incidence of CCR is language contact history. Varieties of English influenced by phonological transfer from languages not having syllable-coda consonant clusters tend to have significantly higher levels of CCR than other varieties. In Wolfram, Childs, and Torbert (2000), we hypothesized that although all varieties of English have substantive levels of CCR in preconsonantal position (e.g., *west side* or *find time*), significant levels of prevocalic CCR seem to be primarily characteristic of varieties influenced historically by phonological transfer from language contact situations rather than through independent, internal linguistic change. For example, in a summary of CCR in representative ethnic and social varieties of English, Wolfram and Schilling-Estes (1998) show that higher levels of prevocalic CCR are found in Hispanic English varieties (Wolfram, 1974b; Galindo, 1987; Santa Ana, 1991), Vietnamese English (Wolfram et al., 1986), and Puebloan Native American English (Wolfram, 1980), all of which involve heritage languages that do not have syllable-coda consonant clusters. Therefore, Wolfram, Thomas, and Green et al (2000) hypothesized that the higher levels of prevocalic CCR observed in Vietnamese English, Hispanic English, and Native American English are probably attributable to native language influence – either direct language transfer in cases of speakers who have learned English as a second language, or to substratal influence passed on to subsequent generations as a defining trait of a social or ethnic variety.

What does CCR reveal about the past and present alignment of African American and European American varieties of English in Hyde County? Is there evidence that these varieties have accommodated to each other with respect to CCR, or has there been a persistent ethnolinguistic divide? What do these data suggest about the historical and current sociolinguistic relationship of these speech communities? In the next section, we examine the empirical evidence for the historical status of CCR in Hyde County and the current trajectory of change, based on an extensive analysis of CCR by Childs (2000) and Wolfram, Childs, and Torbert (2000).

7.2.1 The patterning of cluster reduction

To consider the historic and current role of CCR in the ethnolinguistic alignment of European Americans and African Americans in Hyde County, we compare the incidence of CCR in the speech of 32 different African-American speakers evenly divided among four different generational groups: elderly, born from 1896 to 1917; senior, born from 1927 to 1942; middle, born from 1953 to 1962; and young, born from 1972 to 1984. Four men and four women were selected within each generational group. A baseline European American group of 16 speakers was also selected, eight representing elderly speakers born between the 1902–1916, and eight young speakers born between 1970–1983.[1] We assume that the elderly speakers will give a picture of what the dialect may have been like early in the twentieth century and that the youngest group of speakers will provide a picture of the current state of the dialect.

The analysis of CCR follows fairly well-established procedures for data extraction and analysis. First, all cases of clusters meeting the specifications for the operation of CCR were extracted in terms of actual cases of reduction in relation to all cases where it might have occurred (Wolfram, 1993). That is, all cases of syllable-coda stops preceded by a consonant with alpha voicing were considered as potential candidates for deletion. Type–token relations were controlled in that no more than five cases of one word in a particular environment were tabulated. In addition, items subject to lexicalized reduction – in particular, the conjunction *and* and the unstressed adverb *just* – were excluded from the tabulation. Descriptive statistics were compiled for various social groups of speakers and the VARBRUL statistical

Table 7.3 Consonant cluster reduction in Hyde County African American speech

| | Monomorphemic | | | | | | Bimorphemic | | | | | |
| | Prevocalic | | Prepausal | | Preconsonantal | | Prevocalic | | Prepausal | | Preconsonantal | |
Age/Ethnic Group	% Red	N	% Red	N	% Red	N	% Red	N	% Red	N	% Red	N
European American												
Elderly	10.3	68	35.1	37	53.3	107	4.0	101	3.1	28	46.6	73
Young	9.3	75	30.0	33	64.1	103	4.4	68	10.0	20	31.8	44
African American												
Elderly	52.1	69	78.3	60	81.4	108	29.1	48	72.7	11	85.5	69
Senior	55.1	49	69.5	23	72.2	83	22.4	49	66.6	15	85.0	40
Middle	55.0	80	85.0	27	89.5	134	36.7	79	100.0	10	77.1	49
Young	44.4	54	83.0	36	83.5	85	26.9	26	80.0	5	78.9	19

VARBRUL analysis

Input probability = .53

Ethnicity/Generation
European American
    Elderly = .23; Young = .25
African American
    Elderly = .67; Senior = .61; Middle = .73; Young = 65.
Cluster Status: monomorphemic = .56; bimorphemic = .40
Following Environment: prevocalic = .24; pause = .55; preconsonantal = .72

Total chi square = 51.711; Chi square per cell = 1.436

procedure was applied to the data in order to determine the relative effect of various factor groups on the incidence of CCR.

Table 7.3 gives the raw figures and percentages for the incidence of CCR for the four generational groups of Hyde County African Americans and the two baseline European American groups. Figures are divided into monomorphemic and bimorphemic clusters in three different phonetic environments: preconsonantal, prepausal, and prevocalic.[2] While other linguistic variables might have been included in the analysis, morphemic status and following phonetic environment have proved to be the primary variable effects on CCR in previous analyses. The results of the VARBRUL analysis showing the systematic effects of the different linguistic and social factors are given in table 7.3.

Table 7.3 indicates that CCR is a robust process in the Hyde County African American community, in contrast to the European American community where it is limited largely to preconsonantal contexts. There is a significant difference between European Americans and African Americans in Hyde County regardless of age, but there is little difference across the different generations of African Americans. At the same time, we see the strong favoring effect of CCR in monomorphemic clusters versus bimorphemic clusters and the favoring effect of prepausal and preconsonantal environments over prevocalic contexts. These are, of course, the same ordered effects replicated in virtually all studies of CCR (see table 7.2).

On one level, it may not seem unusual for an African American community to show substantive levels of prevocalic cluster reduction as indicated in table 7.3. CCR is a characteristic trait of AAVE documented in a variety of settings throughout the United States (e.g., Labov et al., 1968; Wolfram, 1969; Guy, 1980; Bailey and Thomas, 1998). But it is, in fact, quite striking when we consider the historic alignment of the vowels for Hyde County European Americans and African Americans discussed in chapter 6; our analysis there showed that elderly African Americans and Anglo Americans are quite congruent in their vowel configuration. CCR differs: there is no indication that Hyde County African Americans and European Americans have ever been aligned with respect to CCR in the diagnostic prevocalic environment. Figure 7.1 shows the incidence of prevocalic CCR compared for the elderly and young European American groups and the four age groups of African Americans in prevocalic environments. Figures for both monomorphemic and bimorphemic clusters are included.

Figure 7.1 suggests that prevocalic CCR has been a stable process in Hyde County AAVE but negligible for European American speakers in the past and present. The consistently high levels of usage across the generations of African Americans hardly appear to be a recent innovation. As noted, older speakers align with the cohort European American community with respect to a number of other phonological traits; furthermore,

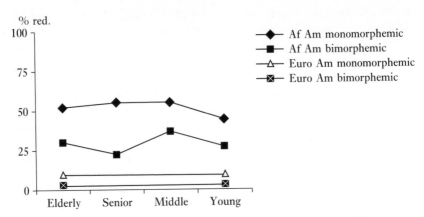

Figure 7.1 Prevocalic CCR for Hyde County African Americans and European Americans

older speakers do not manifest the adoption of AAVE grammatical features now considered to be innovations of the twentieth century, such as habitual *be* (Bailey and Maynor, 1987; Rickford, 1999). Given the age-related distribution of other features, it is unlikely that CCR would be a more recent innovation within African American speech in Hyde County. The evidence clearly points to long-term retention of this phonological process.

7.2.2 Explaining consonant cluster reduction patterns in Hyde County

How do we explain the long-standing, persistent differentiation of European American and African American speech communities in Hyde County with respect to CCR? And how do we reconcile this misalignment with our comparison of other phonological features – in particular, the vowels that show a pattern of historical accommodation? The persistent ethnolinguistic divide in CCR is not only supported by the figures for different age groups of speakers in figure 7.1; there is also evidence from the earlier LAMSAS speakers that this was the case in the mid-1800s. For example, the European American LAMSAS speaker born in 1858 has 21 cases of final consonant clusters meeting the conditions for potential CCR as specified in figure 7.1. None of the cases in prevocalic or prepausal position was transcribed as reduced. There is simply no evidence that earlier European Americans in Hyde County had CCR in prevocalic or prepausal position to any extent. Possible accommodation of an earlier European American trait must clearly be dismissed as a possible reason for CCR among African Americans in Hyde County.

As Wolfram, Childs, and Torbert (2000) hypothesize, extensive prevocalic CCR tends to be a trait of historical contact situation involving transfer from a language not having syllable-coda clusters. This does not mean that CCR cannot result from internal language change, as Wolfram et al. (2000) seem to imply; only that it is more likely to result from a language contact situation when it is found in prevocalic position. We would suggest that historical language transfer is the reason for CCR in Hyde County African American speech, though the transfer is of course now a substratal effect rather than a case of recent phonological transfer. African Americans probably brought this trait with them originally when they were brought to Hyde County – a holdover from the original contact situation involving West African languages. With a few exceptions (Holm, 1988:108), West African languages do not have syllable-coda clusters (Migeod, 1911: 13; Welmers, 1973), and early forms of Africanized English probably exhibited cluster reduction as a product of fossilized language transfer. Furthermore, the developing creoles of West Africa and the Caribbean (Holm, 1988) adopted extensive CCR as a typological trait so that earlier contact with creole speakers (Winford, 1997; Rickford, 1999) may have reinforced the pattern. It is quite reasonable that this early pattern simply was retained as a persistent substratal effect that differentiated African American speech from other varieties of English. Wherever it is spoken in the USA, AAVE seems to distinguish itself from cohort European American varieties in its level of CCR – especially for prevocalic clusters and to a lesser extent for prepausal environments as well (e.g., Labov et al., 1968, Wolfram, 1969; Fasold, 1972; Rickford, 1999). In this respect, Hyde County African American speech simply aligns – and always has – with other varieties of AAVE rather than with the local dialect. If it were a more recently developing trait we would expect it to show increased frequency for younger speakers; we would also expect it to parallel other, more recent, changes in AAVE that are apparently innovations, such as the rise of grammatical features like habitual *be* (Bailey and Maynor, 1987; Dayton, 1996; Labov, 1998).

While we maintain that CCR is due to a persistent substratal effect from West African languages that may have been reinforced through contact with earlier West African and Caribbean Creoles, this is different from maintaining that CCR is evidence for the creole hypothesis as discussed in chapter 2. It is quite possible for influence from phonological transfer to take place quite independently from the adoption of a full-fledged pidgin or creole in the USA. There have been numerous cases in the formation of American English varieties where other languages influenced structures without developing into a pidgin or creole – for example, Minnesota English, Chicano/a English, and so forth. CCR seems to have been such a case, and its persistence hardly implies the development of an expansive creole.

The second question concerns the status of CCR in relation to other phonological features of Hyde County speech. Why would it not accommodate to the Hyde County European American pattern, as did so many features of the vowel system discussed in chapter 6? The possible answer here may relate in part to its level of phonological organization. Phonotactic patterns may be more resistant to accommodation than segmental, paradigmatic patterns (Sabino, 1993, 1994a). Note, for example, that some of the most prominent differences between African Americans and European Americans in Hyde County set forth in section 7.1 involve phonotactic structures. We take up this matter in more detail in section 7.4; for the present discussion it is sufficient to note that there may be a structural linguistic as well as a social reason for the long-standing differentiation of CCR in Hyde County.

7.3 The Case of Postvocalic *r* Vocalization

As mentioned previously, the status of postvocalic *r*-vocalization may be one of the best phonological indicators of the past and current alignment of Hyde County African American and European American speech. Historically, Hyde County was a rhotic region contiguous to the *r*-less inland areas of the Coastal Plain, with the notable exception of *r* when it is after /ð/ and followed by a nonvocalic segment (i.e., a consonant or utterance-final position). This peculiar pattern of post-/ð/ *r*-lessness seems to set apart Hyde County from other dialects of the mid-Atlantic region and other dialects of American English in general (Kretzschmar et al., 1994:349). By contrast, practically all descriptive accounts of African American English in the past and present describe it as a prototypical example of a postvocalic *r*-less dialect (Labov et al., 1968; Wolfram, 1969, 1994b; Bailey and Thomas, 1998). In fact, Feagin (1997) contends that African American English *r*-lessness in the South historically was so extensive that it was probably influential in the adoption and maintenance of *r*-lessness among Southern European American English speakers.

Levine and Crockett (1966), Anshen (1970), Myhill (1988), and Feagin (1990) note that contemporary Southern European American speech is currently transitioning from a primarily *r*-less area to a rhotic region, a change not paralleled in the African American community. In light of the general history of *r*-lessness in the South and the local history of *r* in Hyde County, the detailed examination of this variable may provide essential insight into past and current patterns of consonantal alignment among Hyde County African Americans and European Americans.

7.3.1 The patterning of postvocalic r-lessness

To determine the extent to which African Americans and European Americans have shared postvocalic *r* patterns, we extracted approximately 100 tokens of postvocalic *r* from conversational interviews with 34 African Americans born between 1896 and 1983 and from 13 European Americans born between 1902 and 1983. The African Americans were selected to represent four generations of speakers at the time of the interview (elderly = 77–91; senior = 55–70; middle = 32–43; young = 14–23), with the largest groups of speakers representing the oldest (11 speakers) and the youngest groups (14 speakers). The European American sample was limited to a baseline of six elderly speakers (between the ages of 80 and 94 at the time of their interview) and seven young speakers (between the ages of 15 and 27 at the time of their interview) in order to represent the most distinctive baseline generations in apparent time. For each occurrence of postvocalic *r*, we impressionistically classified it simply as constricted or vocalized.[3]

Several types of *r* were differentiated in the tabulation, following the traditional delimitation (Feagin, 1990; Bailey and Thomas, 1998). These include: (1) nuclear stressed position as in *sir* or *hurt*; (2) syllable-coda, word-stress position as in *car* or *port*; and (3) unstressed nuclear syllable position as in *mother* or *letter*. In addition, the following phonetic context was distinguished in terms of prevocalic versus nonprevocalic (i.e., consonant or utterance-final) phonetic contexts. Table 7.4 gives the raw figures and percentages of *r*-lessness for the three *r* types. For syllable-coda stressed and for unstressed *r*, the following phonetic environment is also distinguished. Following table 7.4 are VARBRUL analyses in terms of two linguistic factor groups: *r* type and following phonetic environment. Social factors included generation and ethnicity, but the VARBRUL analyses for African Americans and European Americans had to be computed separately because of interactive effects between ethnicity and independent linguistic factors. Figure 7.2 charts the incidence of *r*-vocalization in terms of age and the three types of *r* for the two ethnic groups.

Table 7.4 and figure 7.2 clearly indicate the significance of both linguistic and social constraints on the incidence of *r*-lessness in Hyde County. The VARBRUL analyses indicate further that *r*-vocalization operates quite differently for the European American and African American communities. The initial run of VARBRUL, which combined independent linguistic and social factors for both ethnic groups, had to be rejected because of interactive effects among ethnicity, age, and the independent linguistic variables. Thus separate analyses for the African American and the European American

Table 7.4 R-vocalization: Hyde County African Americans and European Americans

| | Syllable Coda | | | | | | Unstressed | | | | | Total | |
| | Nuclear | | Prevocalic | | Non–PreV | | Prevocalic | | Non–PreV | | | | |
Age/Ethnic Group	% Voc	No./Tot.	% Voc	No./Tot.	% Voc	No./Tot.	% Voc	No./Tot.	% Voc	No./Tot.	% Voc	No./Tot.
European American												
Elderly	0.0	0/72	1.4	1/74	3.1	9/291	23.8	5/21	27.4	49/179	10.0	64/637
Young	0.0	0/82	0.0	0/49	2.9	10/341	0.0	0/23	8.6	14/162	3.7	24/657
African American												
Elderly	19.1	31/162	26.7	16/60	25.6	102/399	55.6	25/45	54.0	157/291	34.6	331/957
Senior	4.2	2/48	6.7	2/30	19.3	32/166	50.0	11/22	65.5	76/116	32.2	123/382
Middle	17.9	14/78	21.6	8/37	29.9	53/177	44.4	12/27	74.8	92/123	40.5	179/442
Young	32.5	106/326	50.5	46/91	42.3	247/584	62.0	31/50	64.3	202/314	46.3	632/1365

VARBRUL Results

European American
  Input probability = .05
Generation
  elderly = .63; young = .37
R type
  nuclear = *; syllable-coda = .34;
  unstressed = .79
Following environment
  consonant = .53; vowel = .34

African American
  Input probability = .41
Generation
  elderly = .41; middle = .48; young = .57
R type
  nuclear = .33; syllable-coda = .44;
  unstressed = .71

Total Chi square = 9.931; Chi square per cell = 1.241   Total Chi square = 13.941; Chi square per cell = 1.549
* = knockout constraint

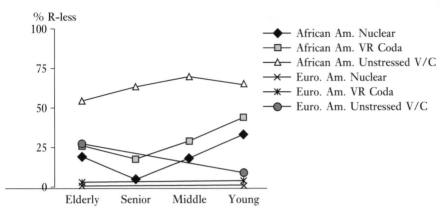

Figure 7.2 Hyde County *r* vocalization, by ethnicity, age, and *r* type

communities of speakers had to be conducted in terms of independent linguistic factors.

The analysis shows important differences in the overall incidence of *r*-lessness (European American input probability = .05; African American = .41), as well as differences in the independent linguistics and social factors. For the European American community, *r*-vocalization is limited primarily to the unstressed syllables; in fact, there is no *r*-vocalization in nuclear stressed syllables at all and very little in syllable-coda stressed syllables. Furthermore, the limited *r*-vocalization once found for European American speakers is now receding even further.

The picture of the African American community is quite different, in terms of both independent linguistic constraints and age. African Americans and European Americans alike show a consistent effect based on syllable stress (unstressed > stressed syllable-coda), but there is a difference between the groups in terms of the following phonetic environment. European Americans show a consistent effect in which following nonvocalic phonetic environment strongly favors *r*-lessness over prevocalic contexts; however, there is no parallel effect for the African American sample of speakers. Consequently, the effect of the following phonetic environment was thrown out in the VARBRUL step-down procedure for African Americans.

The trajectory of change also is quite different for the European American and African American community. While the European American community is moving away from *r*-lessness completely, even in unstressed syllables, the African American community is moving towards more general *r*-lessness, with substantive changes taking place for syllable-coda stressed syllables and even nuclear *r* among younger groups of speakers. The exception to this pattern is the senior group of African Americans; this

Table 7.5   R-vocalization variation within age groups

Age/ethnic group	Mean %	Standard deviation	Range of variation
European American			
Elderly	10.1	7.5	19.2 (2.9–22.1)
Young	3.7	2.8	8.7 (0–8.7)
African American			
Elderly	40.3	31.0	84.9 (8.7–96.9)
Young	48.2	12.1	43 (22–65)

group shows slightly reduced levels of overall *r*-lessness compared with the elderly group. In the VARBRUL analysis, a significant goodness of fit for VARBRUL could only be obtained by eliminating this group from the application.[4] The positioning of the senior generation in terms of language change will be taken up more fully in chapter 9, when we discuss the overall trajectory of language change. At this point, it is sufficient to note that they show a recession in *r*-vocalization, which is reversed by the middle and younger generations of African American speakers. The youngest group of African Americans is clearly moving towards more heightened overall *r*-lessness in comparison with other age groups. So we see quite different paths of change for *r* in the two ethnic communities: European Americans are receding from earlier, limited use of *r*-vocalization whereas African Americans are moving towards more extensive *r*-vocalization.

The figures in table 7.4 and figure 7.2, following the conventional practice in VARBRUL-based variation analysis, are based on aggregate sums for each generational group; therefore, they do not take into account the level of *r*-lessness for individual speakers. However, as we discuss more fully in chapter 9, such aggregate figures can sometimes obscure individual differences that may give insight into the dynamics of change and variation within a community. The patterns of ingroup variation for different generations of speakers seem to be particularly instructive for the differential alignment of *r*-lessness over time. To give an indication of ingroup variation, we provide in table 7.5 the means, the standard deviations, and the range of variation for overall *r*-lessness for the elderly and young European American and the elderly and young African American speakers.

Table 7.5 depicts important differences about in-group variation based on age and ethnicity. For example, both elderly and young groups of European

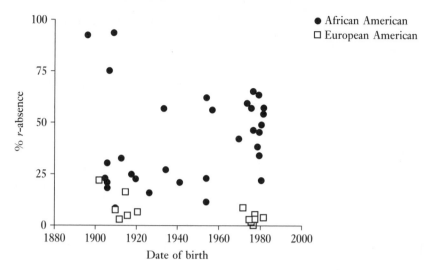

Figure 7.3   Scatterplot of *r*-vocalization, by date of birth and overall *r*-vocalization

American speakers show a limited range of *r*-lessness, unlike the African American groups. The elderly African American speakers, in particular, show a wide range of variation, from 8.7–96.9 percent *r*-lessness, and a high standard deviation (31.0%). Younger African Americans, however, show a narrower range (22–65%), with a much lower standard deviation (12.1%). The degree of individual variation over apparent time is best displayed in a scatterplot (figure 7.3) in which the *x* axis represents each speaker's date of birth and the *y* axis represents the overall percentage of *r*-lessness.

It seems clear from the scatterplot in figure 7.3 that the African American speech community in Hyde County is following a course of change quite different from that of the European American community. Elderly African Americans show great individual variation, from those who show very high levels of overall *r*-lessness to those who seem to align with the overall rhotic pattern exhibited by elderly cohort European American speakers (under 10%). In fact, elderly African Americans exhibit a bimodal distribution, with speakers showing a very high or low incidence of *r*-lessness. Over time, however, the Hyde County African American speakers appear to have moved toward a more cohesive norm in which *r*-lessness has been adopted as a general trait of their phonological system that brings them more in line with AAVE elsewhere. Thus, the pattern of great individual variation in alignment exhibited by the oldest group of speakers appears to be replaced by a more unified norm. We take up the issue of individual variation in earlier African American English more fully in chapter 9.

Table 7.6   Post-ð *r*-vocalization: Hyde County African Americans and European Americans

	Post-ð		Non-Post-ð Unstressed	
Age/ Ethnic Group	*% Voc*	*N/ T*	*%*	*N/ T*
European American				
Elderly	78.7	37/47	11.1	17/153
Young	27.3	15/55	0.0	0/142
African American				
Elderly	84.9	73/86	43.6	109/250
Senior	69.8	37/53	58.1	50/86
Middle	89.7	26/29	62.0	75/121
Young	85.6	77/90	57.0	156/274

VARBRUL Results

European Americans
Input probability = .08

Generation
   Elderly = .78; Young = .22

Post-ð Status
   Post-ð = .94; Other Unstressed Syllables = .28

Total Chi square = 1.707; Chi square per cell = .427

African Americans
Input probability = .63

Generation
   Elderly = .43; Senior = .48; Middle = .59; Young = .54

Post-ð Status
   Post-ð = .75; Other Unstressed Syllables

Total Chi Square = 9,545; Chi square per cell = 1.193

7.3.2 Post-/ð/ r vocalization

The patterning of post-/ð/ *r* vocalization, an apparent localized trait of Hyde County speech according to LAMSAS records, can provide a more specific picture of dialect alignment over time and across ethnicities in Hyde County. In table 7.6 we summarize the incidence of post-/ð/ *r*-vocalization for elderly and young European Americans and for the four generations of African Americans. To control for the effect of /ð/, preceding *r* in an unstressed syllable (e.g., *mother, together, either*), we compare the

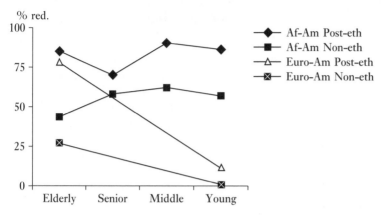

Figure 7.4 Post-ð and non-Post ð *r* vocalization: Hyde County African Americans and European Americans

figures for post-/ð/ with the incidence of *r*-lessness in other, nonpost-/ð/ unstressed syllables (e.g., *over*, *letter*). VARBRUL analyses of the effects are given following the table. Separate runs of VARBRUL were conducted for the European American and the African American groups. In figure 7.4 the descriptive data are summarized graphically.

The descriptive data and VARBRUL analyses indicate that the distinctive local pattern of post-/ð/ *r* vocalization is most clearly exhibited among elderly European Americans. While the input value on *r*-lessness in un- stressed syllables is low overall (.08), the constraining effect of post-/ð/ position is highly significant (.94), with the effect of this pattern still evident among young European Americans. At the same time, the African Amer- ican speech community, with a much higher incidence of overall *r*-lessness in unstressed position (input probability .63), accommodates the local pat- tern by maintaining post-/ð/ status as a constraining effect on the incidence of *r*-vocalization. In this respect, elderly African Americans are the group most accommodating to the local norm; the incidence of post-/ð/ r-lessness is almost double that of *r*-lessness in other unstressed syllables. However, all age groups of African Americans show significantly higher frequencies of *r*-lessness in post-/ð/ contexts compared with other unstressed syllables. We thus see that there is a persistent effect from this local dialect pattern even as the African American community moves towards a more consolid- ated, external norm of *r*-lessness. The overall pattern of *r*-lessness in the Hyde County African American community may obscure the distinctiveness of this peculiar dialect pattern, but it is still manifested in the systematic variable constraints on the incidence of *r*-lessness.

7.4 Conclusion

What can we conclude about the alignment of earlier African American English and European American English based on our examination of consonants? How do the patterns for consonantal alignment compare with other levels of linguistic alignment, including different subsystems of phonology? And what is the significance of our findings for the reconstruction of earlier African American phonology and its contemporary course of change?

While the consonantal dialect traits of African Americans in Hyde County obviously show some historical alignment with their European American cohorts, such as the accommodation of the distinctive pattern of post-/ð/ *r*-vocalization, prenasal fricative stopping, unstressed /w/ deletion, and so forth, it is also apparent that there have been some long-standing ethnolinguistic differences. Our analysis of consonant cluster reduction, for example, revealed that prevocalic cluster reduction has been significantly different in the African American and European American speech communities of Hyde County for as long as we can reasonably project. There is no indication that these communities were ever aligned with respect to this trait and they continue to exhibit an ethnolinguistic divide in the most diagnostic phonetic environment, prevocalic position.

There are a couple of reasons why CCR might be perpetuated as a distinctive trait of AAVE while other aspects of phonology became more aligned with local dialect traits over time. Part of the explanation is probably related to phonological structure, but the reason may also partly be embedded in a sociopsychological explanation. As a highly marked syllable structure, there would be a natural inclination to reduce final consonant clusters to a more natural and more unmarked sequence. The reduction of syllable-coda consonant clusters is a well-known trait of first language development (Ingram, 1976), second language acquisition interlanguage (Tarone, 1980, 1988), and phonological transfer (Weinreich, 1953; Odlin, 1989). Furthermore, by comparison with segmental inventories, phonotactic structures tend to be particularly susceptible to persistent language transfer. Sabino's studies of Negerhollands (Sabino, 1988, 1993, 1994a, 1994b), for example, show the long-term persistence of phonotactic patterns; she notes (1994a:16) that "250 years after the arrival of the first slave ship, a substrate phonotactic constraint was still partially evident in the language of the last speakers of the language." As it turns out, some of the most socially marked, continuous differences in African American and European American speech in Hyde County are found in the phonotactic system. For example, traits such as *skr* for *str*, *aks* for *ask*, and a more generalized unstressed syllable deletion process (*'member* for *remember*) are among the most durable and prominent ethnic distinctions between African Americans and European Americans in

Hyde County.[5] Perhaps more importantly, these distinctions were maintained at the same time that other phonological features, in particular, the vowel systems, converged (see chapter 5). Though we may be surprised at their long-term maintenance, we are hardly surprised that traits involving marked phonotactic sequences would be perpetuated as a substratal effect of an earlier language contact situation.

The persistence of some long-term phonotactic effects might also be reinforced by a type of *camouflaging* in phonology that is comparable to that discussed for some syntactic structures in AAVE (Spears, 1982; Baugh, 1984; Wolfram, 1994a). Wolfram and Schilling-Estes (1998:347) define camouflaging as "a form in a vernacular variety that looks like a standard counterpart but is used in a structurally or functionally different way." Although the notion of camouflaging has not previously been applied to phonological structures, some parallels seem apparent. With respect to consonant clusters, we noted that CCR is quite common in standard varieties in some phonetic contexts – for example, in preconsonantal position (e.g., *tes' case, col' person*), in unstressed syllables (e.g., *breakfas' at*), and function words such as *an'* for *and*. In cases of such overlap in a phonological process, the social obtrusiveness of a form might be reduced in the selected environments where there is a diagnostic difference. This, of course, is analogous to how camouflaging works with syntactic structures. Prevocalic CCR may not be as socially conspicuous in the selected environments where it is ethnolinguistically distinctive because of the shared cross-dialectal process of CCR in other phonetic environments. Partial overlap in phonological processes may be one of the language internal factors that leads to reduced saliency in a phonological feature.[6]

In the sociolinguistic literature, the notion of camouflaging has only been applied to cases where similarities in standard and vernacular forms obscure a distinctive vernacular use. But it seems obvious that this construct can be applied to other kinds of sociolinguistic relations as well, such as the effect of local dialect peculiarities in relation to other vernacular varieties. For example, as we discuss more fully in chapter 10, the trajectory of change for African American English in Hyde County is moving it away from the local norm and towards a supralocal AAVE norm. In such a change, distinctly local features of Hyde County would naturally be abandoned in favor of the contemporary norms of urban AAVE. With respect to postvocalic *r* vocalization, we see that there is a developing trend towards more general postvocalic *r* vocalization that is taking AAVE away from the overall Hyde County rhotic character. In such a transition, however, we see the lingering influence of the peculiar local post-/ð/ *r*-vocalization trait in the systematic constraint effects on variability, where *r*-lessness continues to be favored in post-/ð/ contexts over other unstressed contexts for all generations of African Americans, including the youngest generation of speakers, who are most likely to abandon local dialect traits. The fact that Hyde County AAVE is now characterized by overall postvocalic *r*-lessness certainly obscures this historical effect, now manifested only in differential frequencies of post-/ð/ *r*-lessness. Nonetheless, the effect is still present, though camouflaged by the overall movement towards *r*-lessness in the African American speech community.

The picture of consonant alignment offered in this chapter clearly shows some differences from that found for the description of vowels in chapter 5. In part, we may attribute these to the structural dynamics of phonotactic hierarchies involving consonants, but differences do not appear to be a simple matter of structural composition. We have also suggested that social and psychological factors may be implicated in explaining the earlier and current development of African American English in Hyde County as it manifests both past and present patterns of convergence and divergence.

Notes

1   The figures for the African American sample are taken from Childs (2000); Childs' original sample was supplemented with additional tabulations for European American speakers in this analysis.

2   For the sake of this tabulation, the intermediate category in which tense marking includes both an internal change and suffix (e.g., *kept*, *slept*) are eliminated because their incidence was so low in the corpus.

3   Dan Beckett and Walt Wolfram extracted *r*-lessness for African American speakers, whereas Wolfram extracted the data for the European American population. No more than seven tokens of one word were taken in the extraction process in order to control for type–token relations.

4   For the VARBRUL analysis including the senior group, the Chi square score per cell was 2.504, which is generally considered to be nonsignificant. Excluding the senior group of speakers, the Chi square score per cell was 1.549, thus indicating a better fit without this group.

5   It is also quite possible that the sequence *skr* for *str* may be related to indirect substrate influence, given the inherent complexity of *sCr* clusters for non-Germanic speakers (Sabino, 1994a:21). In this instance, however, the sequence *skr* would be an intermediate phase in the interlanguage transition process vis-à-vis the less natural sequence *str*.

6   Hickey (forthcoming b) is one of the few serious attempts to seriously discuss the role of system-internal factors on saliency in terms of language change Although he does not specifically discuss the role of overlapping processes as discussed here, this dimension might fall under the rubric of what he refers to as system conformity.

8

Intonational Alignment in Hyde County English

Thus far we have presented a variety of different types of linguistic differences between African Americans and European Americans in Hyde County including morphosyntactic, vocalic, and consonantal variables. Other possible differences remain, however. Differences in discourse style undoubtedly exist (see, e.g., Kochman, 1981; Goodwin, 1990) but lie beyond the scope of our methods. Differences in mean fundamental frequency, or F_0 (Hollien and Malcik, 1962; Hudson and Holbrook, 1981, 1982; Hawkins, 1993; Walton and Orlikoff, 1994) and in other voice quality traits (Walton and Orlikoff, 1994) have also been found between these two ethnic groups in other parts of the United States. Outside of these factors, though, intonation represents the major linguistic category for which African American/European American differences are poorly understood. At present, little research has been conducted on how African American and European American intonation differ. Nevertheless, we were able to investigate one apparent intonational difference involving the frequency of high pitch accents in connected speech.

8.1 African American and European American Intonation

Intonational differences between African Americans and European Americans have received surprisingly little attention, even though they are often named as a likely difference between the two groups (e.g., by Lass et al., 1980). The first major study of African American intonation was that of Loman (1967, 1975). He examined conversations spoken by African Americans, mostly 10-year-old children, in Washington, DC, and discussed intonation in conjunction with stress. He named three prosodic features that set African American prosody apart from European American prosody: (1)

African Americans show a higher frequency of primary stresses; (2) they show a "constant and marked shift" between higher and lower pitches, which he attributed to stronger and weaker stress, respectively; and (3) they (especially men) use falsetto frequently (Loman, 1975:242). He mentioned a few other features of African American prosody as well. For example, he observed that *wh*-questions and imperatives tend to show overall falling intonation, in part because *wh*-words at the beginning of *wh*-questions generally show high pitch (Loman, 1975:228–9).

Another important early inquiry was that of Tarone (1972, 1973), who focused specifically on black and white intonational differences. Based on her analysis of spontaneous speech recorded in Seattle, she proposed that African Americans and European Americans show four general differences related to intonation: (1) African Americans show a wider pitch range, or key, than European Americans. This finding is undoubtedly related to the use of falsetto observed by Loman. (2) African Americans show level and rising final pitch contours more often than European Americans, who show falling final contours more consistently. (3) Unlike European Americans, African Americans often show falling final contours in yes/no questions in formal situations. (4) Finally, African Americans often mark conditional clauses by intonation instead of by *if*.

Hudson and Holbrook (1981, 1982), using subjects from universities in Florida, found that African Americans showed a wider range of F_0 values than European Americans, corroborating Tarone's first conclusion. They also noted that the range was wider in spontaneous speech than in reading. In addition, they reported that African Americans showed a greater range of pitch above their mean modal F_0 value than below it while European Americans showed a greater range below their mean modal value.

More recently, Jun and Foreman (1996) and Foreman (2000) analyzed African American/European American intonational differences using subjects who lived in California. Jun and Foreman (1996) designed an ingenious procedure in which African American and European American subjects acted out dialogues designed to mimic real conversations. Recordings of these dialogues were then analyzed both instrumentally – using pitch tracking – and impressionistically in the Tone and Break Index (ToBI) notation (see Silverman et al., 1992), a special transcription system designed for English intonation. A number of differences in intonation patterns emerged between African Americans and European Americans: (1) European Americans showed consistent patterns for boundary tones of yes/no questions, *wh*-questions, and declarative sentences, while African Americans showed more variation. (2) When high boundary tones occurred, European Americans placed them on the final syllable, while African Americans placed them at the beginning of the final word and then showed a slight pitch fall. (3) In yes/no questions, European Americans consistently showed low pitch accents (pitch prominences), while African Americans variably produced low or high pitch accents. (4) African Americans were more likely than European Americans to show pitch accents after the nucleus of the sentence. (5) African Americans were more likely than European Americans to show a high tone at the beginning of sentences. (6) Finally, as with the earlier studies, Jun and Foreman found that African Americans showed a wider pitch range than European Americans.

Foreman (2000) used excerpts from the recordings in Jun and Foreman (1996) as stimuli in a perception experiment. The subjects in the experiment consisted of African Americans and European Americans who were divided according to their level of exposure to black and white culture. They were asked to identify the ethnicity of the speakers they heard. The results showed not only that listeners with exposure to both cultures were the best at identifying the speakers, but also that stimuli featuring intonational characteristics typical of only one ethnicity were the easiest to identify. This result suggests that intonation may play a role in real-life ethnic identification.

In a study conducted without knowledge of Loman's or Jun and Foreman's work, Thomas (1999) conducted an acoustic analysis of recordings, made in 1989 in Silsbee, Texas, of high school students reading a story. The story consisted entirely of declarative sentences. Three general findings emerged from this study. (1) African Americans showed more high pitch accents than European Americans. This finding matches Loman's observation that African Americans show more primary stresses. (2) African Americans were more likely to show a pitch accent on the first syllable of a sentence. (3) European Americans showed a greater fall in pitch through the course of a sentence. The last finding appears to contradict the conclusions of the earlier studies that African Americans show a wider pitch range, but it may be explicable. First, Thomas' study used a reading passage, and Tarone (1973) had noted that the wider pitch range of African Americans appeared chiefly in certain other forms of speech, such as verbal play. Second, Tarone had stated that African Americans often showed level and rising final boundary tones, which would decrease their pitch range in sentences with such tones. Third, the European Americans in the previous studies, in all likelihood, predominantly spoke non-Southern dialects. Tarone's subjects were from Seattle, Washington, and Jun and Foreman's from California; although Hudson and Holbrook's subjects were from Florida, peninsular Florida, where the bulk of the state's population lives and thus where most of the subjects presumably originated, shows distinctly non-Southern speech features (Labov et al., 2001). Thomas's speakers, conversely, were from a rural community in the southeastern corner of Texas and showed many diagnostically Southern dialect features, such as monophthongal /ai/ and /e/ with a lowered nucleus. Wide pitch ranges have been named as a feature that sets European American speech in the South off from European American speech in other regions (Feagin, 1987).

Thomas's second conclusion, that African Americans were more likely to produce pitch accents on initial syllables, may be simply a correlate of the first finding, that they showed more pitch accents overall than European Americans. Nevertheless, it matches Jun and Foreman's finding that African Americans were more likely to show high initial tones. As noted above, Thomas's first finding squares perfectly with Loman's finding that African Americans show more primary stresses. However, it also fits well with Jun and Foreman's conclusion that African Americans are more likely to show additional pitch accents after the nucleus of the sentence.

However, Thomas's first conclusion may also relate to some of Jun and Foreman's other findings. Although Thomas did not state it, his findings suggested that African American and European American intonation are organized according to different underlying principles. European American intonation is clearly organized by intonation groups, which tend to coincide with sentences or clauses in scripted speech and reading. Within each intonation group, one syllable – the nucleus – shows the strongest pitch prominence. Other prominences correspond to word stress patterns. Different sentence types show characteristic patterns, with declaratives and *wh*-questions ordinarily exhibiting downdrift and yes/no questions exhibiting rising pitch. Stressed syllables generally show higher pitch than unstressed syllables except when a low pitch accent or a rising pitch is involved. African American intonation, in contrast, seems to show a pattern in which successive stressed syllables show alternating high and low pitches. Other factors, such as word stress and emphasis of particular words (i.e., nucleus placement), are overlaid on the basic alternating pattern. This alternating pattern appears to represent the same phenomenon as the "constant and marked shift" between high and low pitches that Loman (1975:242) described and which, he added, "may give the impression of a 'musical rhythm'" in AAVE. It may be reflected in the characteristic rhythms of certain types of music associated with African Americans, such as rap, versus those associated with European Americans, such as Country-Western.

If our proposal that African American intonation and European American intonation are organized in fundamentally different ways holds true, then the inconsistency that Jun and Foreman found among African Americans for boundary tones and for pitch accents in yes/no questions can be explained. Jun and Foreman discussed intonational patterns in terms of sentences, and because sentences (insofar as they correspond to intonation groups) are how European American intonation is organized, their European American speakers naturally showed consistent patterns. If African American intonation is organized according to a different principle, it should not be surprising that Jun and Foreman's African American speakers appeared to show inconsistency when the patterns were described according to sentence boundaries.

For the purposes of this study, we investigated whether intonational differences occurred between African Americans and European Americans in our Hyde County corpus. In order to do so, it was necessary to find a quantifiable variable. The interviewers asked the questions during the interviews and the subjects gave answers, so the subjects' speech consisted almost entirely of declarative sentences. The main exceptions were insertions such as "Huh?" when the subject could not hear a question. It was therefore necessary to exclude variables that previous studies had found to pertain only to questions. The speaking style in the interviews was also restricted, so variables relevant primarily to verbal play also had to be excluded. As a result, we focused on one intonational variable that occurs in declarative sentences and regardless of speaking style: the relative frequency of high pitch accents.

8.2 Analytical Methods

Recordings of 32 Hyde County speakers were selected for the quantitative analysis. The sample consisted of eight African Americans born before 1920, eight European Americans born before 1920, eight African Americans born after 1960, and eight European Americans born after 1960. The two elderly groups each consisted of five women and three men; the two younger groups each consisted of four women and four men. As with the samples used for other variables, it was impossible – given the social constraints of a rural Southern community – to construct samples of African Americans and European Americans of equal social standing, but all groups in the sample include some vernacular speakers.

A transcript containing at least 500 syllables of the subject's speech was made for each subject. The occurrence of high pitch accents was then marked on the transcripts. We defined a high pitch accent as a stressed syllable whose pitch was higher than that of the immediately preceding stressed syllable. The marking of high pitch accents was conducted impressionistically by Thomas using a Sanyo Memo–Scriber, Model TRC-8080, cassette tape player. All signals were listened to at least twice (and often many more times) before decisions about the location of pitch accents were reached. Some of the recordings were checked later for intratranscriber reliability as well.[1] Although autocorrelation pitch tracking as a means of measuring F_0 is now conventional in studies of intonation, it is plagued by errors caused by pitch doubling and pitch halving. It is also troublesome when applied to field recordings because of the effects of background noise.

F_0 can be calculated from harmonic values in narrow-band spectrograms or power spectra as well, but this method is painfully slow and thereby more suitable for small-scale studies. The volume of speech examined here, totaling 20,062 syllables, made calculation of F_0 from harmonics impractical.

The number of high pitch accents and the total number of syllables were tallied for each subject. In addition, the number of stressed syllables was tallied. Numerous function words, such as *and*, *in*, *just*, and *he*, can occur in discourse in both stressed and unstressed forms. These words were counted as stressed or unstressed mostly on the basis of vowel quality, though the presence or absence of [h] proved useful for *he*, *him*, and *her* as well.

8.3 Results and Implications

When all subjects are weighted equally, the results are as follows. Elderly African Americans produced high pitch accents on 27.5 percent of all syllables and 39.0 percent of stressed syllables; elderly European Americans on 23.6 percent and 35.2 percent, respectively; young African Americans on 27.7 percent and 39.7 percent, respectively; and young European Americans on 22.3 percent and 33.9 percent, respectively. These figures suggest that the two ethnicities differ substantially, both in the proportion of total syllables with high pitch accents and in the proportion of stressed syllables with high pitch accents. Because we defined high pitch accents as stressed syllables, the analysis here will focus on the proportion of stressed syllables bearing high pitch accents. Figure 8.1 shows the means of those proportions and 99 percent confidence intervals, with subjects grouped according to ethnicity and age.

The 99 percent confidence interval for the elderly African Americans overlaps broadly with that of the young African Americans. Likewise, the 99 percent confidence interval for the elderly European Americans overlaps that of the young European Americans. In striking contrast, the 99 percent confidence intervals for the two African American age groups do not overlap at all with those of the two European American age groups. Thus it seems clear that African Americans in Hyde County do show more high pitch accents in their speech than their European American neighbors. Furthermore, the difference appears to be long-standing. Although the means for the two elderly groups are closer to each other than those for the two young groups, the age group means do not differ significantly for either ethnicity.

The small difference in the mean values for elderly and young European Americans seems to be due to the fact that some elderly European American females occasionally exhibited contours similar to those described

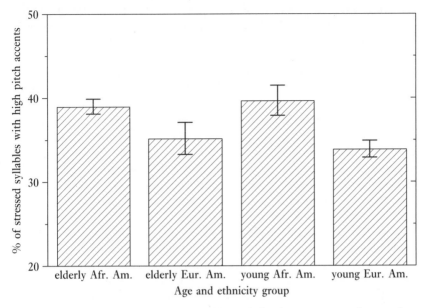

Figure 8.1   Means and 99% confidence intervals for the percentage of stressed syllables with high pitch accents produced by Hyde County speakers

elsewhere as "high rising terminals" (e.g., Guy et al., 1986; Britain, 1992). These contours differed from the high rising terminal pattern in that they seemed to be spread more broadly across intonation groups; as such, the pattern might best be called "updrift." This pattern inflated the number of syllables counted as high pitch accents for elderly European Americans, but it was absent among young European Americans of either sex. It is quite distinct from the typical patterns shown by African Americans, who rarely exhibited updrift across entire intonation groups.

European Americans produced high pitch accents on just over a third of their stressed syllables. This figure may appear rather high. Word stress accounts for many of the pitch accents. Another important factor is that the pervasiveness of hesitations and incomplete sentences in spontaneous speech causes intonation groups to generally be shorter than sentence length in spontaneous speech. As a result, there are more nuclei than in the scripted speech used by Jun and Foreman (1996) or the reading used by Thomas (1999). The results for the African Americans may also seem incongruous with the model, but in the opposite way. They produced high pitch accents on just under 40 percent of their stressed syllables. This figure is considerably lower than the 50 percent expected from the pattern of alternating high and low tones described earlier. However, this discrepancy is explicable, too. First, word stress and nucleus placement often disrupt the alternating pattern. Since the African Americans in our sample usually avoided successive upsteps, the result was successive stressed syllables with low pitch. Second, weakly stressed syllables – in such function words as *my* – are often passed over in the pattern. Thus, a high pitch accent may be followed by a strongly stressed and a weakly stressed syllable, both of which show lower pitch.

Although it is clear that African Americans and European Americans are aligned differently for intonation, the findings reported here open up a variety of new questions. The first question is whether the intonational difference found between African Americans and European Americans in Hyde County is a local phenomenon or a widespread one. Studies of ethnic intonation patterns in other parts of the country are necessary to resolve this question, but the similar findings by Loman (1967, 1975) in Washington, DC, by Jun and Foreman (1996) in California, and by Thomas (1999) in Texas suggest that this difference may be widespread.

Another question is the origin of the difference. The difference appears for both young and elderly Hyde County subjects, suggesting that it is a long-standing ethnic marker. However, unlike for some other variables, there is no prior evidence for the intonational patterns of Hyde County. The small drop between elderly and younger European Americans might suggest that European Americans are moving away from an earlier system more like that of African Americans, but, as explained above, it is more likely due to the disappearance of an updrifting pattern in the local European American vernacular. More data from other regions on the proportion of high pitch accents are certainly needed. Information from other parts of the South would illuminate the issue, as might data from the British Isles and perhaps from West Indian creoles. The distinctive African American pattern is somewhat reminiscent of tonal patterns in West African tone languages, which often consist of only two tones. In fact, Loman (1975), citing Herskovits (1941), suggested that the African American pattern could derive from West African languages. There are, then, multiple possibilities. The African American pattern could be an old development of Pamlico Sound or of the South in general that is preserved in African American speech. It could have its origins in the British Isles. It could be a creole feature. It could result from interference from West African languages. Or it could be an innovation in African American speech. It is our hope that other researchers can produce evidence that would narrow this list of possibilities.

There are other questions as well. Why is the frequency of pitch accents, like copula deletion, one of the features for which Hyde County African Americans of all ages do not accommodate to the local European American vernacular? Or, perhaps, is the difference greater elsewhere such that they have accommodated to a degree? Are intonational differences greater in some parts of the country than in others? How is the difference evaluated, both for ethnic identity and for ethnic identifications?

8.4 Conclusions

We have attempted to quantify one intonational difference between African Americans and European Americans, the frequency of high pitch accents. As it turns out, the difference is robust and does not appear to be new. Although a few previous studies have described intonational differences between those two groups, only Loman (1967, 1975) and Tarone (1972, 1973) applied quantitative analysis of intonation to a sociolinguistic study, and no other study of AAVE has examined intonation in conjunction with nonprosodic features. Our findings, while promising, require corroboration from further work elsewhere. There are a number of intonational variables, including some that apply specifically to yes/no questions, that we could not investigate. These variables also deserve further study. We do not expect our study to be the last word on ethnic differences in intonation. Instead, we prefer to see it as helping to lay a foundation for future work.

Note

1 It was determined that one listener who was experienced in impressionistic phonetic transcription should conduct the marking of pitch accents because it was found that inexperienced listeners missed a large fraction of the pitch accents.

9

The Individual and Group in Earlier African American English

In previous chapters, we focused on the dialect characteristics of different groups of speakers rather than individual speech behavior. Even when presenting individual profiles, we were highlighting how these speakers represented different age and ethnic groups of speakers. But the relation of the individual to the group in sociolinguistics is hardly a settled issue. As Romaine (1982b:15) notes, "We scarcely know how heterogeneous some speech communities are." At this point, we turn specifically to the role of the individual and group, both as a general issue in sociolinguistic variation and as a specific issue in reconstructing earlier African American English.

Our discussion focuses on two primary issues. One is the role of intra-community individual variation in earlier African American English. Certainly the original transition from African languages to English was not seamless to begin with and has endured continued variation throughout the development of AAVE, but we have little information about the range of variation at earlier stages. The question is not whether there was diversity in earlier African American speech, but the nature of the variation and the degree to which relevant sociolinguistic, sociohistorical, and sociocultural factors might – or might not – have accounted for it.

An equally important question for sociolinguistic study is the role of individual variation in small, historically isolated communities. To what extent is there individual variation in small communities where "everybody knows everybody?" Recent research by Dorian (1994) in a small, homogeneous community has pointed to patterns of individual variation rather than an intricate array of social and stylistic factors that correlate with language differences in most sociolinguistic studies of large metropolitan areas (e.g., Labov, 1966, 1972a; Wolfram, 1969). At the same time, studies of other isolated communities indicate that there may be important sociolinguistic and ethnolinguistic boundaries in such speech communities just as there are in larger, metropolitan areas (Wolfram, Hazen, and Tamburro, 1997). The question of diversity in small enclave dialect communities thus remains an open one, as does the question of variation in earlier African American speech.

9.1 The Individual and Group in Variation Studies

One of the persistent theoretical and methodological questions facing current variation studies is the relationship of the individual to the group (Bailey, 1973; Wolfram, 1973; Romaine, 1982a, 1982b; Guy, 1980). It is often assumed, tacitly if not explicitly, that the individual and the group are one and the same in studies of linguistic and social covariation. This assumption that speakers who are sociologically similar can be expected to be linguistically similar, which we will call the *homogeneity assumption*, has been named as a basic tenet of the "quantitative paradigm" (Romaine, 1982a:11), that is, the investigative framework established by Labov, and it pervades much sociolinguistic work. Under the homogeneity assumption, data are presented for a set of speakers as if they are a homogenous group. Such groups may be designated by demographic characteristics, for example, an elderly group of working-class lifetime African American Hyde County residents; by social networks, for example, "the poker game network" of Ocracoke (Wolfram and Schilling-Estes, 1995); or by some other means of designation. Theoretically, the homogeneity assumption implies that individual variation is insignificant in terms of the description of linguistic and social covariance. Methodologically, it implies that data from a grouped set of individuals may be treated as an "undifferentiated mass" (Chambers, 1995:100), provided that meaningful social boundaries have been used to delimit the group to begin with. When the congruity of a particular group is characterized by too much ingroup variance, it is typically replaced with what Chambers (1995:100) describes as more "numerous small groups with subtle, special relationships to the whole," thus preserving the notion of homogeneity within the social group.

The acceptance of the homogeneity assumption does not preclude the possibility of anomalous individuals within socially designated groupings, but these are clearly seen as exceptional cases. On occasion, individual speakers may not fit the overall profile of their given social group; however, in these cases the anomalous speakers are either removed from the data that are statistically skewed by the inclusion of the speakers or simply discussed separately as "atypical" speakers – as in the well-known case of Nathan B. in Labov's *Social Stratification of English in New York City* (1966). Notwithstanding such cases, the guiding rule of variationist investigation remains the assumption that socially meaningful divisions of groups of speakers will not be linguistically heterogeneous.

An alternative to the homogeneity assumption/quantitative paradigm is what Romaine (1982b:19) calls the "dynamic paradigm." The dynamic paradigm, promoted by Charles-James N. Bailey (e.g., Bailey, 1973) and favored by many creolists (e.g., Bickerton, 1971, 1975), "take[s] the individual rather than the group as the starting point for analysis" (Romaine, 1982b:19). According to Romaine (1982a:11), this paradigm assumes that there are "internally consistent lects," called *isolects* by Bailey (1973), that differ for one or more variables. This notion is opposed to the quantitative paradigm's assumption that variability, in the form of variable rules, is encoded in lects. Each speaker may command several isolects for stylistic purposes. Implicational scales figure prominently in defining what constitutes an isolect. Under the dynamic paradigm, "it is the behavior of the individual which is of linguistic significance" Romaine (1982a:240). Regarding idiolects instead of sociolects as primary is nothing new in linguistics, of course. Romaine (1982b) notes that the primacy of idiolects was assumed by nineteenth century neogrammarians, and it has certainly been assumed by structuralists and generativists. However, sociolinguists have predominantly favored sociolectal approaches. Romaine (1982a:282–3), it should be added, finds both paradigms – quantitative and dynamic – deficient in that they treat models based on quantitative data as explanations for linguistic change when in fact they are only descriptions of data.

The general acceptance of the homogeneity assumption by sociolinguists has not been accompanied by much testing of it. This fact is something of a blind spot for sociolinguists. Romaine (1982b:20) writes that "[t]he variability of individual idiolects, or their lack of isomorphism with the group, is a problem, or at the very least an embarrassment which a number of sociolinguists . . . have tried, but not successfully, to explain." One explicit attempt to investigate the homogeneity assumption is that of Guy (1980), who examined final stop deletion among speakers in Philadelphia and New York. He asks, "is variation in the speech community the result of diversity of the group, reflecting the organization of society into a number of discrete lects within which variation is at a minimum, or is this variation present with identical uniform structure in the speech of every individual?" (Guy, 1980:2) Although his data initially seem to support an individualistic structuring of constraint patterns, he shows that as the number of tokens per speaker increases, so does the probability that their constraint patterns will be equivalent to the majority pattern. His conclusion is clear: "group norms are not just artifacts of the macrocosmic viewpoint, representing mere averages of a collection of widely scattered individual norms. Rather, they recapitulate the generally uniform norms of individuals" (Guy, 1980:12).

Not everyone has remained as satisfied as Guy with the homogeneity assumption, though. Questions about it have now been raised from a number of different perspectives. For example, Johnstone (1996), in her discourse-level investigation of individual voice, maintains that contemporary linguistics continues to replicate the Saussurean *langue/parole* (de Saussure, 1959) distinction and dismiss intracommunity individual variation as *parole*. Johnstone contends, in a criticism similar to Romaine's complaint, that typical language study involves

> something that is by definition superindividual and self-replicating, . . . [resulting in a] fundamental incompatibility of the linguistic individual with Saussurean structuralism . . . The object of study for linguistics is thus social: societies and social groups, dialects and languages. These are sometimes treated not as convenient abstractions but as real entities. (Johnstone, 1996:11)

This framework is often adopted in sociolinguistics as well, following Labov's edict that "idiosyncratic habits are not a part of language so conceived" (1972b:277). In opposition to this prevailing assumption, both Johnstone and researchers such as Le Page and Tabouret-Keller contend that language is "essentially idiosyncratic," and that the individual is foremost "the locus of his language" (Le Page and Tabouret-Keller, 1985:116).

From a different perspective, Schilling-Estes (1998) challenges the homogeneity assumption based on data from isolated speech communities. One of the fundamental problems for Schilling-Estes is the belief that contact alone can explain linguistic heterogeneity in socially isolated groups, whether the change is linguistic or cultural. She maintains that in investigating the language of a speech community,

> . . . there are also identificational considerations to bear in mind . . . a community's sense of ethnic identity may undergo shifts over time; and in addition, individuals and groups within a community may have quite different senses of what it means to "belong" to that community at any given time, and so they may use language quite differently to express their differential senses of group (and personal) identity. (Schilling-Estes, 1998:5–6)

While Johnstone attempts to shift the center of attention to the individual and away from social organization, Schilling-Estes seeks to refine the conception of this relationship so that the individual is not seen as a simple reflection of a group. Nonetheless, both perspectives share a focus on individual choice in relation to the system of linguistic variables by highlighting the speaker's ability to produce and display certain conceptions of self through the use of language. Embedded in this idea of personalized identity is the notion that linguistic and dialectal systems constrain but do not predict, and that agent speakers more or less consciously position themselves within a self-expressive frame. Variant usage is ultimately thus correlated with individual expression as well as group affiliation.

From yet another perspective, grounded in her long-term studies of moribund Gaelic speech in East Sutherland, Scotland, Dorian (1994) introduces the concept of *personal pattern variation*. She argues that the standard sociolinguistic descriptive paradigm has limited the possible theoretical expression of individual variation by assuming *a priori* that any two speakers "whose speech is found to vary either live in different areas from one another or represent different age-groups, sexes, socioeconomic groups, or social networks" (1994:633). Contra this assumption, Dorian has found a large amount of variation that correlates with none of these variables. Furthermore, the linguistic structures do not appear to be involved in language change. Her data thus challenge the notion that community homogeneity necessarily correlates with linguistic homogeneity. Her data further refute the notion that dense, multiplex social networks (Milroy, 1987) must have a normative effect on linguistic variation. The variants found in her detailed study of the East Sutherland community over three decades do not appear to carry social meaning or stylistic significance; in fact, different variants of the same variable are found to be used at different points in the discourse of one speaker without any evidence of a stylistic shift. Dorian (1994:633) concludes that "a profusion of variant forms can be tolerated within a small community over a long period without a discernible movement toward reduction of variants and also without the development of differences in the social evaluation of most variants."

Furthermore, although East Sutherland Gaelic is moribund, Dorian denies the interpretation that the variation she found is nothing more than an unusual distortion of a dying language. Many of her speakers were fluent only in Gaelic and not in English. Gaelic is dying in East Sutherland because fewer speakers among the younger generations are fluent in Gaelic, but the same individual variation is reported across generations and various levels of fluency. Accordingly, she concludes that personal-pattern variation must be recognized as being separate from stylistic, geographic, and proficiency-related variation.

Data challenging the homogeneity assumption are not limited to isolated communities. Thomas (1996a) examined a variety of linguistic variables in the speech of sixth-graders and their parents in Johnstown, Ohio, a commuter town near Columbus. When speakers were grouped by sex and generation, familiar patterns emerged: children and females showed more innovative forms than parents and males. However, when a different analysis was conducted that took individuals into account, a completely different picture emerged. Linear regression was used to compare the usage of individual sixth graders with that of the friends with whom they spent the most time and that of their parents. Of the 12 variables examined, only two showed a statistically significant correlation ($p < 0.05$) with the usage of close friends. It was clear that the sixth graders were not emulating the speech of the members of their networks at school, at least for most of the variables. Instead, they appeared to be exhibiting individualistic patterns. In a follow-up analysis, Thomas (1996b) rank ordered for each variable the members of one particularly close-knit clique of eight girls from the earlier study. It turned out that the members of this group showed almost as much variation for each variable as the sixth-grade class as a whole, indicating that while they were socially cohesive, they were not linguistically cohesive at all. Moreover, the rank ordering revealed that each member of the clique was innovative for different variables, suggesting that they were not responding to the same norms. Though the eight girls may have functioned as a group in some ways, they were clearly behaving as individuals in other ways.

The kinds of arguments and the empirical data offered by Romaine, Johnstone, Schilling-Estes, Dorian, and Thomas underscore the need to re-examine the role of the individual in language variation on a methodological and theoretical level. The homogeneity assumption has been applied to data related to earlier African American English as well as to other variationist analyses. For example, studies of African American transplant communities that are assumed to reflect the state of earlier African American speech, such as those in Samaná (e.g., Poplack and Sankoff, 1987) and Nova Scotia (Poplack and Tagliamonte, 1991), usually report only aggregate data for groups of speakers and thus ignore the possible role of individual differences in earlier African American speech. Likewise, our examination of different generations of speakers in the Hyde County population in previous chapters adopted a similar procedure in the analysis of many diagnostic structures, particularly in the treatment of the morphosyntactic variables. The question of individual diversity thus remains an important issue in reconstructing earlier African American speech as well as for general variation studies in sociolinguistics. An examination of individual variation can have significant import for reconstructing the earlier state of AAVE and for understanding the role of speakers from enclave communities in our assessment of its historical development.

9.2 The Sample of Elderly African American Speakers

Our examination of individual variation includes the speech of 11 elderly lifetime African American residents of Hyde County born between 1896 and 1920. At the time of the interviews with staff members of the North Carolina Language and Life Project, their ages ranged from 77 to 102. All of the speakers were born and raised in Hyde County, as were their parents and grandparents, so they represent long-standing continuity within the community. Most never even traveled outside the county until they were well into adulthood, and they have spent little time outside of the region. Demographically, they are also similar in that they have had only a few years of formal schooling, and all worked as laborers – as tenant farmers, fishers, domestics, and the like. In terms of traditional socioeconomic indices, they would be ranked at the lower end of the scale. All of them would also be rated as vernacular dialect speakers, as they exhibit a range of socially stigmatized structures. In many respects, they would thus appear to fit a fairly neat social group division for an examination of linguistic and social homogeneity – a congruent group of vernacular-speaking, elderly African American lifetime residents of rural Hyde County.

The presumption that the sample of elderly speakers represents an earlier stage of African American speech in Hyde County is based on a couple of additional premises. First of all, it is grounded in the apparent time construct (Bailey, Wikle, Tillery, and Sand, 1991), which maintains that speakers' fundamental language variety reflects their community's language variety at the time they acquired their language – at least with respect to phonology and morphosyntax. On this basis, then, we would assume that their dialect phonology and morphosyntax would at least represent that of Hyde County African American speech in the early twentieth century. There are a number of important qualifications about the apparent time construct (Wolfram and Schilling-Estes, forthcoming) that apply to this study, as they do to other variation studies of language change based on this assumption, but this construct is used as an operational procedure in the absence of counterevidence.

Another assumption that guides the interpretation of data with respect to earlier African American speech is the founder principle, as discussed in chapter 3. Given the continuity of the Hyde County community over almost three centuries, we would assume that the founder effect is certainly as applicable to this situation as it is to expatriate transplant communities such as those discussed in Poplack and Sankoff (1987), Poplack and Tagliamonte (1989), and Poplack (1999). Our projective assumption is that the variety exhibited by speakers who learned their language early in the twentieth century would at least give us an idea of the language spoken by the parents and grandparents of contemporary Hyde County African Americans (therefore giving us apparent data from speakers who lived in the area during the mid–1800s, and perhaps earlier).

9.3 Some Diagnostic Variables

The examination of intragroup variation is based on a subset of representative dialect structures associated exclusively with African American speech in Hyde County, as well as structures that represent the distinctive Pamlico Sound dialect that is characteristic of the cohort European American community in Hyde County. In particular, it includes variables we analyzed on a group level in previous chapters.

We first examine each of the selected variables in terms of their distribution among the 11 individual speakers in the sample of elderly African Americans in Hyde County. Then we consider some possible co-occurrence relationships among structures to determine if there are subsets of linguistic structures that cohere for subgroups of speakers. Finally, we consider the broader implications of our findings for reconstructing the history of AAVE and the notion of individual variation in insular enclave communities.

9.3.1 Rhoticity

As noted in Chapter 7, the status of postvocalic *r* is particularly diagnostic in the Hyde County region. On the one hand, European American varieties of English spoken in this region were traditionally typified by their rhoticity (e.g., Howren, 1962; Wolfram and Schilling-Estes, 1997) while adjacent mainland dialects such as those of the Coastal Plain participated in a pattern of postvocalic *r* vocalization that has typified many regions of the South over the past century (cf. Kurath and McDavid, 1961, map 156). On the other hand, both rural and urban AAVE are largely *r*-less, regardless of regional location (Labov et al., 1968; Wolfram, 1969; Pederson et al., 1986–92; Myhill, 1988; Bailey and Thomas, 1998). How do individual elderly residents of Hyde County accommodate the local pattern vis-à-vis the general AAVE pattern of postvocalic *r*-lessness? In figure 9.1, we present a bar chart and the raw figures and percentages for *r*-lessness for each of the 11 elderly speakers in our sample, following the procedures for extraction set forth in chapter 7. We thus have figures for *r* vocalization in nuclear stressed position as in *sir* or *hurt*; syllable-coda, word-stress position as in *car* or *port*; and unstressed nuclear syllable position as in *mother* or *letter*.

Although figure 9.1 shows that the majority of elderly African American speakers may have relatively low figures for *r*-lessness in the most diagnostic environments, especially as compared with other AAVE-speaking communities, several speakers clearly deviate from this norm. In fact, the overall figures of *r*-lessness range from under 8.7 percent overall *r*-lessness to 93.6 percent, with a mean (M) of 40.3 percent and a standard deviation (SD) of 31.0 percent. We thus find fairly dramatic variation among some elderly African Americans in the incidence of rhoticity. The three speakers with the highest levels of *r*-lessness are all females, whereas the speakers with the three lowest levels of *r*-lessness are males. Although this might suggest that

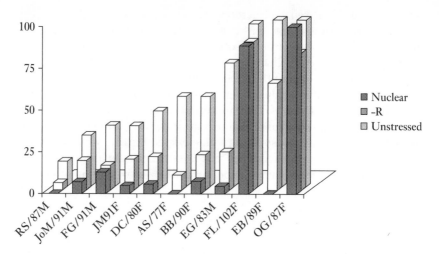

Speaker	Nuclear		Stressed Coda		Unstressed		Overall %
	%	No.	%	No.	%	No.	r-less
FG; 91m	13.0	23	14.8	61	36.8	19	18.4
JuM; 91f	5.0	20	18.6	43	36.6	41	23.1
JoM; 91m	7.1	14	17.6	51	30.8	39	21.2
BB; 90f	7.7	13	21.4	56	54.5	33	30.4
AS; 77f	0.0	14	9.1	55	54.5	33	23.1
RS; 87m	0.0	13	4.4	45	15.2	46	8.7
EG; 83m	4.8	21	23.2	56	74.1	27	32.7
DC; 80f	5.9	17	20.0	25	45.5	22	25.0
FL; 102f	88.9	18	88.9	36	97.6	41	92.6
EB; 89f	0.0	2	64.3	14	100.0	12	75.0
OG; 87f	100.0	7	82.4	17	100.0	23	93.6

Figure 9.1   The incidence of postvocalic *r*-lessness, by individual speaker

there may be a meaningful gender-based division within the community for
r-lessness, there is too much individual variation among both the men and
the women to establish statistical significance for a gender boundary (t score
= 2.26, p = .11). Whereas the aggregate tabulation of postvocalic *r* might
lead to the conclusion that elderly African Americans accommodated to
local rhotic norms by comparison with other African American communities, it is clear that this is not a homogeneous pattern. There is significant
individual variation in both the type and the extent of *r*-lessness in the
elderly Hyde County African American community.[1]

9.3.2 Syllable-coda consonant cluster reduction

As noted in chapter 7, syllable-coda cluster reduction in prevocalic position (e.g., *wes en', col' out*) is one of the hallmark phonological features of AAVE (Labov et al., 1968; Wolfram, 1969; Fasold, 1972; Guy, 1980). The analysis presented there, based on Childs (2000), shows that that the Hyde County African American community aligns with other AAVE communities in having relatively high levels of prevocalic consonant cluster reduction, whereas the European American community in Hyde County, like vernacular European American varieties such as Southern White Vernacular English, Appalachian English (Wolfram and Christian, 1976), and Outer Banks Vernacular English (Wolfram, Hazen, and Tamburro, 1997), shows very low levels of prevocalic consonant cluster reduction.

To what extent is there variation in prevocalic cluster reduction among elderly African Americans in Hyde County, and what might this suggest about earlier African American speech in Hyde County? In figure 9.2, we display the figures for cluster reduction for each of the 11 elderly speakers in our corpus. Unfortunately, for some of the speakers, the number of tokens is limited so that we cannot obtain a meaningful measure of variation for all of the individuals in our sample.[2] We have therefore determined to include in the graphic display only the nine speakers who have at least eight tokens of prevocalic clusters in their speech sample. We include figures for prevocalic monomorphemic and prevocalic bimorphemic clusters.

The overall range of prevocalic cluster reduction shows some individual variation, from 23.5 to 55.6 percent overall reduction (M = 37.6%; SD = 11.1%), with more variation exhibited for monomorphemic clusters (M = 56.3%, SD = 16.1%) than for bimorphemic clusters (M = 22.5%; SD = 13.3%). Though exhibiting a range of individual variation in the overall incidence of cluster reduction among elderly African Americans, all of the speakers differentiate themselves from the normative European American speakers in Hyde County (Childs, 2000), who have virtually no consonant cluster reduction for prevocalic bimorphemic clusters and very limited reduction for monomorphemic clusters.

9.3.3 The vowel system

In Chapter 6 we discussed the different traits that characterize the Hyde County vowel system. In figures 6.1a–c, vowel formant plots were shown for three elderly African Americans: a female born in 1906, a female born in 1909, and a male born in 1910. Although we have not normalized the vowel formant values for cross-speaker comparison, several observations

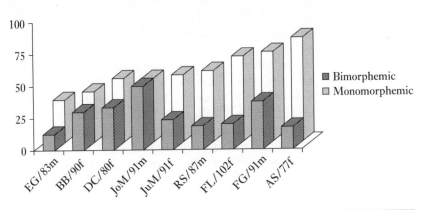

Speaker	Bimorphemic		Monomorphemic		Prevocalic Bi. + Mono.	
	%	N	%	N	%	N
FG; 91m	0.0	5	76.9	13	55.1	18
JuM; 91f	23.5	17	52.6	19	38.8	36
JoM; 91m	45.5	11	62.50	9	50.0	20
BB; 90f	30.0	10	40.0	20	36.6	30
AS; 77f	17.4	23	81.2	11	38.2	34
RS; 87m	18.6	43	55.5	20	30.1	63
EG; 83m	12.5	8	33.3	9	23.5	17
DC; 80f	33.3	6	50.0	2	37.5	8
FL; 102f	20.0	5	66.7	6	45.4	11
EB; 89f	—	—	—	—	—	—
OG; 87f	20.0	5	—	—	20.0	5

Figure 9.2   The incidence of prevocalic cluster reduction, by individual speaker

can be made about variation based on the overall configuration of each speaker's vowel plots. The speakers charted in figures 6.1a–c show some variation in the relative degree of backing of the nucleus of the /ai/, the relative fronting of the back vowels /u/, /ʊ/, and /o/, and the raised, essentially monophthongal production of /ɔ/, but all three speakers show some alignment with the vowel configuration of the traditional Outer Banks vowel system as compared to the vowel configuration described for most southern-based AAVE systems (Thomas and Bailey, 1998; Thomas, 2001). Other variables, such as the fronted glide of /au/ (*brown, south*) and the lowering of the nucleus of /er/ (*bear, there*; represented as *eʳ* in the plots), indicate more individual variation. The speaker in figure 6.1a has a fronted, unrounded glide for /au/ and a quite low /er/ nucleus. The speaker in figure 6.1b shows a central-gliding /au/ and also has a low /er/ nucleus.

The speaker in figure 6.1c shows a back-gliding /au/ and a raised rather than lowered /er/ nucleus.

As discussed in chapter 6, there is a relatively uniform base for elderly African American vowel variants, but certain speakers, such as the one featured in figure 6.1c, show patterns more typical of AAVE elsewhere (described in Thomas and Bailey, 1998). It is noteworthy that most of our elderly African Americans seem more aligned with the European American Outer Banks system described in Chapter 6 than with the prototypical AAVE system.

9.3.4 Verbal -s concord

As noted in chapter 5, there are two dimensions of verbal -*s* concord that are notable in Hyde County speech: (1) the well-attested Outer Banks pattern that marks -*s* on verbs occurring with plural subjects such as *The dogs barks at the ducks* (Hazen, 1996, 2000b; Wolfram, Hazen, and Schilling-Estes, 1999) and (2) the absence of 3rd sg. -*s* absence. In chapter 5, we showed that that elderly African Americans in Hyde County distinguish themselves from their elderly European American cohorts with respect to 3rd sg. -*s* absence, but that they may share the plural -*s* attachment pattern.

In figure 9.3, we show the incidence of 3rd pl. -*s* marking as well as 3rd sg. -*s* absence. In addition, we note whether speakers also have attachment of -*s* on verbs occurring with 1st person subjects such as *I goes down there all the time* or *We takes it when we get a chance*, although we have not tabulated the relative frequency of -*s* verbal attachment with 1st person subjects. Speakers who have less than five potential cases of nonpast 1st person are indicated by parentheses. While the number of tokens is relatively low for some speakers, authentic patterns of variation can sometimes be indicated by relatively few tokens, particularly with respect to verbal concord patterns.

Several observations can be made on the basis of figure 9.3. Although there is considerable variability in the rates, all of the elderly African Americans in the corpus have substantive levels of 3rd sg. -*s* absence, ranging from 30.8 to 100 percent (M = 70.2%, SD = 26.6%). In contrast, we find a different pattern of variation for 3rd pl. -*s* attachment. Several speakers do not manifest 3rd pl. -*s* attachment at all, and other speakers have quite variable application, with up to half of all examples attaching 3rd pl. -*s* (M = 22.4%, SD = 20.9%). Furthermore, speakers with the highest incidence of 3rd sg. -*s* absence are among those who use the lowest levels of 3rd plural -*s* attachment. It is possible that some speakers may have accommodated to the local vernacular variety – which attaches 3rd person -*s* to verbs with plural subjects – while other speakers have not, and that speakers who accommodate the local pattern are more likely to reduce the indigenous AAVE pattern of 3rd sg. -s absence. But it may also be the case that some speakers simply have lower overall frequency of -*s* verbal marking as a

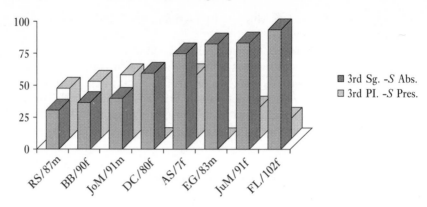

Speaker	3rd -s *Abs.*		3rd pl. -s		1st pers. -s
	% Abs	No.	%	No.	
FG; 91m	(100.0)	2	(0.0)	3	–
JuM; 91f	83.3	6	25.0	4	+
JoM; 91m	40.0	5	50.0	4	–
BB; 90f	36.8	19	45.0	20	+
AS; 77f	75.0	4	50.0	4	–
RS; 87m	30.8	26	39.4	33	+
EG; 83m	82.6	23	0.0	17	–
DC; 80f	59.5	37	0.0	6	–
FL; 102f	93.8	16	16.7	6	+
EB; 89f	—	—	(0.0)	1	(–)
OG; 87f	(100.0)	2	20.0	5	(–)

Figure 9.3   The incidence of third singular -*s* attachment, by individual speaker

generalized optional rule regardless of the subject, since there are some speakers who do not show this inverse relationship between 3rd sg. -*s* absence and 3rd pl. -*s* marking. It is further possible that some speakers have adopted an even more sweeping -*s* attachment rule in which all sub-jects, regardless of person, may attach verbal -*s*. Verbal -*s* thus shows wide variation among speakers at the same time that it reveals shared dimensions, most notably, the absence of 3rd sg. -*s*, albeit at different frequency levels.

9.3.5 Copula absence

As noted in chapter 5, the absence of copula and auxiliary for contractible forms of *is* and *are* as in *She nice* for "She's nice" or *They acting silly* for

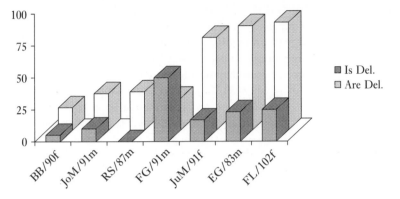

Speaker	% is Del.	Tot. (F + C)	% are Del.	Tot. (F + C)	% is/are Del.	Tot is/are Del.
FG; 91m	50.0	4	25.0	4	37.5	8
JuM; 91f	16.7	6	72.7	11	52.9	17
JoM; 91m	10.0	10	28.6	7	17.6	17
BB; 90f	5.0	20	50.0	8	17.9	28
AS; 77f	0.0	5	(100.0)	1	16.7	6
RS; 87m	0.0	27	30.0	10	8.1	37
EG; 83m	23.1	13	81.8	11	50.0	24
DC; 80f	25.0	16	(100.0)	2	33.3	18
FL; 102f	25.0	16	84.6	13	51.7	29
EB; 89f	(50.0)	2	—	—	(50.0)	2
OG; 87f	—	—	—	—	—	—

Figure 9.4 The incidence of copula absence, by individual speaker

"They're acting silly" is one of the most scrutinized structures of AAVE. Our previous comparison of European American and African American speech in Hyde County indicated that copula absence was found only in the African American community, thus sharply distinguishing the local varieties from each other.

In figure 9.4, we summarize the incidence of copula absence for *is* and *are* forms, and graphically display these figures for the seven speakers who meet our threshold criterion for quantitative measurement: four or more potential cases of deletable items for both *is* and *are*, following the procedures we outlined in chapter 5.

Figure 9.4 shows uniformity in the manifestation of copula absence in that all the individual speakers have copula absence, at least for are, though there is considerable individual variation in the relative frequency of usage

(M = 33.6%; SD = 17.3%). Most speakers show relatively low levels of *is* deletion, with a couple of speakers having no deletion of *is* at all. For example, one speaker (born in 1910) who has 27 cases eligible for *is* deletion does not exhibit any copula absence.[3] All of the speakers show deletion of *are*, but again there is considerable individual variability in the relative frequency (M = 63.6%; SD = 30.7%). There are no apparent social boundaries that correlate with different levels of copula absence. For example, there is no apparent differentiation based on gender; both men and women are among both the lowest and highest users of copula absence and there is no significant difference in the scores for women and men in the sample for this variable (t = 2.447; *p* = .431). Although all speakers participate in the general pattern of copula absence, the levels of variation seem to be individualistic rather than group-related.

9.3.6 Past tense be *leveling*

As discussed in chapter 5, the remorphologized pattern of past tense *be* regularization in which leveling to *was* takes place in positive constructions (e.g., *The dogs was down there* or *We was down there*) and leveling to *weren't* in negative constructions (e.g., *I weren't there*; *It weren't nice*) is a distinctive regional dialect pattern that elderly African Americans have participated in to a considerable extent. Whereas leveling to *was* is quite common in English vernaculars around the world (Chambers, 1995:243), including AAVE (Labov et al., 1968; Wolfram and Fasold, 1974; Weldon, 1994), Hyde County English participates in a more regionalized, remorphologized version of leveling based on polarity (Trudgill, 1990; Cheshire, 1982; Wolfram and Sellers, 1999). Figure 9.5 indicates the incidence leveling to *was* for positive constructions and leveling to *weren't* for negative constructions for the individual, elderly African American speakers in our sample; the bar chart is given for the eight speakers who have at least 10 potential cases of leveling.

The distribution shows considerable interspeaker variation for leveling to *weren't*, with less variation for leveling to *was*. Most speakers have robust levels of *was* leveling in positive constructions (M = 77.2% percent, SD = 23.6%) but the variation in *weren't* leveling is noteworthy (M = 38.8%, SD = 41.2%). While some speakers level the negative paradigm categorically to *weren't*, others don't level at all. Furthermore, the leveling between paradigms are not correlated. One speaker levels to *was* 96.3 percent of the time (27 tokens) and to *weren't* categorically (9 tokens), whereas another speaker levels to *was* 81.8 percent of the time (11 tokens) and to *weren't* just 25 percent of the time (8 tokens). Moreover, several speakers don't level to *weren't* at all. Thus, one speaker levels to *was* 61.1 percent of the time, but never levels to *weren't* in the 14 potential occurrences for *weren't* leveling. The data indicate great individual variation and perhaps a complex system of

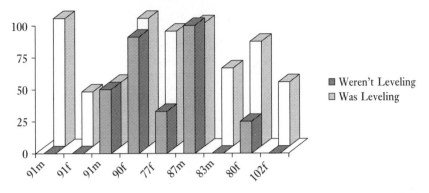

Speaker	Positive Leveled to was		Negative Leveled to weren't	
	%	No.	%	No.
FG; 91m	(100.)	2	87.5	8
JuM; 91f	42.9	14	0.0	6
JoM; 91m	50.0	12	50.0	8
BB; 90f	100.0	26	91.7	12
AS; 77f	90.0	10	33.3	12
RS; 87m	96.3	27	100.0	9
EG; 83m	61.1	18	0.0	14
DC; 80f	81.8	11	25.0	8
FL; 102f	50.0	2	0.0	2
EB; 89f	(100.)	2	—	—
OG; 87f	—	—	(0.0)	2

Figure 9.5   The incidence of *was* and *weren't* leveling, by individual speaker

sociolinguistic marking related to the regional Pamlico Sound dialect pattern and the core AAVE pattern. Elderly African Americans in Hyde County, and by extension, earlier AAVE in this region, probably varied widely in patterns of leveling to *weren't*, based to a large extent on a speaker's alignment with the European American dialect. At the same time, the vernacular has maintained relative uniformity in the more widespread pattern of *was* leveling.

9.4 Patterns of Correlation and Individuation

In the previous section, we examined a subset of diagnostic structural items independently to reveal the range of variation for a set of speakers representing

Table 9.1   Summary of rank frequency order for vernacular dialect structures

Speaker	r-*lessness*	*PreV* CCR	*3rd* -s *Abs*	*Cop* *Abs*	was Lev.	weren't level	*Mean* *rank*
FG; 91m	8	1	—	4	—	3	4
JuM; 91f	5	4	2	1	7	7	4.3
JoM; 91m	7	2	6	7	6	4	5.3
BB; 90f	3	7	7	6	1	2	3.8
AS; 77f	5	5	4	8	3	5	5
RS; 87m	9	8	8	9	2	1	6.2
EG; 83m	2	9	3	3	5	7	4.8
DC; 80f	4	6	5	5	4	6	5
FL; 102f	1	3	1	2	—	7	3.6

a demographically defined group. We now turn to relations among structures to see if there are coherent patterns of subgroup covariance. Are there diagnostic structures that may cluster together, indicating linguistically defined subgroups within the set of speakers? Are there speakers who might be subgrouped in some meaningful way other than the demographically based definition we used for grouping elderly African American speakers? Are there social boundaries that might be ferreted out and correlated with some of the intragroup variation, or is the variation simply a case of "personal pattern variation" as defined by Dorian (1994)? What might the variation say about the role of intragroup and intergroup variation in earlier AAVE?

To determine if we could find correlations among the variables, we first ranked the speakers in terms of relative frequency level on each of the variables.[4] That is, levels of usage for each variable were rank-ordered from highest to lowest in terms of the incidence of vernacular variants, with 1 representing the most vernacular speaker in terms of the use of the variant. For this exercise, we only included nine of the 11 subjects in the original subject pool, as there were not sufficient tokens for some of the variables in the interviews of two of the speakers included in the original corpus.[5] The rank order of frequency for each speaker on each variable is summarized in table 9.1. On the basis of the frequency ranking for each of the variables, we then computed a mean rank score for each speaker, which is given in the rightmost column of table 9.1. A wide range in the mean rank orders would suggest that the speakers exist on a unified vernacular continuum for the overall set of diagnostic features whereas a narrower range would indicate greater individual variation in terms of the set of variables.

The rank orders for the entire set of variables in table 9.1 do not show a coherent overall ranking profile. The range in the mean rank scores is less

Table 9.2 Rank order of frequency usage for three AAVE features in Hyde
County

Speaker	r-*lessness*	3rd -s *Abs*	Cop *Abs*	Mean rank
FG; 91m	8	—	4	6
JuM; 91f	5	2	1	3
JoM; 91m	7	6	7	6.7
BB; 90f	3	7	6	5.3
AS; 77f	5	4	8	5.7
RS; 87m	9	8	9	8.6
EG; 83m	2	3	3	2.6
DC; 80f	4	5	5	4.6
FL; 102f	1	1	2	1.3

than 3.5 (from 2.8 through 6.2), and it is clear that speakers rank quite
differently from variable to variable. However, there do appear to be some
correlated subsets of rankings within the variables. For example, one group
of variables that shows correlation in the rank frequency includes several
hallmark AAVE features such as copula absence, third person -s absence,
and r-lessness. Speakers who rank high in terms of one of these variables
tend to rank high on the others. For example, consider table 9.2, which is
restricted to the frequency rankings for r-lessness, 3rd sg. -s absence, and
copula absence – features that are found only in the African American
community in Hyde County.

The rank order for the subset of traditional AAVE features in table 9.2
shows a correlation in the ranking, with a mean range from 1.3 through 8.6.
An application of a Pearson r correlation coefficient to the scores for the
incidence of copula deletion and 3rd sg. -s absence shows a high correlation
($r = .851$). The incidence of r-lessness also correlates positively with copula
absence ($r = .610$). We thus conclude that there is a correlated continuum
related to some of the uniquely AAVE Hyde County features. The existence of traditional AAVE structures on a continuum is not surprising; it has
been a fundamental observation about AAVE for some time now (Wolfram,
1969).

At the same time, the profile does not reveal expected correlations
for some variables that might be included within the AAVE vernacular
continuum. It also shows a couple of important negative correlations with
other diagnostic dialect variables of Hyde County. For example, the relative
frequency levels for prevocalic cluster reduction do not seem to correlate
with other, exclusively AAVE structures in Hyde County. Our correlation analyses of prevocalic cluster reduction with copula deletion ($r = -.074$)
and -s 3rd sg. absence ($r = .019$) do not reveal significant correlation

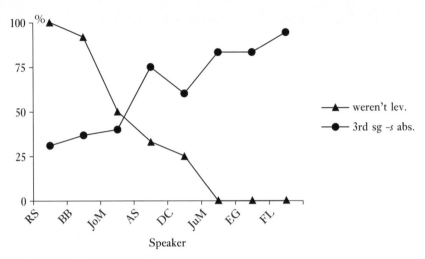

Figure 9.6   The inverse relationship of *weren't* Leveling and 3rd sg. -*s* absence

coefficients. So there is also some selective, individualized patterning of variation for particular structures within the context of a core AAVE continuum.

There are also a couple of significant negative correlations for AAVE structures and regional dialect features of Hyde County. For example, there is a strong negative correlation between leveling to *weren't* (e.g., *It weren't me*), and 3rd sg. -*s* absence ($r = -.927$), and a strong negative correlation between *weren't* leveling and copula absence ($r = -.753$), with a weaker negative correlation between *weren't* leveling and *r*-lessness as well ($r = -.515$). The inverse relationship of *weren't* leveling and 3rd sg -*s* absence is shown in figure 9.6 for the eight speakers who have sufficient tokens of both variables for quantitative analysis.

Figure 9.6 clearly demonstrates that leveling to *weren't*, a highly localized feature of the regional European American dialect, correlates inversely with a classic AAVE trait such as 3rd sg. -*s* absence. Again, this is not true for all of the distinctive AAVE and Hyde County regional features; for example, we do not find a significant negative correlation between *weren't* leveling and prevocalic cluster reduction.

Finally, we see that localized dialect features may be correlated with one another. For example, there is a positive correlation ($r = .607$) between leveling to *weren't* and 3rd pl. -*s* marking, both distinctive traits of the local regional variety. This suggests that there is some clustering of speakers and features with reference to local dialect features. At the same time, some variables seem to show independence, suggesting that there is an individual dimension to the variation as well.

9.5 Variation in Earlier AAVE

What does this analysis of elderly African American speakers in Hyde County indicate about variation in earlier African American speech and variation in long-standing insular situations? First, we must recognize that there is considerable intragroup variation even within long-standing, relatively stable insular enclave communities. Within this context, social groupings based on conventional demographic profiles, such as the delimitation of a group of "elderly working-class Hyde County African Americans" may obscure significant variation. What subgroup and individual dimensions need to be recognized within a group of elderly vernacular-speaking African Americans?

On the one hand, we are impressed with the uniformity exhibited by the speakers in our corpus with respect to some core AAVE features. For example, all of our subjects exhibited 3rd -*s* absence, copula absence, and significant levels of prevocalic consonant cluster reduction. These data provide evidence for positing a core set of vernacular dialect structures at an earlier stage of African American English even in regionalized, insular dialect contexts in the South. Given the assumption that the oldest living speakers in a continuously insular, rural community would be expected to show continuity with an earlier time period – or at least with the speech of their parents and grandparents – it may be hypothesized that some core structures of AAVE were well established, at the latest, by the mid- and late 1800s.

On the other hand, we need to recognize significant variation with respect to some AAVE features and the existence of a vernacularity continuum – even among speakers with common demographic profiles living in long-standing insular situations. Although we have illustrated the vernacularity continuum here primarily in terms of a quantitative dimension, it is obvious that the range of vernacular structures encompasses a qualitative dimension as well. A qualitative examination of the speech samples thus reveals some significant within-group differences not revealed in this quantitatively based analysis. One of the speakers in the sample, for example, uses object pronoun forms as subjects, as in *Us went down there* for *We went down there*. She and another speaker use *me* for possessives (e.g., *It's me house*) and *meself* for *myself* (e.g., *I did it meself*); others do not.[6] Furthermore, a couple of speakers use perfective *be* as in *I'm been there* for *I've been there* or *She be took it out* for *She has taken it out* whereas others do not. Both inherent quantitative and qualitative variation exist in the AAVE of an isolated regional dialect variety. It seems clear that insularity did not breed homogeneity within the African American community; nor did it result in complete convergence with the dialect of the European American community. If a long-standing insular dialect situation indicates robust intragroup variation, we would certainly expect no less for other situations in which AAVE existed historically.

This analysis also forces us to recognize an accommodation continuum in terms of the local European American regional cohort variety. For some variables, this accommodation axis seems to be related inversely to unique structures in the AAVE continuum, so that higher frequency levels of a local, European-American dialect structure correlates with lower levels of an AAVE structure. This is the case for 3rd sg. *-s* absence, a uniquely AAVE structure in Hyde County, and *weren't* leveling, a predominantly regional, traditionally European American structure. But the relationship between the two scales is much more complex than this simple inversion equation. Thus, the inverse relationship does not hold for other features, such as prevocalic cluster reduction and *weren't* leveling, even though prevocalic syllable coda cluster reduction is also uniquely African American in Hyde County. To some extent, then, the relationship between the AAVE vernacular index and local accommodation index is based on the particular linguistic variable and the individual speaker.

Although we do not yet have enough background information on all of the speakers in our corpus to conduct a detailed analysis, it is tempting to explain the accommodation continuum in terms of the extent and type of social contact that different African Americans might have with members of the cohort European American community. For example, one speaker with high levels of *weren't* leveling, substantial levels of *-s* 3rd pl. attachment, and a fairly traditional Pamlico Sound vowel system is a gregarious elderly man (born in 1910) who has had ongoing contact with a variety of European Americans in different contexts over his lifetime. For one period of his life he worked on the water, which necessitated regular work-related interaction with European American watermen; he also worked on a farm and as a maintenance worker for European Americans in town. Comments by some of the European American interviewees in our sample indicate that he is well-known and highly regarded by many European Americans in the community; the subject's remarks also tend to be fairly conciliatory in terms of race relations. However, his demographic profile in terms of traditional socioeconomic factors such as level of education, occupation, and residency do not set him apart from other elderly African Americans in our sample. Some work activities in a biracial setting may involve cooperative work activities as in commercial fishing, as opposed to other work activities that may be more independent, such as farm work in the fields.

Even if we were able to neatly subdivide the sample in terms of a kind of racial isolation index, such as that originally posited in Wolfram (1969) or the ethnically based social network profile of Edwards (1992), there are some personal attributes of speakers that go beyond contact *per se*. Thus, a couple of elderly women in the sample worked as domestics in the homes of

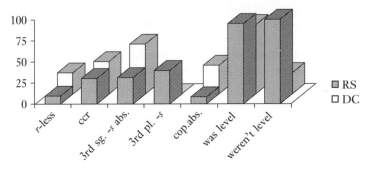

Figure 9.7   Comparison of two speakers, by diagnostic dialect structures

European Americans and were in fairly regular contact with Europeans Americans as well, but their speech does not reveal the same level of accommodation as that noted for the elderly man described above. So there may well be factors related to attitudes and personal values as well as contact *per se.*

To demonstrate the overall range of quantitative variation for individual speakers, we compare in figure 9.7 the relative use of the set of dialect features considered here for two individual speakers, the elderly man described above (RS) and a cohort elderly woman born in 1918 (DC). The elderly woman worked in the fields and in a seafood packing plant and, based on conversations with her and others in the community, had less personal contact with people in the European American community than the elderly man. Several hours of interviews have been conducted at different times with both of these speakers over a period of a couple of years, and these serve as the basis for the comparison.

As indicated in figure 9.7, some features show quite parallel patterns of variation whereas others do not. For example, the levels of consonant cluster reduction usage and leveling to *was* are comparable. At the same time, they vary widely on two local dialect features of Hyde County, leveling to *weren't* and 3rd pl. *-s* marking. And there are some marked qualitative differences as well; for example, the elderly woman uses the object pronoun form *us* regularly in subject position whereas the elderly man never does.

Our data clearly suggest that some variation may be a function more of personal history, interactional relations, and attitudes and values than conventional social divisions, or even constructed social identities. This does not discount the role of various social identities – for example, men but not women could fish and interact cooperatively with European Americans in this local community of practice – but it simply factors these into a much more complex array of variables that must be considered in explaining intragroup diversity. Among these are individualized life histories and personal identities. Although some differences certainly exist along the AAVE and the local accommodation continua, and the demographically defined group might be subdivided into finer subgroups that show covariance with linguistic variables, there remain patterns of inexplicable individual variation that seem to fall into Dorian's (1994) description of personal pattern variation.

This chapter clearly demonstrates the robust variation of earlier African American speech in terms of intra- and intercommunity dimensions. Some of the variability is due, no doubt, to the broad-based regional Southern context of earlier AAVE, some to the localized relations with cohort European American contact communities, and some due to social boundaries and identities within these communities. But there still is an idiolectal residue that must be recognized. Sorting out which kind of structural variation fits with systematically defined social and sociopsychological categories may be a complex and elusive analytical challenge, but it seems apparent that a realistic reconstruction of earlier (and contemporary) African American speech must appeal to a broad range of social and personal explanations.

Descriptions that ignore the individual – theoretically, descriptively, and methodologically – cannot provide an adequate explanation of synchronic and diachronic sociolinguistic variation. The recognition of individual variation does not, however, negate the extensive patterning of linguistic variation in terms of group affiliations and social boundaries – in small, rural, insular settings as well as large, urban settings. There is obviously a range of social factors, including social boundaries of various types and varied interactional relationships, that correlate with some of the linguistic variation. But even when the group is broken down into smaller subgroupings based on different permutations of demographic, sociocultural, and sociopsychological factors, there remain individual dimensions of variation. Speakers are both individuals with idiosyncratic life histories and affiliated members of a complex array of social groups. This dualistic perspective seems essential for describing variation – for earlier African American speech, for speakers from small, long-standing insular communities, and for sociolinguistics in general.

Notes

1 Although we have not done a VARBRUL analysis for any of our variables (see chapter 5 and Wolfram, Thomas, and Green, 2000), our speakers do exhibit a constraint pattern of *unstressed* > *coda* > *nuclear* for *r* vocalization.

2 The limited number of tokens seems to be a problem for studies of individuals. However, we support the integrity of our data on the basis of strong individual variation across linguistic environments, and among speakers with higher numbers

of tokens. If our patterns of variation were merely a function of low token totals, we would expect to find individual variation only among speakers with lower tokens, but this is not the case; they exist for speakers who have been interviewed several times and therefore have much more substantive numbers of tokens.

3   In our tabulations, we have not adjusted the figures for the leveling of *are* to *is* (e.g., *The dogs is here* for *The dogs are here*) as suggested by Green (1998). If we had done so, we might have posited that all speakers exhibited copula absence for both *is* and *are*.

4   Although we might have done a factorial analysis or a principal components analysis of our data to examine the clustering effect of linguistic variables, the relatively small number of speakers and limited set of diagnostic variables examined in this study preclude these procedures at this point in the analysis.

5   A lack of a ranking indicates an inadequately low number of tokens for the speaker and variable in question.

6   The form *me* may also result from a phonological reduction process (i.e., [maI] → [mə] → [mɨ]) in unstressed position. In most cases possessives occur in unstressed phrase position, as in the phrase *in my bóok*.

10
Beyond Hyde County: The Past and Present Development of AAVE

In the previous chapters we considered some empirical evidence for the past and present development of African American English in a unique biethnic enclave setting. At the outset of this discussion, we maintained that this situation had implications for the development of African American speech well beyond the localized context of Hyde County. We now return to some of the general questions that we raised in our earlier discussion, particularly in chapter 2. What did earlier African American English look like and how did it develop? What is the current trajectory of change for this variety and how does it align with the speech of regionalized cohort European American vernacular varieties? What is the relationship of the past to the present in the development of AAVE? While our study answers some of these questions more fully than others, it provides some of the most compelling evidence provided to date on the nature of the past and present development of African American speech and its relationship to developing regional varieties of English.

10.1 The Origin of African American English

On one level, the origin of African American English in the USA will always be a matter of speculation. Written records are sporadic and incomplete, and open to interpretation; demographic information about language use is also selective and largely anecdotal. Furthermore, great variation was exhibited in the speech of Africans when they were first brought to the "New World" and to colonial America, as indicated in references to black speech in slave advertisements and court records (Brasch, 1981). It is also indisputable that English-lexifier creole languages developed and continue to flourish in the African diaspora – from coastal West Africa to coastal North America – and that the middle passage for some Africans brought to colonial America included exposure to these creoles (Kay and Cary, 1995; Rickford, 1997, 1999; Winford, 1997). Beyond these acknowledgements, however, the origin and status of early African American speech has been and continues to be vigorously disputed.

Recent discussions of a possible widespread plantation protocreole as the structural base for the development of AAVE have included the scrutiny of both linguistic evidence (Poplack, 1999; Poplack and Tagliamonte, 2001; Rickford, 1998, 1999) and population ecology (Mufwene, 1999, 2001; Rickford, 1997; Winford, 1997). As noted in chapter 2, linguistic evidence from some enclave communities has led to the conclusion that earlier African American speech was largely indistinguishable from the speech of European Americans. Furthermore, the racial density of blacks and whites in most regions in colonial America (Mufwene, 1999, 2001) was apparently not conducive for the development of a creole, excepting some areas of coastal South Carolina and Georgia where Gullah developed.

Our study of Hyde County, as well as other isolated situations involving African Americans (Wolfram et al., 1997), raises cautions about both the linguistic facts and the sociohistorical circumstances related to earlier African American English. While we acknowledge the partial alignment of earlier regional European American and African American speech, we also find evidence for long-term substrate influence that has perpetuated an ethnolinguistic divide. Furthermore, our evidence suggests that the development and maintenance of linguistic divergence is more than a simple matter of population ecology. Although the numbers game may provide an important context for reconstructing the existence of a creole (Mufwene, 1999, 2001), it is not the only sociohistorical game in town. The strength of racial and ethnic division, the nature of social relations, and the dynamics of interethnic interaction are also critical factors to consider in reconstructing earlier African American English and may, in fact, outweigh factors related to population ecology. As Wolfram et al. (1997) observed in their analysis of a sole African American family who lived on Ocracoke for over a century, an ethnolinguistic divide can sometimes be maintained against seemingly overwhelming demographic odds. Notwithstanding such cautions, sociohistorical and demographic evidence is lacking to support the contention that an extensive plantation creole existed in the antebellum South, as originally posited by Stewart (1967, 1968) and Dillard (1972). At most, there may have been isolated pockets of creole speakers in colonial America (Rickford, 1997).

Although we do not find support for a widespread protocreole, we must acknowledge that speakers within particular communities certainly exhibited a wide range of vernacular variation that may have included some features associated with creoles as well as other language contact phenomena.

Recall, for example, the fact that a couple of elderly Hyde County African Americans considered in chapter 9 used object pronoun forms as subjects (e.g., *Us went down there* for *We went down there*) and possessives (e.g., *It's me house*; *I did it meself*) while others did not. Our observation about this variation is not intended to imply that some Hyde County African American speakers once spoke a creole; rather, it is meant to recognize a continuum of vernacularity in isolated rural communities that exhibited varying degrees of influence from earlier linguistic backgrounds.

In studies of the genesis of AAVE, evidence for substrate influence has often been linked directly to the creole-origin hypothesis. Accordingly, structural correspondence between undifferentiated pronoun use or copula absence in AAVE and in creoles of the African diaspora has sometimes been interpreted as supportive evidence for the existence of a creole in Colonial America. But this is not necessarily the case. The attribution of a structure to a creole source does not necessarily entail the position that AAVE *per se* developed from a creole language that underwent decreolization in arriving at its current form, as originally posited by Stewart (1967, 1968) and Dillard (1972). It is quite possible to maintain that contact with speakers of English-based creoles influenced developing varieties of English without adoption of the creole as a primary means of communication. Thus, Schreier (forthcoming), in his discussion of the development of English on the isolated island of Tristan da Cunha in the South Atlantic, shows that an earlier contact situation between British and American expatriates and a small group (six) of apparently creole-speaking women brought from the island of St Helena resulted in a substantive restructuring of Tristan da Cunha English. This variety now reflects fairly extensive substrate influence from the mixing of creole speakers and monolingual English speakers from England and the USA, but the historic records of the island, settled originally in the early 1800s, do not indicate that the residents of the island ever adopted a creole as a primary means of communication. It is indeed quite possible for creole substrate influence to exist apart from the widespread adoption of a creole.

It is also possible for creole language transfer to converge with influences from other types of language contact situations, including typological transfer from noncreole heritage languages and generalized interlanguage restructuring. For example, in our discussion of consonant cluster reduction (CCR) in chapter 7, we argued that substantive prevocalic CCR is most often traceable to a language contact situation involving a language that does not have syllable-coda clusters, as was the case for most West African languages spoken by African slaves (Welmers, 1973; Alleyne, 1981; Holm, 1988). Thus, a native speaker of one of these languages might adopt this phonological trait whether or not their learning of English involved a middle passage through a pidgin or creole. Of course, the developing creoles of West Africa and the Caribbean (Holm, 1988, 1989) adopted CCR as a typological trait, so that creole transfer, language transfer from African languages, and even generalized interlanguage strategies involving CCR (Tarone, 1980) would reinforce one another in the development of a less phonologically marked syllable structure.

Naturally, we cannot rule out the possibility that AAVE features such as prevocalic CCR, copula absence, or inflectional -*s* absence might have developed independently as a product of natural language change. However, such independent development has not been documented for long-term isolated, monolingual English situations (e.g., Wolfram, Thomas, and Green, 2000; Wolfram and Schilling-Estes, forthcoming). It thus seems most reasonable to conclude that our Hyde County evidence argues for durable substrate influence that was part of earlier African American English and perpetuated in the contemporary version of AAVE. Multiple causation would have reinforced these structural traits, including fossilized transfer from African languages, transfer from African diaspora creoles, generalized interlanguage strategies, and even independent language development.

Two observations from the Hyde County sociolinguistic situation support our argument that contemporary AAVE exhibits persistent substrate effect from its past language contact history. One is the long-term ethnolinguistic dichotomy exhibited by Hyde County European American and African American residents with respect to selected AAVE structures. For example, -*s* 3rd sg. absence was clearly a part of earlier African American speech in Hyde County but not of earlier Hyde County European American speech. The Pamlico Sound region is an area that has been, and continues to be, an -*s* 3rd sg. marking region rather than a region characterized by 3rd sg. -*s* absence. Although regions of colonial America and contemporary European American English elsewhere might have been characterized by 3rd sg -*s* absence, there is simply no indication that this pattern extended to Hyde County. Further, it is improbable that the lack of -*s* 3rd sg. marking would have once typified European American speakers in the region only to be lost among subsequent generations of speakers, since the community exhibits the overall retention of a number of other earlier traits. We contend, instead, that 3rd sg. -*s* absence was brought to the region at the turn of the 1700s by the earliest African Americans as a vestige of an earlier contact situation and was simply perpetuated over the centuries as a distinctive trait, as were other traits such as copula absence and extensive syllable-coda CCR.

The second bit of evidence for persistent substrate effect comes from the overall profile of accommodation. We have provided ample evidence that African Americans in Hyde County accommodated many of the regional dialect features of Hyde County speech historically, to the point of being perceptually indistinguishable from corresponding European Americans to outside listeners (see section 10.2). The fact that a small set of ethnically distinctive features would persist in an overall context of earlier accommodation suggests that these distinctive traits were strongly embedded in the speech of African Americans when they came to the area to begin with. Whereas younger Hyde County speakers are clearly influenced by external urban AAVE norms, there is no evidence for selective borrowing from outside African American groups in earlier generations of speakers who otherwise accommodated local dialect norms. We discuss some possible explanations for this selective maintenance in section 10.3; for our purposes here, it is sufficient to observe that the sociolinguistic context and the sociohistorical background of Hyde County support the contention that substrate influence is responsible for the perpetuation of some ethnolinguistic differences in AAVE and European American vernaculars – in Hyde County and elsewhere in the USA.

10.2 The Regional Context of Earlier African American English

The results of this study show that earlier Hyde County African Americans accommodated the regional dialect much more than the current generation of African Americans. Most of the salient dialect traits of Pamlico Sound English are manifested in the speech of older generations of speakers regardless of ethnicity. Thus, the distinctive vowel system presented in chapter 6, regional consonant variables such as the highly localized pattern of post-/ð/ *r*-lessness discussed in chapter 7, and the morphosyntactic variables of *weren't* leveling and 3rd pl. -*s* marking considered in chapter 5 showed elderly African American speakers to be aligned with their European American cohorts. This alignment, however, is not maintained by younger European Americans and African Americans, who differ markedly in their dialect norms.

The general recession of traditional Pamlico Sound dialect features is, of course, not unique to the African American community in Hyde County. For example, European Americans show a parallel decline in the use of traditional Pamlico Sound vowel features and the distinctive pattern of post-/ð/ *r*-lessness. Similarly, the European American community reveals attrition in the use of the 3rd pl. -*s* marking pattern that was once a prominent feature of the local variety. But there are two important differences that suggest that a significant ethnolinguistic divide has developed, or more accurately, widened over time. First, we see that African Americans do not participate in the pattern of local dialect focusing that we uncovered for European Americans. In chapter 5 we showed that older European American and African American speakers were quite similar in their use of *weren't* leveling but that younger generations of speakers diverged dramatically. Younger vernacular European American speakers intensified their use of *weren't* leveling whereas younger African American speakers abandoned the use of this dialect structure. This divergence, in which European Americans accentuate their use of a prominent local dialect structure while African Americans relinquish it, suggests that the older pattern of local dialect accommodation by African Americans has been replaced by a different normative model.

African Americans are clearly supplanting the traditional Pamlico Sound English with core AAVE features that are shared with external communities of African Americans, whereas European Americans, notwithstanding a couple of cases of dialect focusing, are replacing these features with a combination of Southern and Midland vernacular structures (Wolfram and Schilling-Estes, 1997). The younger generation of African American speakers in Hyde County is intensifying some of the core AAVE features that were evident in the older generations of speakers, as well as adding some evolving features of AAVE not found among previous generations of speakers. Frequency levels of copula absence and *r*-vocalization, for example, which are prime traits of core AAVE throughout the USA, are higher for the younger speakers than for the older, and the use of habitual *be*, largely absent in the speech of the older cohorts, has now been adopted by younger speakers (Addy, 2000). Not only are African Americans in Hyde County abandoning the regional dialect of Pamlico Sound, they are also adjusting their linguistic orientation towards an external norm.

Without extensive study of the regional context of Earlier African American English in other representative locales, it is difficult to say how applicable these findings might be to earlier African American English in general. However, there is some emerging evidence that suggests that the picture we have painted here is not unique to Hyde County. Studies of ex-slave written documents by Montgomery and his colleagues (Montgomery et al., 1993; Montgomery and Fuller, 1996) reveal regional dialect patterns more than they do the features considered to be core AAVE structures. Montgomery's data, for example, show that -*s* 3rd pl. -*s* marking is well represented in the letters but that -*s* 3rd sg. absence is not particularly prominent.

From a somewhat different vantage point, the detailed phonetic analysis of the vowel system of an ex-slave from Charlottesville, Virginia, born in 1848 (Thomas, 2001a) also indicates regional vowel accommodation – in particular, the raising of the nucleus in the /au/ diphthong, a prominent regional trait of this region at the time of the subject's residency. Further support comes from an emerging study of an isolated black and white enclave Appalachian mountain community of former feldspar miners in Beech Bottom, North Carolina, located by the Tennessee border, where older African American speakers strongly accommodated the local dialect norms (Mallinson, Wolfram, and Fried, 2001). Such evidence suggests that the earlier versions of African American English were probably much more locally aligned with regional dialects than the twentieth century counterpart. In fact, Thomas and Bailey (1998), speaking of the monophthongal forms of /e/ and /o/ found in the "Low Country" of South Carolina, argue that local alignment could include accommodation of European Americans to the speech of African Americans in areas of high African American density.

One of the by-products of the earlier regionalization of African American speech is that it may have obscured ethnolinguistic distinctiveness – at least to outside listeners.[1] The speech of elderly African American speakers in Hyde County, for example, tends to be more readily associated with European American speech than that of their younger speakers. To examine the empirical basis for this observation, we constructed two speaker identification experiments involving recorded speech samples representing several types of speakers. For the first experiment, we extracted passages of 20–30 seconds each from conversational interviews with seven different speakers.[2] The content of the passages consisted of human-interest stories that were neutral with respect to ethnic content so that they precluded ethnic identification based on the content of the passage rather than speech *per se*. The speakers included a middle-aged European American speaker from Hyde County (born 1945), an elderly (born 1910) and younger (born 1975) African American from Hyde County, an older African American speaker from the Piedmont area of North Carolina located near Raleigh, North Carolina, the ex-slave from Charlottesville, Virginia, mentioned above, and a Native American and European American speaker from the coastal plain of North Carolina. For the purposes of this investigation, we concern ourselves only with the first five speakers.

We played the sample passages to group of listeners in Raleigh, North Carolina, and asked them simply to identify the ethnicity of each speaker. Of the 29 listeners who participated in the task, 13 were African American and 16 European American; none of the listeners was originally from Hyde County, and most knew very little about it. The results of the task for the five speakers of relevance to this study are summarized in table 10.1. Significant differences in correct identification (Chi square test of significance) are shaded.

Note, in particular, the contrast between the correct identification of the elderly and young African American speaker from Hyde County. The elderly speaker is correctly identified as African American by only 10 percent of the listeners and the young speaker is correctly identified by 90 percent of the listeners, and there is not a significant difference based on the ethnicity of the listeners. The generational difference takes on more significance when we consider the background of the two speakers with such contrastive scores. Not only are these two speakers lifetime residents of

Table 10.1 Results from the first speaker identification experiment

Listener identification	Outer Banks Euro. Am.	Elderly Coastal NC Af. Am.	Young Coastal NC Af. Am.	Mainland NC rural Af. Am.	Ex-slave Charlottesville VA
Total correct ethnic identification (N = 29)	100%	*10.4%	89.7%	100%	*69.0.6%
Correct ethnic identification Euro. Am. judges (N = 16)	100%	15.4%	84.6%	100%	76.9%
Correct ethnic identification Af. Am. judges (N = 13)	100%	6.3%	93.8%	100%	62.5%

* = Significant difference in correct identification (Chi square).

Hyde County, but they lived in the same home and are related; in fact, the elderly speaker is the great-grandfather of the young speaker. The great-grandfather, whose speech shows many of the regional dialect features found in the speech of cohort European Americans, is overwhelmingly identified by both African American and European American listeners as "white" while his great-granddaughter, whose speech exhibits many traits of contemporary AAVE, is overwhelmingly identified as African American.

The generational split in ethnic identification within a single Hyde County family should not be taken to mean that earlier African American English was always indistinguishable from European American speech. The elderly African American speaker from the Piedmont area of North Carolina (taken from the subject pool of Hazen, 2000a) was, in fact, categorically identified as African American by the same listeners who misidentified the elderly African American from Hyde County as white. Meanwhile, the correct ethnic identification of the ex-slave from Charlottesville, Virginia, was more inconsistent, probably due to the regional production of the /au/ diphthong with a raised nucleus. It may be that this distinctly regional /au/ production moderates the ethnic classification of the speaker, since highly regionalized dialect traits tend to be associated, for the most part, with European American varieties in the USA.

The second experiment was a more controlled procedure on the role of specific features in triggering ethnic identification and was carried out by

Thomas and Reaser (2001). A review of literature on features used for black/white ethnic identification is found in Thomas (2001b). For this experiment, five-second excerpts were extracted from NCLLP recordings of 24 speakers: 12 Hyde County African Americans, six Hyde County European Americans, four inland African Americans, and two inland European Americans. The inland speakers were included as controls. The Hyde Countians were selected to represent a range of ages. For each of the Hyde County speakers, two excerpts were included, one featuring diagnostic Pamlico Sound vowel variants (usually fronted /o/) prominently and the other not doing so. Distinctive morphosyntactic variants and content that might reveal the speaker's ethnicity were avoided in the excerpts. Once all the excerpts were collected, the signals were subjected to three treatments. The first treatment was to leave them unmodified. The second treatment was monotonization – that is, conversion of F_0 to a constant value for the entire signal (120 Hz for males and 200 Hz for females). Monotonization was accomplished with the Kay Analysis Synthesis Laboratory, Model 4304, which is a linear predictive coding (LPC) synthesizer. The purpose of monotonization was to eliminate intonation and other F_0-related cues from the signal. The third treatment was lowpass filtering at 325 Hz, which was accomplished using the Kay CSL. Lowpass filtering eliminates segmental information from the signal. Each group of respondents who participated in the experiment heard stimuli with only one of the three treatments.

The stimuli were placed in random order. The first three stimuli were repeated at the end and the results from the initial playing of these stimuli were excluded from the analyses. The stimuli were divided into sets of five, and before each set a voice on the recording announced "Group One," "Group Two," and so forth. Each stimulus was repeated once on the recording, with a two-second pause between the first and second instances of a stimulus and between different stimuli. The same order of stimuli was used for each of the three treatments.[3] Results are given in table 10.2. Figures for African American subjects are shown only for the monotonal stimuli because too few African American subjects listened to the other two treatments.

Overall, the unmodified and monotonal stimuli were identified much more accurately than the lowpass filtered stimuli. In fact, identifications of the lowpass filtered stimuli were close to random (50%). This result might suggest that intonation was not a factor in the identifications. However, the filtering may have eliminated so much information as to make the filtered stimuli unrecognizable. It is also possible that prosodic elements in the individual stimuli, such as intonation, overall F_0 level, and rhythm, were atypical of the ethnicity that each one represented and thus misled the subjects.

Another important trend is that Hyde County European Americans and the inland speakers were identified far more accurately than Hyde County African Americans. Identification accuracy for the Hyde County African

Table 10.2   Percentages of correct ethnic identifications in the second speaker identification experiment

	European American respondents			Afr. Am. respondents
Stimuli	unmodified (N = 29) % Correct	monotonal (N = 40) % Correct	lowpass filtered (N = 35) % Correct	monotonal (N = 13) % Correct
Hyde Co. African Am.				
all stimuli	56.3	59.7	53.0	47.7
diagnostic vowels prominent	44.3	51.9	47.1	36.8
diagnostic vowels not prominent	68.4	67.7	58.8	58.7
Hyde Co. European Am.				
all stimuli	89.1	89.2	47.1	89.1
diagnostic vowels prominent	88.5	89.2	45.7	89.7
diagnostic vowels not prominent	89.7	89.2	48.6	88.5
Inland African Am.	92.2	91.2	66.4	90.4
Inland European Am.	98.3%	80.0%	52.9%	88.5%

Americans did not exceed 60 percent for any of the treatments. In contrast, identification accuracy for the other speakers never dropped below 80 percent for the unmodified or monotonized treatments. It is clear that listeners found the speech of the Hyde County African Americans ambiguous as to ethnic markers. It should also be pointed out, though, that there were twice as many African American stimuli in the experiment as European American stimuli, and subjects were not told what the ratio was. It is likely that the accuracy rates would have differed if there had been an equal number of African American and European American stimuli or if subjects had been informed about the ratio.

Nevertheless, the results from the experiment provide important evidence about what cues the subjects were responding to. The results for the unmodified and monotonized treatments are virtually the same for all the stimuli, which suggests that listeners did not require intonation or overall F_0 level to make their identifications. However, subjects could also have been responding to possible differences in timing, shimmer (local amplitude variation), or global amplitude variation, none of which monotonization filters out. The difference in accuracy for the stimuli that featured diagnostic vowels prominently and those that did not provides further evidence for our conclusions about the effect of regional dialect features in assessing ethnic identification. For the Hyde County African Americans, the stimuli featuring diagnostic vowels were identified significantly less accurately than those that did not feature these vowels (p < .001 on Chi square test in all treatments for African American respondents). In contrast, accuracy rates for identifications of Hyde County European Americans were almost exactly the same for stimuli featuring diagnostic vowels prominently and those not doing so. These findings demonstrate that the subjects in the experiment were reacting to vowel variants. It does not rule out the possibility that they were responding to other cues as well, but it is clear that vowel variants – mainly fronted /o/ – were misleading the subjects. The distinctive Pamlico Sound vowel variants are associated with European American identity and dissociated with African American identity. As Hyde Countians have gained more contact with outside regions, they have surely gained more exposure to inland norms.

Evidence from the speaker identification experiments, along with the cross-generational linguistic analysis of dialect features in Hyde County, clearly supports the contention that some earlier varieties of English spoken by African Americans were probably quite regionalized. Younger speakers in these regions, however, are losing their regional dialect identities as they acquire structures representing the common core features found in AAVE speakers throughout the USA. We discuss the broader sociocultural and sociopolitical implications of this change in 10.6.

10.3 Levels of Linguistic Alignment

The phonological and morphosyntactic variables examined in this study reveal a pattern of mixed alignment for earlier Hyde County English. For as long as we could project into the past history of Hyde County, African Americans and European Americans shared some distinctive regional dialect features at the same time that they also revealed an ethnolinguistic division for other features. On a phonological level, both ethnic speech communities shared the distinctive vowel traits of the Pamlico Sound dialect (chapter 6) as well as some distinctive consonantal traits, such as the distinctive pattern of post-/ð/ r-vocalization (chapter 7). At the same time, there have been some long-standing differences between the groups, such as consonant cluster reduction; prevocalic cluster reduction has been significantly different in the African American and the European American speech communities of Hyde County for as long as we could document. There have also been long-term differences in syllable-onset clusters such as *skr* for *str*, as well as other syllable structure differences. For morphosyntactic phenomena, we established that earlier African American and European American speech shared the distinctive Pamlico Sound version of past tense *weren't* leveling as well as the pattern of verbal -*s* marking with plural subjects. As with phonology, however, there are a couple of features of AAVE in Hyde County that have apparently always been and continue to be dissimilar – both in earlier and in contemporary vernacular varieties in Hyde County. These include the optional marking of 3rd sg. -*s* and copula absence. So even as African Americans accommodated some regional dialect traits, there was evidence of residual differences that distinguished African Americans from the norms of their cohort European American vernacular speakers.

How do we explain these patterns of long-standing congruity and divergence? In our specific discussion of diagnostic structures, we offered several possible explanations. Part of the reason for the alignment pattern may be related to the linguistic system itself. With respect to phonology, we suggested that highly marked syllable-coda clusters and other marked phonotactic phenomena such as initial *str* clusters might be predisposed towards perpetuating long-term language contact effects. Although not many studies have examined the potential for differential substrate phonological effects based on the distinction between syntagmatic versus paradigmatic patterning, there is some evidence that phonotactic patterns may be more likely to exhibit long-standing substrate effects than paradigmatic ones (Sabino, 1994b). There is also support for this explanation from first language and second language acquisition, where marked syllable structure phenomena tend to be acquired later than paradigmatic segmental features (Ingram, 1989; Tarone, 1980; Odlin, 1989). Of course, the explanation is hardly as simple as the distinction between paradigmatic versus syntagmatic patterning, since they entail the relative marking of phonological structures. Though specific ranking hierarchies of markedness may be difficult to motivate formally, there seems to be little question that some kinds of structures are more highly marked than others, regardless of the criteria or the notational scheme used to represent marking hierarchies (Battistella, 1990). Certainly, structures like syllable-coda clusters and three-segment syllable-onset clusters such as *str* would be among the most marked phonotactic sequences regardless of the formal ranking schemata, and these are precisely the kinds of items that show persistent effects from the historical contact situation.

We also posit an internal-systemic explanation for some of the long-term morphosyntactic effects. There is ample evidence that inflectional processes such as 3rd sg. -*s* verbal attachment, as well as suffixation of possessive and plural -*s*, are predisposed towards leveling or simplification based on their status within the English morphosyntactic system. Thus, 3rd -*s*, a redundant inflectional suffix with no thematic syntactic role within a relatively weak subject–verb concord system, is highly vulnerable to unmarking. This vulnerability is evidenced in a number of independent situations where contact or independent development has led to the loss of 3rd sg. -*s* in varieties of English in the British Isles and elsewhere (Trudgill, 1990; Cheshire, 1991; Schreier, forthcoming), to say nothing of creole situations (Alleyne, 1980; Holm, 1988, 1989) and other conditions (e.g., language impairment) that affect morphosytnactic composition (Myers–Scotton, 1998; Myers–Scotton and Jake, forthcoming). Myers–Scotton's 4-M model, for example, posits a hierarchy of morphemes vulnerable to loss or transfer based on internal levels of systemic organization; in this scheme, redundant inflectional morphemes would be most likely to be vulnerable in various kinds of language adaptation situations regardless of the internal or external stimulus.

While we recognize the role of internal systemic factors in predisposing structures for adaptation, we have also suggested that linguistic organization alone is not sufficient for explaining patterns of accommodation and divergence. Part of the explanation may reside in sociopsychological factors as well. Thus, the social marking of dialect structures may be involved. Distinguishing vowel traits and characteristic Pamlico Sound morphosynatctic structures were among the features adopted by Hyde County African Americans over the centuries of biethnic coexistence. In this respect, there seems to have been a symbolic accommodation of the most locally marked dialect features. The sociopsychological basis for this symbolic adoption is supported by the observation (chapter 9) that elderly African American speakers who had more regular interaction with members of the European American community and expressed more accommodating cultural values tended to display higher levels of local dialect features. We also observed that for many elderly speakers, the exclusive Pamlico Sound dialect represented additive rather than replacive features. That is, it seemed quite possible to add local dialect features alongside traits that exhibited long-term contact effects, especially when the features were not in direct structural conflict with each other. Thus, we could observe a kind of synergism in which substrate effects that perpetuated ethnolinguistic distinctiveness could be combined with the accommodation of local dialect structures. The most noteworthy example of this dialect synergism is verbal -*s* marking, where both -*s* 3rd sg. absence and 3rd pl. -*s* marking were accommodated within the verbal paradigm of elderly African American speakers. We hypothesized in chapter 5 that 3rd sg. -*s* absence was a persistent substrate effect while the application of -*s* marking to plurals was indicative of local dialect accommodation. Although a kind of ebb and flow (Hickey, forthcoming a) of substrate and accommodation effects may be reflected in some of the quantitative differences over time and for particular individuals, there is clear evidence for long-term, mixed alignment that reflects both the past and the present state of African American English.

Although it has been noted that morphosyntactic features are more likely to show persistent ethnolinguistic differences than phonological ones because of the level of structural integration (Rickford, 1985), this observation is moderated by two observations. First, it must be noted that there is a range of structural complexity within both phonology and grammar, so that the particular level of complexity may mitigate the grammar–phonology dichotomy or markedness reflected in particular structures. In fact, part of our argument for the long-term ethnolinguistic division in prevocalic consonant cluster reduction was related to the highly marked nature of syllable-coda consonant clusters. This suggests that it is the level of structural integration *per se* rather than module of language organization that is central in the argument about linguistic levels of alignment.

As noted above, social marking may also be a mitigating factor in understanding alignment patterns. Thus, the symbolic significance of various phonological and morphosyntactic phenomena may play a role in explaining patterns of congruence and divergence. For example, in the Pamlico Sound dialect, phonological features have been assigned much more symbolic value than grammatical ones. In their study of a lone African American family that lived on the island of Ocracoke for over a century, Wolfram, Hazen, and Tamburro (1997) showed that phonological structures tend to be more diagnostic than morphosyntactic structures as indicators of ethnolinguistic alignment among the different members of the family. Accordingly, diagnostic phonological structures are manipulated to indicate social congruity and dissonance. We thus see that the level of linguistic alignment is not only sensitive to linguistic composition but is responsive to social marking as well. Phonological and morphosyntactic structures may therefore be implicated differentially in the alignment of African American speakers based on their symbolic status as social markers.

10.4 The Trajectory of Language Change

One of the most instructive findings of this study concerns the trajectory of language change revealed for the African American and European American populations in Hyde County. Several different paths of convergence and divergence have been charted for particular structures in terms of the models of change outlined originally in chapter 2. First, we have found parallel paths of development for dialect items that were shared by African Americans and European Americans in the past. For example, 3rd pl. *-s* marking (e.g., *The dogs barks*) was once a prominent dialect pattern for both African Americans and European Americans although there were some differences in the constraints on -*s* marking detailed in chapter 5 (viz., the NP vs. pronoun subject constraint). However, this -*s* marking pattern has receded so that neither young African Americans nor young European Americans mark verbal -*s* with plural subjects to any extent. A number of the vowel traits of Hyde County are also receding for both groups of speakers, such as lowering of /e/ before *r* (e.g., *bear, there*) and the raised nondiphthongal production of /ɔ/.

A second path of change involves divergence for dialect structures that were once shared. These routes of change may involve primary divergence on the part of either the European American or the African American community, or, in a couple of cases, mutual divergence. In the case of *weren't* leveling (e.g., *I weren't there*) we find the European American community accentuating a feature that has receded completely for the African American community, thus showing a type of mutual divergence. In the case of habitual *be* in *be* + verb + *ing* (Addy, 2000), there is primary divergence by the African American community. Neither ethnic group used habitual *be* to any extent in the past; European Americans have stayed the course while African Americans show grammatical innovation. In this case, we find African Americans taking the lead in terms of divergence.

Other features show more complicated paths of change for once-common dialect traits. We observed in chapter 6 that the backed nucleus of the iconic Pamlico Sound diphthong /ai/ of *tide, time*, and *right* was – unexpectedly – stable among European Americans, though it was undergoing fronting among African Americans. The glide showed a great deal of individual variation. However, in general, it was being weakened before voiced obstruents, as in *tide* (and presumably before other voiced consonants, as in *time*) between both ethnicities. This development brings Hyde County speech in line with general Southern norms and with general AAVE norms. Before voiceless obstruents, as in *right*, European Americans showed no clear overall direction of change but considerable individual variation. African Americans seemed to be lowering the glide before voiceless obstruents, which would represent a departure from the general AAVE norm. Thomas and Bailey (1998) and Thomas (2001a) show prevoiceless glide weakening to be a feature of white Southern American English but not of African American Southern speech (but see Anderson and Milroy, 1999; Anderson, 2002). One potentially important finding is that younger European American speakers who reduce the /ay/ glide before voiceless obstruents also tend to use *weren't* leveling. It may well be the case that these features work in tandem in their ethnolinguistic effect, perhaps serving as an identity marker for a particular subgroup of European Americans. The shifting vernacular norms for European Americans and African Americans in Hyde County will be discussed more extensively in section 10.5. At this point it is sufficient to note that a number of different trajectories of change have been documented in relation to features that were once shared by both speech communities.

Different routes of change have also been documented for dialect features that were historically differentiated by ethnicity. In some cases, we have found the stable maintenance of differences so that prevocalic consonant cluster reduction has been maintained at a fairly parallel level across the generations of European American and African American speakers. There are also cases where the groups follow parallel courses of change, as in the case of *was* leveling; older speakers in both ethnic groups had higher levels of leveling while younger speakers have lower levels by comparison. Structures that are particularly sensitive to mainstream standard English norms often tend to show this path of change. Although we have not considered irregular verb use in this study in quantitative detail, we would expect a similar patterning in the reduction of regularization (e.g., *growed* for *grew*), bare root pasts (e.g., *run* for *ran*, *come* for *came*), and other types of changes in irregular verb (e.g., *done* for *did* or *seen* for *saw* as a past) use over time.

At the same time, we have found some cases where earlier dialect disparities between the African American and European American communities have been accentuated. For example, overall levels of postvocalic *r*-lessness and copula absence, particularly for *are*, have increased for younger African Americans. Although differences between the two speech communities existed to begin with, the quantitative gap has widened. This finding is similar to the pattern of divergence found by Rickford (1992, 1999) in his examination of some of the core structures of African American English in Palo Alto, California, a sociolinguistic setting quite different from the one under consideration here. We have already mentioned how the use of *weren't* is intensifying for European Americans as it recedes for African Americans, showing that European Americans can also proactively lead the way toward ethnolinguistic divergence.

Our study shows that the course of change for African Americans in Hyde County does not follow a simple regression slope across different generations. For a number of characteristic traits of Pamlico Sound English, we have found that the oldest group of African Americans shows a high level of alignment with Pamlico Sound English which is followed by a period of even more intensified accommodation, only to be followed by a sharp regression slope in the use of Pamlico Sound features by successive generations of speakers. Over the same time span, some core AAVE features showed a mirror image in their change trajectories, with the oldest group of speakers showing moderate levels of core AAVE features, the next generation showing a reduction of these features, and the two younger generations showing a progressive increase. The idealized trajectory of change across

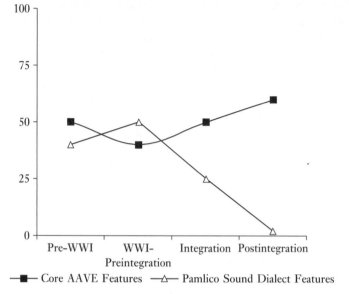

Figure 10.1   Idealized model of change for African Americans in Hyde County

the generations in terms of specific Pamlico Sound features and core AAVE feature is plotted in figure 10.1. For convenience, the four periods are broken down on the basis of different sociohistorical periods: speakers who were born and raised in the early twentieth century up through World War I; speakers born and raised between World War I and school integration in the late 1960s; speakers who lived through the early period of school integration as adolescents, and those who were born and raised after integration.

    Although the change trajectory in Pamlico Sound and core AAVE structures might be attributed to the size of our sample (particularly for the senior and middle age groups), the fact that some of these speakers represent different generations within the same family militates against this explanation. Instead, we turn to the social history of Hyde County for a potential explanation. The middle group of speakers in our sample represents those born in the middle 1950s through the mid 1960s – the group most directly affected by the racial conflict brought about by court-ordered school integration. As children and adolescents they experienced the social upheaval of school integration firsthand. The reader may recall from our discussion in chapter 4 that this integration did not come easily, with protests and marches to preserve the integrity of the historically black schools of Hyde County and the cohesion of the Hyde County African American community. In this sociopolitical milieu, and in the integrated schools that followed, African Americans started intensifying the ethnolinguistic divide between the groups – by reducing the alignment with local Pamlico Sound features and increasing the adoption of core AAVE structures. We thus see that the integration period actually corresponded with a reduction rather than an increase in dialect accommodation by the African American community. Following that period, we also find dialect focusing of local features by the European American speech community. On one level, this path of change speaks to the limited effects of institutionally mandated integration in circumscribed settings on dialect convergence. On another level, however, it speaks to the growing consciousness of the role of language in maintaining ethnolinguistic identity in the face of sociopolitical pressure and legal coercion to integrate – by both African Americans and European Americans. For the study of African American English over time, it speaks further to the significant effect of social circumstances and change as we consider the context for the development of AAVE. Language change cannot be divorced from the social and historical events that affect general populations and specific communities of speakers.

Our examination of change in apparent time shows a number of different trajectories. Furthermore, it offers important cautions with respect to discussions of the divergence hypothesis as set forth over the past couple of decades. First, it underscores the need for the examination of a full range of structures in charting the empirical course of change in AAVE. A very different picture of change in African American speech might emerge if a researcher focused on the vowel system, selected consonant structures, *weren't* regularization, 3rd pl. *-s* marking, 3rd sg. *-s* absence, or copula absence. While single-structure studies may reveal significant insights into a particular linguistic process and/or on a particular dimension of an ethnolinguistic boundary, such studies may obscure or even distort our understanding of the relationship of African American speech to other varieties. Our investigation of fairly broad ranges of phonological and morphosyntactic structures has certainly demonstrated the need for extending the range of variables in the study of ethnolinguistic boundaries.

Second, this study cautions us against the reduction of change in AAVE and European American vernaculars to categorical assessments in terms of convergence or divergence. The empirically documented profile of change is much more complicated than that; in fact, most of the possible paths of convergence and divergence outlined in chapter 2 have been documented within Hyde County, including divergence by the African American speech community, divergence by the European American speech community, mutual divergence, parallel change, and even some convergence. Depending on the variable under examination, the picture of language change in the respective vernacular communities may be very different indeed. At the same time, there is an indisputable and significant overall change taking place in how the African American and European American vernacular speech communities are defining themselves in relation to each other, as well as in relation to other communities. It is therefore essential to keep both the linguistic trees and the sociolinguistic forest in view as we attempt to capture a clear picture of change in earlier and contemporary AAVE.

10.5 The Norming of AAVE

All language communities engage in language norming, that is, the establishment of appropriate models of language behavior for members of the speech community. In this respect, socially subordinate, vernacular-speaking communities are no different from their socially dominant, "mainstream" counterparts. Although there is a substantial base of knowledge about the development and codification of standard English norms, sociolinguistics has paid little attention to the process of instantiating, transmitting, and regulating vernacular norms within indigenous speech communities. Most descriptions of vernacular dialects, including the one offered here, are content to describe dialect forms simply by comparing them with a codified or implicit standard English norm, even when describing the patterns of vernacular varieties as linguistically independent rules or processes. Little attention has been given to the process whereby vernacular norms are instantiated and regulated within a community. Notwithstanding the lack of attention, the norming of vernacular varieties should be a central question in sociolinguistic inquiry. We thus conclude our investigation of AAVE by opening up the discussion of vernacular language norming – in Hyde County and in other locations within the USA.

10.5.1 Issues in vernacular dialect norming

At least four major issues need to be recognized in the construction of vernacular dialect norms: (1) the actuation issue, (2) the embedding issue, (3) the diffusion issue, and (4) the dynamic issue.[4] The *actuation issue* refers to the process whereby vernacular dialect structures are initiated to begin with. What internal and external forces give rise to the emergence of vernacular dialect forms and norms? Linguistic explanations for the initiation of vernacular dialect structures may include differential language change, language contact, and independent language development. In differential language change, structural features once shared by the speakers of the language at large may be retained and established as part of the normative vernacular by some speech communities, while other groups of speakers lose or change these structures in different ways. Structures associated with vernacular varieties also may be activated through the linguistic negotiation of language contact situations, including direct and indirect language transfer as well as accommodation. Some of the vernacular language norms of AAVE, for example, are attributable to the long-term substratal effects of an earlier language contact situation in the African diaspora, just as dialect norms in other ethnic communities may reflect the residual effects of their heritage languages. It is also important to observe that some normative vernacular structures are actuated by internally motivated language changes, as we discussed in chapter 3. These may involve parallel independent development, or Sapir's (1921) "drift," due to the operation of general processes of analogy and the universal tendency to move toward unmarked forms. Such developments result from natural processes that guide change quite independently from diffusion or language contact.

The *embedding issue* concerns the social processes whereby linguistic features are incorporated into and ratified as part of the vernacular norm, including the assignment of sociolinguistic significance. On one level, the establishment of vernacular variants appears to be a relatively straightforward case of covariance in which particular linguistic variants become established as vernacular norms by virtue of their association with particular socially subordinate groups. On another level, however, the instantiation is a complex, selective process. There are *social indicators* (no conscious recognition), *social markers* (conscious recognition without overt comment), and *stereotypes* (conscious recognition and the object of overt commentary) within vernacular dialect communities, just as there are in the socially favored dialects (Labov, 1966, 1972b:178–80). Furthermore, there may be an interactive effect between the linguistic principles that drive language change and the social mechanisms that ascribe social meaning to particular forms in the construction of vernacular norms.

The *diffusion issue* concerns the spread of vernacular norms, both within the social networks of localized speech communities and across larger populations of vernacular-speaking communities. Differential patterns of settlement and resettlement, migration patterns, and intra- and inter-community interaction patterns are involved. Traditional models of dialect diffusion focus on the *contagious model*, in which the spread of features follows a straightforward wave-like time and distance relation; the *hierarchical model*, in which features spread from areas of denser population to areas of sparser population; or the *contrahierarchical model*, in which features spread from more sparsely populated areas to more densely populated ones (Bailey, Wikle, Tillery, and Sand, 1991). As useful as these macro models may be, we cannot simply assume that they will apply to the spread of change among socially subordinate, vernacular-speaking groups as they do to socially favored, superordinate population groups. It is also possible that these models related to population ecology may be insufficient to explain how vernacular normativization takes place on a community level. In fact, we hypothesize that mechanistic models of diffusion do not adequately account for some of the supraregional, normative developments taking place in contemporary AAVE.

The *dynamic issue* relates to the fact that vernacular varieties, like all other dialects, are constantly undergoing change. Accordingly, their language norms shift as well. What kinds of structural features change and how do such changes affect the reconfiguration of vernacular norms? How have the norms of different vernaculars changed over time, and what social mechanisms are used to transmit and regulate these changing norms? With reference to norming, there appears to be an essential difference in the establishment of norms for overtly sanctioned varieties recognized as standard varieties and the establishment of nonmainstream vernacular norms. Usage books, orthoepical guides, Internet grammar hotlines, and other venues provide for the codification of standard English, and various language agents, including recognized language experts, teachers, parents, and caretakers, serve as gatekeepers for the standard norm. However, no comparable codification of vernacular norms exists, and their transmission and regulation takes place on a much more covert, informal regulatory level. At this point, we know little about the regulatory procedures and social mechanisms used to instantiate and perpetuate vernacular dialect norms.

There may also be important differences in the rate of normative change for vernacular varieties as compared with their standard counterparts. Codified norms of socially dominant varieties tend to be relatively conservative and resistant to ongoing change. But this is not necessarily the case for some vernacular norms. According to Chambers (1995:246), a standard norm is "more restricted or tightly constrained in its grammar and phonology" due to the social pressures to resist some natural linguistic changes. Standard varieties therefore may resist the natural pull of some natural processes because socially sanctioned, mainstream norms tend to emphasize permanency and conscious resistance to some natural linguistic changes. By the same token, however, some characteristic traits of vernacular English norms have existed for centuries, therefore showing a kind of permanency in their own right.

While not all of the issues raised here can be addressed in detail, they should prove essential for future discussions of vernacular dialect norming. Perhaps more importantly, they point to the need for recognizing that the construction of vernacular norms involves a complex array of intersecting linguistic, social, psychological, and ideological factors fully deserving of careful sociolinguistic scrutiny.

10.5.2 Vernacular language norming in Hyde County

Our empirical evidence suggests that the roots of vernacular norms in AAVE were established early in the history of African American English, and that many of the current features associated with AAVE were well established in Hyde County by the beginning of the 1800s. In the process, these traits mixed readily with local dialect features represented in cohort European American varieties. Given the distinctiveness of the local dialect, the regional character tended to become a prominent reference point in the dialect identity of earlier Hyde County African Americans. In the twentieth century, however, AAVE intensified some of its ethnically marked features as it distanced itself from local dialect traits found in the cohort European American communities. In effect, African American speech in Hyde County turned away from local, rural norms toward the norms of AAVE found in other settings throughout the USA, particularly urban contexts. It is now well established that there is a core set of AAVE structures regardless of where AAVE is spoken in the USA (e.g., Fasold and Wolfram, 1970; Labov, 1972a; Bailey and Thomas, 1998; Rickford, 1999). This generalized core of features seems to be the norm that younger African American speakers are turning to as their vernacular model at the same time they are moving away from the Hyde County regional dialect norms. Young European American vernacular speakers, on the other hand, are accentuating selected local features and diverging from the normative path adopted by their African American counterparts. Meanwhile, there is an overall recession in some traditional dialect traits of Pamlico Sound English. An illustrative profile of some of the diagnostic linguistic structures in this normative shift is given in table 10.3. The table includes five different age/ethnic groups of speakers: elderly Hyde County European Americans, elderly Hyde County African Americans, younger Hyde County European Americans, younger Hyde County African Americans, and contemporary urban AAVE speakers. The structural characteristics of the contemporary urban norms are based on summaries such as Rickford (1999:4–9), which is in turn based on earlier studies such as Labov et al. (1968), Wolfram (1969), and Fasold and Wolfram (1970). Changes in structural features are organized according to the following categories: receding dialect traits, persistent dialect traits, and newly acquired traits. In the table, + indicates the presence of a trait, − the absence of a trait, and +/− or −/+ the limited occurrence of the trait, with the preferred value indicated by the order of the values.

The most noteworthy pattern in table 10.3 is the alliance of the speech of younger Hyde County African American speakers with contemporary urban AAVE norms. This is exhibited both in the change away from local dialect norms as well as the persistence and adoption of structures associated

Table 10.3   Summary of vernacular dialect alignment

Dialect feature	Elderly Hyde Euro. Am.	Elderly Hyde Af. Am.	Young Hyde Euro. Am.	Young Hyde Af. Am.	Urban AAVE
Receding features					
NP 3rd pl. subj. verbal -s e.g., *The dogs barks*	+	+	−	−	−
Pro3rd pl. verbal -s e.g., *The dog go*	−	+	−	−	−
Weren't regularization e.g., *It weren't nice*	+	+	+	−	−
Post-/ð/ r-lessness in *bother*	+	+	−	−	−
Backed /ay/ nucleus in *tide, right*	+	+	+	−	−
Front-gliding /aw/ in *town*	+	+	−	−	−
Lowered /er/ in *bear*	+	+	−	−	−
Raised, unglided /ɔ/ in *caught*	+	+	−/+	−/+	−
Persistent features					
Prevocalic CCR in *bes' egg*	−	+	−	+	+
Relatively high frequency of pitch accents	−	+	−	+	+
Copula absence e.g., *She nice*	−	+	−	+	+
3rd sg. -s absence e.g., *The dog bark_*	−	+	−	+	+
Possessive -s absence e.g., *the dog_ bone*	−	−/+	−	+	+
Was regularization e.g., *The dogs was nice*	+	+	+	+	+
Fronted /o/ nucleus in *coat*	+	+	+	+	−
Fronted /o/ glide in *coat*	+	−	+	−	−
Stopping of /ð/ to [d] e.g., *dat* for *that*	−	+/−	+/−	+/−	+
Newly adopted features					
Prevoiced /ay/ glide reduction in *tide*	−	−	+/−	+/−	+
Generalized postvocalic r-lessness in *fear*	−	−/+	−	+	+
Habitual *be* V -*ing* e.g., *They be laughing*	−	−	−	+	+

with contemporary AAVE. In part, the recession of distinctive Pamlico Sound structures is shared with the European American community, but persistent and accentuated features for younger European Americans, such as *weren't* regularization, diverge sharply from the innovative processes found in the African American community. At the same time, innovative features of AAVE such as habitual *be* take AAVE on a course away from the Pamlico Sound variety.

In part, the explanation for the change in alliance for African American speech may be attributed to the expanded mobility and contact with other communities now characteristic of Hyde County residents. Contact with other communities and external varieties became much more extensive for Hyde County African Americans during the middle and latter half of the twentieth century (see chapter 4), and the increasing movement of Hyde County African Americans toward the widespread AAVE norm may be due, in part, to the increased mobility and expanded contact of Hyde County African Americans with other AAVE-speaking communities, particularly in urban areas. As AAVE developed in the twentieth century, it became much more of an urban than a rural phenomenon (Bailey and Maynor, 1985a, 1987).

While the emerging structural delimitation of African American speech is becoming associated with a core set of features associated with broad-based AAVE, it is also characterized by the avoidance of features that are associated with "white speech" (Ash and Myhill, 1986; Graff et al., 1986). Local rural dialects such as the traditional Pamlico Sound dialect carry strong associations with white, rural speech, as indicated by identification tasks that lead listeners to identify African Americans as white when they are characterized by local dialect traits. In this respect, the association of a regional Hyde County dialect with white speech is not unlike the ethnic associations often accompanying regional dialect traits in other areas. For example, the Northern Cities vowel shift tends to be strongly associated with white speech (Labov, 1991). Furthermore, this shift has not been adopted on a wide-scale basis by African Americans living in metropolitan areas where it is currently in progress (Jones, 2000; Gordon, 2000). Younger speakers who identify strongly with African American culture contra "white culture" would therefore be inclined to change their speech both by moving toward the more generalized norms of AAVE and by moving away from the local regional norm. In effect, the ethnic marking of speech in Hyde County is now superseding a former regional locus.

10.5.3 Explaining the supraregional norms of contemporary AAVE

How do we explain the development and maintenance of a supraregional norm for AAVE? Several factors seem to converge in such an explanation.

First, there is a historical, linguistic explanation. Although the speech of earlier African Americans showed considerable accommodation to regional variation in English, some distinctive, long-term ethnolinguistically distinct structures obviously existed in earlier AAVE. Even in highly regionalized contexts where African Americans adopted many local dialect traits, structures such as prevocalic consonant cluster reduction, copula absence, and optional inflectional -*s* marking have marked the speech of African Americans for as long as we can project into the past. We have argued that the most reasonable explanation for the existence of some of these structures is substrate influence from the earlier contact situation between speakers of African languages and speakers of English in the African diaspora. A series of long-term, ethnolinguistically distinctive features thus provided an embryonic base for some of the structures characteristic of the past and contemporary vernacular (see also Thomas and Bailey, 1998). But historical preservation is obviously not the whole story. There is also evidence that a few of the important features of the contemporary AAVE norm were creations of the twentieth century (Bailey and Maynor, 1985a, 1987; Dayton, 1996; Labov,1998), and these features have been integrated into the supraregional norm that now typifies AAVE.

As noted previously, a partial explanation for the supraregional status of AAVE is the expanded mobility and interregional, intraethnic contact situation characteristic of African Americans in the twentieth century (Johnson and Campbell, 1981). African Americans in isolated rural regions of the South, including Hyde County, have much more expanded contact with other African Americans outside of the area than they did a century ago. Whereas the elderly Hyde County African American used in the first ethnic identification experiment did not leave the county until he was in his mid-30s, his great-granddaughter has traveled outside of the county on a regular basis, including trips to some urban areas outside of the state. Along with this is the observation that residents who leave isolated, rural areas of the South often visit relatives and friends back home. In fact, various "homecoming" events and family reunions bring together those living within and outside of the local community on a semiregular basis. This steady interregional contact is more typical of African American communities than it is of many European American communities. Patterns of interregional contact and mobility thus play a role in the transmission of a supraregional vernacular norm.

At the same time, the continuing *ex facto* segregation of American society serves as a fertile environment for developing and maintaining a distinct ethnic variety. Many Northern urban areas are, in fact, more densely populated by African Americans today than they were several decades ago (Graff et al., 1986), and the informal social networks of many urban African

Americans remain quite segregated (Stack, 1996), providing both a macro and micro social context for maintaining ethnolinguistic distinctiveness.

Along with explanations based on population movement and segregation patterns, however, there is the role of cultural identity. Over the past half century, there has been a growing sense of ethnic identity now associated with AAVE. This identity is supported through a variety of informal and formal social mechanisms that range from community-based social networks to stereotypical media projections of African American speech (Lippi-Green, 1997). Language has clearly been a part of the construction of this identity. Fordham and Ogbu (1986), for example, suggest that the adoption of standard English is at the top of the list of behaviors listed as "acting white." The creation of an *oppositional identity*, in which African Americans avoid conduct with strong associations of white behavior (Fordham and Ogbu, 1986), including language, may thus be an important part of the explanation for the rejection of regional dialect features that have strong white connotations. In this developing ethnolinguistic milieu, traditional rural dialects such as the Hyde County dialect – or any other regional dialect that would carry strong associations of white speech – would be avoided. In fact, a number of younger African American subjects in our study describe the speech of older Hyde County African Americans as "sounding country" and more white-sounding than the younger African Americans. Younger speakers who identify strongly with African American culture contra "white culture" would therefore be inclined to change their speech toward the more generalized version of AAVE and away from the localized regional norm. An essential ingredient of the contemporary supraregional norm for AAVE is thus the heightened symbolic role of language as an ethnic emblem of African American culture. Such an identity would accordingly enhance the role of a widespread supraregional AAVE norm with regard to accommodation to a regional dialect norm that bears strong connotations of white identity.

10.6 Conclusion

The empirical study of vernacular language development and change in Hyde County underscores the kinds of factors that need to be included in any account of vernacular dialect formation and development. First, there is a *linguistic dimension*, which involves the molding of a vernacular variety such as AAVE through both specific language influence from its heritage languages and generalized language change. Certainly, the early contact history of Africans with English in the African diaspora has left a unique linguistic imprint on the speech of African Americans. At the same time, AAVE also shares vernacular features that cannot be accounted for simply on the basis of language transfer or diffusion. It is apparent that some vernacular forms arise through parallel, independent development due to the operation of general processes of analogy and a universal tendency to move toward unmarked forms. Thus, surveys of various socially subordinate vernacular varieties in the USA (Wolfram and Schilling-Estes, 1998), England (Trudgill, 1990) and around the world (Cheshire, 1991) show the uniform tendency to expand the regularization of once-irregular plurals (e.g., *two sheeps*), the regularization of past tense forms (e.g., *They growed up*), and the adoption of negative concord (e.g., *They didn't do nothing*), along with the stopping of syllable-onset, interdental fricatives (e.g., [dIs] "this"). The unifying dimension of such common vernacular traits, referred to in chapter 3 under the *principle of vernacular dialect congruity*, seems to be the operation of natural linguistic processes in a social context less constrained by the overt prescriptive norms impeding naturally occurring changes (Chambers, 1995:246).

There is also a *sociohistorical component*. Patterns of population settlement, migration, and diffusion are as vital for understanding the growth and maintenance of vernacular varieties as they are for socially sanctioned dialects. Thus, the migration of African Americans from the South in the early and mid-twentieth century (Johnson and Campbell, 1981; Grossman, 1989), as well as the maintenance of interregional connections and family ties, provides a communication network for the diffusion of vernacular norms from the South to the North and West. In more recent decades, the return of some African Americans to the South (Stack, 1996) no doubt has also provided for the diffusion of vernacular norms from urban areas, the current focal point for AAVE, back to rural areas that were once the primary regions for earlier vernacular development. The dynamics of migration, along with the regular maintenance of interregional family ties has no doubt afforded a convenient transmission route for contemporary supraregional AAVE norms.

In addition, a *sociolinguistic component* to vernacular norming exists in the sense that some vernacular structures are socially marked and instantiated for specific speech communities. Communities may differ significantly in their social embedding of dialect structures, selectively focusing on some variants as dialect icons while ignoring others. Thus, Schilling-Estes and Wolfram (1999) show how two isolated island communities in the mid-Atlantic with similar dialect profiles, Smith Island in the Chesapeake Bay area and Ocracoke on the Outer Banks, differ significantly in their social marking of the same structures. Similarly, AAVE appears to have adopted some symbolic icons to mark its current ethnolinguistic status, including, for example, structures such as habitual *be*.

There is a *sociopsychological component* as well in that individual and group identities are constructed and maintained through dialect variation. We have seen, for example, that the appeal to oppositional identity (Fordham and Ogbu, 1986) helps explain why younger African Americans who have lived all of their lives in relatively isolated, distinctive dialect areas such as Hyde County are abandoning their regional dialect roots in favor of an external, nonwhite supraregional AAVE norm. Present-day African American youth want to sound neither "white" nor "country," reflecting the strong urban, ethnic association of the current version of AAVE.

Finally, there is *an ideological dimension* to the construction of vernacular norms. Underlying assumptions and beliefs about ethnic group membership influence the establishment of vernacular norms. Part of the reason that AAVE is so strongly defined along ethnic lines is no doubt the biracial ideology that defines US society (Milroy, 1999). Accordingly, the primacy of ethnolinguistic distinctiveness has to be factored into the development of a supraregional norm for AAVE as African Americans in Boston, Los Angeles, the rural South, and elsewhere in the USA distinguish themselves from European Americans regardless of their regional context.

Perhaps the most essential lesson to be learned from this discussion is that the construction of vernacular norms cannot be reduced to a single, static dimension or circumstance. As demonstrated in the case of Hyde County, linguistic, demographic, sociohistorical, sociopsychological, and ideological factors all enter into the construction of vernacular norms. In various permutations, we would expect these same factors to be involved in the construction of both vernacular and standard norms, although they would, of course, be instantiated and regulated in quite different ways in different situations. The development of AAVE into an ethnolinguistically distinct variety with a transregional base is one of the strongest arguments for the robustness of vernacular language norming.

The linguistic birthmark of African American English was indelibly imprinted during the early contact between Africans and European speakers of English centuries ago. Though the ethnolinguistic distinctiveness that emerged from this original dynamic was seemingly superseded by accommodation to regional dialect norms in the development of this variety at earlier stages in the linguistic socialization of African Americans, the vestiges of the early contact influence were amazingly resilient. In the ebb and flow of language change, the demographic, social, and ideological dynamics of the twentieth century have converged to bring to the sociolinguistic fore some of these original features, along with some contemporary innovations so that local regional accommodation has taken a back seat to a new display of ethnolinguistic distinctiveness. There is, in effect, no greater testament to the persistence and vitality of African American culture in the USA than the past and present voice of African American Vernacular English.

Notes

1 We cannot say for certain how local listeners might identify the ethnicity of speakers, but there is some basis for maintaining that the correct ethnic identification of speakers might differ for community members and outsiders. For example, Wolfram (2001) shows that Robeson County residents correctly identify Lumbees from Robeson County whereas listeners from other areas do not. At this point, we have only administered our ethnic perception test to outsiders located in Raleigh, North Carolina

2 The first experiment was constructed by Becky Childs and administered by Amy Gantt to students in introductory composition classes at North Carolina State University.

3 Listeners were recruited from various undergraduate and introductory graduate linguistics classes at North Carolina State University. Stimuli were played to respondents from a CD player placed at the front of the classroom, with the volume set to a level that everyone in the room could hear comfortably. The use of headphones was ruled out because it was impractical. Subjects filled out a short questionnaire and signed a release form before participating in the experiment. Only European American and African American respondents who spoke English as their first language and who reported no hearing impairments were included in the analysis.

4 Some of these issues obviously are connected to Weinreich, Labov, and Herzog's (1968) taxonomy of problems for an empirical theory of language change (viz., the *actuation, constraint, transition, embedding, and evaluation* problem). Our focus on the construction of vernacular norms leads us to emphasize a slightly different but complementary set of issues.

References

Addy, Dede Awula (2000) Invariant be in current African American English. Unpublished paper, North Carolina State University.

Allegood, Jerry (1997) A county in need of jobs is jubilant about its new prison. *The News and Observer* 5 May, p. 3A.

Allen, Harold B. (ed.) (1973–6) *The Linguistic Atlas of the Upper Midwest*, 3 vols. Minneapolis: University of Minnesota Press.

Allyene, Mervyn (1980) *Comparative Afro-American*. Ann Arbor, MI: Karoma.

Andersen, Henning (1988) Center and periphery: Adoption, diffusion, and spread. In Jacek Fisiak (ed.), *Historical Dialectology*. Berlin: Mouton de Gruyter, pp. 39–83.

Anderson, Bridget L. (2002) Dialect leveling and /ai/ monophthongization among African American Detroiters. *Journal of Sociolinguistics* 6:86–98.

Anderson, Bridget, and Lesley Milroy (1999) Southern sound changes and the Detroit AAVE vowel system. Paper presented at NWAVE 28, Toronto, ON, 15 October.

Anshen, Frank (1970) A sociolinguistic analysis of a sound change. *Language Sciences* 9:20–1.

Ash, Sharon, and John Myhill (1986) Linguistic correlates of inter-ethnic contact. In David Sankoff (ed.), *Diversity and Diachrony*. Philadelphia: John Benjamins, pp. 33–44.

Atwood, E. Bagby (1953) *A Survey of Verb Forms in the Eastern United States*. Ann Arbor: University of Michigan Press.

Bailey, Beryl (1965) A new perspective in American Negro dialectology. *American Speech* 11:1–11.

Bailey, Charles-James N. (1973) *Variation and Linguistic Theory*. Arlington, VA: Center for Applied Linguistics.

Bailey, Guy, and Natalie Maynor (1985a) The present tense of *be* in Southern Black folk speech. *American Speech* 60:195–213.

Bailey, Guy, and Natalie Maynor (1985b) The present tense of *be* in white folk speech of the southern United States. *English World-Wide* 6:199–216.

Bailey, Guy, and Natalie Maynor (1987) Decreolization? *Language in Society* 16:449–74.

Bailey, Guy, and Natalie Maynor (1989) The divergence controversy. *American Speech* 64:12–39.

Bailey, Guy, Natalie Maynor, and Patricia Cukor-Avila (1989) Variation in subject–verb concord in Early Modern English. *Language Variation and Change* 1:285–300.

Bailey, Guy, Natalie Maynor, and Patricia Cukor-Avila (eds.) (1991) *The Emergence of Black English*. Philadelphia/Amsterdam: John Benjamins.

Bailey, Guy, and Erik Thomas (1998) Some aspects of African-American English phonology. In Salikoko Mufwene, John R. Rickford, Guy Bailey, and John Baugh (eds.), *African American English: Structure, History, and Use*. London/New York: Routledge, pp. 85–109.

Bailey, Guy, Tom Wikle, Jan Tillery, and Lori Sand (1991) The apparent time construct. *Language Variation and Change* 3:241–64.

Bailey, Guy, Tom Wikle, Jan Tillery, and Lori Sand (1993) Some patterns of linguistic diffusion. *Language Variation and Change* 5:359–90.

Battistella, Edwin (1990) *Markedness: The Evaluative Superstructure of Language*. Albany: State University of New York Press.

Bayley, Robert (1994) Consonant cluster reduction in Tejano English. *Language Variation and Change* 6:303–27.

Baugh, John (1980) A reexamination of the Black English copula. In William Labov (ed.), *Locating Language in Time and Space*. New York: Academic, pp. 83–106.

Baugh, John (1983) *Black Street Speech: Its History, Structure, and Survival*. Austin: University of Texas Press.

Baugh, John (1984) *Steady*: Progressive aspect in Black Vernacular English. *American Speech* 59:3–12.

Beckett, Daniel (2001) Sociolinguistic individuality in an enclave community. Unpublished master's thesis, North Carolina State University.

Bernstein, Cynthia (1993) Measuring social causes of phonological variation in Texas. *American Speech* 68:227–40.

Bickerton, Derek (1971) Inherent variability and variable rules. *Foundations of Language* 7:457–92.

Bickerton, Derek (1975) *Dynamics of a Creole System*. Cambridge, UK: Cambridge University Press.

Brandes, Paul D., and Jeutonne Brewer (1977) *Dialect Clash in America: Issues and Answers*. Netuchen, NJ: Scarecrow.

Brasch, Walter M. (1981) *Black English in the Media*. Amherst: University of Massachusetts Press.

Breen, T. H., and Stephen Innes (1980) "Myne Owne Ground:" *Race and Freedom on Virginia's Eastern Shore, 1640–1676*. New York/Oxford: Oxford University Press.

Brewer, Jeutonne (1996) The syntactic and discourse features of AAVE in new ex-slave recordings. Paper presented at NWAVE 25, Las Vegas, 19 October.

Britain, David (1992) Linguistic change in intonation: The use of high rising terminals in New Zealand English. *Language Variation and Change* 4:77–104.

Britain, David (forthcoming) *Was/weren't* leveling in Fenland English. *Essex Research Reports in Linguistics*.

Browman, Catherine P., and Louis Goldstein (1991) Gestural structures: Distinctiveness, phonological processes, and historical change. In Ignatius G. Mattingly and Michael Studdert-Kennedy (eds.), *Modularity and the Motor Theory of Speech Perception*. Hillsdale, NJ: Lawrence Erlbaum, pp. 313–38.

Brown, Cecil Kenneth (1931) *The State Highway System of North Carolina: Its Evolution and Present Status*. Chapel Hill: University of North Carolina Press.

Butters, Ronald R. (1989) *The Death of Black English: Divergence and Convergence in White and Black Vernaculars*. Frankfurt: Lang.

Carawan, Sandra S. (2000) Hyde County's largest plantation owner of 1850 and 1860: John R. Donnell. *High Tides* 21.1:36–41.

Cecelski, David S. (1994a) *Along Freedom Road: Hyde County, North Carolina, and the Fate of Black Schools in the South*. Chapel Hill: University of North Carolina Press.

Cecelski, David S. (1994b) The shores of freedom: The maritime underground railroad in North Carolina, 1800–1861. *The North Carolina Historical Review* 71:174–206.

Cedergren, Henrietta J., and David Sankoff (1974) Variable rules: Performance as a statistical reflection of competence. *Language* 50:333–55.

Census Bureau (1850) *Slave Population Schedule*. Raleigh: North Carolina State Archive.

Chambers, J. K. (1995) *Sociolinguistic Theory*. Cambridge, MA: Blackwell.

Chater, Melville (1926) Motor-coaching through North Carolina. *National Geographic* 44:475–523.

Cheshire, Jenny (1982) *Variation in an English Dialect*. Cambridge, UK: Cambridge University Press.

Cheshire, Jenny (ed.) (1991) *English Around the World: Sociolinguistic Perspective*. Cambridge, UK: Cambridge University Press.

Childs, Rebecca L. (2000) A Hyde County clusterfest: The role of consonant cluster reduction in a historical isolated African-American community. MA thesis, North Carolina State University.

Christian, Donna, Walt Wolfram, and Nanjo Dube (1989) *Variation and Change in Geographically Isolated Communities: Appalachian and Ozark English*. Publication of the American Dialect Society, No. 74. Tuscaloosa: University of Alabama Press.

Clark, Walter (ed.) (1895–1906) *The State Records of North Carolina*, 16 vols. Goldsboro, NC: Nash Brothers.

Clarke, Sandra (1997) English verbal -*s* revisited: The evidence from Newfoundland. *American Speech* 72:227–59.

Cloud, Ellen Fulcher (1995) *Custom Records: Port of Ocracoke, 1815–1866*. Ocracoke, NC: Live Oak Publications.

Compendium of the Enumeration of the Inhabitants and Statistics of the United States, as Obtained at the Department of State, from the Returns of the Sixth Census. (1841) Washington, DC: Thomas Allen.

Cooley, Marianne (1997) An early representation of African American English. In Cynthia Bernstein, Thomas Nunnally, and Robin Sabino (eds.), *Language in the South Revisited*. Tuscaloosa: University of Alabama Press, pp. 51–8.

Cooley, Marianne (2000) Literary dialect in *The Yorker's Stratagem*. *Journal of English Linguistics* 28:173–92.

Corbitt, David Leroy (1950) *The Formation of the North Carolina Counties, 1663– 1943*. Raleigh: Division of Archives and History, North Carolina Department of Cultural Resources.

Dannenberg, Clare J. (1999) Sociolinguistic constructs of identity: The syntactic delineation of Lumbee English. Unpublished PhD dissertation, University of North Carolina at Chapel Hill.

Dayton, Elizabeth (1996) Grammatical Categories of the Verb in African American Vernacular English. PhD dissertation, University of Pennsylvania.

Debose, Charles (1994) Creole English in Samaná. In Frances Ingemann (ed.), *1994 Mid-America Linguistic Conference Papers*, vol. 2. Lawrence: University of Kansas Department of Linguistics, pp. 341–50.

Dillard, J. L. (1970) Principles in the history of American English – paradox, virginity and cafeteria. *Florida FL Reporter* 7, Spring/Fall: 32–3.

Dillard, J. L. (1972) *Black English: Its History and Usage in the United States*. New York: Random House.

Dorian, Nancy (1981) *Language Death*. Philadelphia: University of Pennsylvania Press.

Dorian, Nancy (1994) Varieties of variation in a very small place: Social homogeneity, prestige norms and linguistic variation. *Language*: 70:631–96.

Dorrill, George T. (1986) *Black and White Speech in the South: Evidence from the Linguistic Atlas of the Middle and South Atlantic States*. Bamberger Beiträge zur englischen Sprachwissenschaft, 19. Frankfurt am Main: Peter Lang.

Downes, William (1998) *Language in Society*, 2nd edn. Cambridge, UK: Cambridge University Press.

Edwards, Walter F. (1992) Sociolinguistic behavior in a Detroit inner-city black neighborhood. *Language in Society* 21:93–115.

Ewers, Traute (1996) *The Origin of American Black English: Be-forms in the Hoodoo Texts*. Berlin/New York: Mouton de Gruyter.

Fasold, Ralph W. (1972) *Tense Marking in Black English: A Linguistic and Social Analysis*. Arlington, VA: Center for Applied Linguistics.

Fasold, Ralph W. (1976) One hundred years from syntax to phonology. In Sanford Steever, Carle Walker, and Salikoko Mufwene (eds.), *Papers from the Parasession on Diachronic Syntax*. Chicago: Chicago Linguistics Society, pp. 79–87.

Fasold, Ralph W. (1981) The relation between black and white speech in the South. *American Speech* 56:163–89.

Fasold, Ralph W. (ed.) (1987) Are Black and White vernaculars diverging? Papers from the NWAVE 14 panel discussion. *American Speech* 62:3–80.

Fasold, Ralph W., William Labov, Faye Boyd Vaughn-Cooke, Guy Bailey, Walt Wolfram, Arthur K. Spears, and John Rickford (1987) Are black and white vernaculars diverging? Papers from the NWAVE 14 Panel Discussion. *American Speech* 62:3–80.

Fasold, Ralph W., and Yoshiko Nakano (1996) Contraction and deletion in vernacular Black English: Creole history and relationship to Euro-American English. In Gregory R. Guy, Crawford Feagin, Deborah Schiffrin, and John Baugh (eds.), *Towards a Social Science of Language, Vol. 1: Variation and Change in Language and Society*. Amsterdam/Philadelphia: John Benjamins, pp. 373– 95.

Fasold, Ralph W., and Walt Wolfram (1970) Some linguistic features of Negro dialect. In Ralph W. Fasold and Roger W. Shuy (eds.), *Teaching Standard English in the Inner City*. Washington, DC: Center for Applied Linguistics, pp. 41–86.

Feagin, Crawford (1979) *Variation and Change in Alabama English: A Sociolinguistic Study of the White Community*. Washington, DC: Georgetown University Press.

Feagin, Crawford (1987) A closer look at the Southern drawl: Variation taken to extremes. In Keith M. Denning, Sharon Inkelas, Faye C. McNair-Knox, and John C. Rickford (eds.), *Variation in Language: NWAVE-15 at Stanford. Proceedings of the Fifteenth Annual Conference on New Ways of Analyzing Variation*. Stanford, CA: Department of Linguistics, Stanford University, pp. 137–50.

Feagin, Crawford (1990) The dynamics of sound change in Southern States English: From *R*-less to *R*-ful in three generations. In Jerold A. Edmonson, Crawford Feagin, and Peter Mäullhausler (eds.), *Development and Diversity: Variation across Time and Space*. Dallas: Summer Institute of Linguistics, pp. 29–46.

Feagin, Crawford (1997) The African contribution in Southern states English. In Cynthia Bernstein, Thomas Nunnally, and Robin Sabino (eds.), *Language Variety in the South Revisited*. Tuscaloosa: University of Alabama Press, pp. 123–39.

Fischer, David (1989) *Albion's Seed*. Oxford: Oxford University Press.

Fordham, Signithia and John Ogbu (1986) Black students' school success: Coping with the burden of "acting white." *Urban Review* 18:176–206.

Foreman, Christina (2000) Identification of African-American English from prosodic cues. *Texas Linguistic Forum* 43:57–66.

Forrest, Lewis C., Jr. (1989) The Lake Mattamuskett drainage project. *High Tides* 10.2:4–14.

Fortescue, Zacharia Thomas, Jr. (1923) History of Hyde County. Typescript, University of North Carolina.

Galindo, Letticia (1987) Linguistic influence and variation on the English of Chicano adolescents in Austin, Texas. Unpublished PhD dissertation, University of Texas, Austin.

Godfrey, Elisabeth, and Sali Tagliamonte (1998) The missing link in the verbal -*s* quandary? Evidence from Devonshire English in Southwest England. Unpublished manuscript, University of York, UK.

Goodwin, Marjorie Harness (1990) *He-Said-She-Said: Talk as Social Organization Among Black Children*. Bloomington/Indianapolis: Indiana University Press.

Gordon, Matthew J. (2000) Phonological correlates of ethnic identity: Evidence of divergence?. *American Speech* 75:115–36.

Graff, David, William Labov, and Wendell A. Harris (1986) Testing listeners' reactions to phonological markers of ethnic identity: A new method for sociolinguistic research. In David Sankoff (ed.), *Diversity and Diachrony*. Philadelphia: John Benjamins, pp. 45–58.

Green, Elaine Weslee (1998) A marshland of ethnolinguistic boundaries: Conflicting past and present *Be* paradigms in Coastal Carolina speech. MA thesis, North Carolina State University.

Greet, William Cabell (1933) Delmarva speech. *American Speech* 8:56–63.

Grenoble, Lenora A., and Lindsay J. Whaley (eds) (1998) *Endangered Languages: Current Issues and Future Prospects*. Cambridge/New York: Cambridge University Press.

Grossman, James R. (1989) *Land of Hope: Chicago, Black Southerners, and the Great Migration.* Chicago: University of Chicago Press.

Guy, Gregory R. (1980) Variation in the group and the individual: The case of final stop deletion. In William Labov (ed.), *Locating Language in Time and Space.* New York: Academic Press, pp. 1–36.

Guy, Gregory R. (1991) Explanation in variable phonology. *Language Variation and Change* 3:1–22.

Guy, Gregory R. (1992) Contextual conditioning in variable phonology. *Language Variation and Change* 3:223–39.

Guy, Gregory R. (1997) Violable is variable: Optimality theory and linguistic variation. *Language Variation and Change* 9:333–48.

Guy, Gregory R., and Charles Boberg (1997) Inherent variability and the obligatory contour principle. *Language Variation and Change* 9:149–64.

Guy, Gregory R., Barbara Horvath, Julia Vonwiller, Elaine Daisley, and Inge Rogers (1986) An intonation change in progress in Australian English. *Language in Society* 15:23–51.

Hall, Joan Huston (1976) Rural Southeast Georgia Speech: A phonological analysis. Unpublished PhD dissertation, Emory University, Atlanta, GA.

Hall, Joseph S. (1942) The phonetics of Great Smoky Mountain Speech. *American Speech* 17.2.2:1–110.

Hannah, Dawn (1997) Copula absence in Samaná English: Implications for research on the linguistic history of African-American Vernacular English. *American Speech* 72:339–72.

Harkers Island United Methodist Women (1991) *Island Born and Bred: A Collection of Harkers Island Food, Fun, Fact, and Fiction.* Morehead City, NC: Herald Printing Co.

Harris, Morgan H. (1995) *Hyde Yesterdays: A History of Hyde County.* Wilmington, NC: New Hanover Printing & Publishing, Inc.

Hawkins, Francine Dove (1993) Speaker ethnic identification: The roles of speech sample, fundamental frequency, speaker and listener variations. Unpublished PhD dissertation, University of Maryland at College Park.

Hazen, Kirk (1996) Dialect affinity and subject-verb concord. *SECOL Review* 19:25–53.

Hazen, Kirk (2000a) *Identity and Ethnicity in the Rural South: A Sociolinguistic View through Past and Present* be. Publication of the American Dialect Society, 83. Durham, NC: Duke University Press.

Hazen, Kirk (2000b) Subject-verb concord in a post-insular dialect: The gradual persistence of dialect patterning. *Journal of English Linguistics* 28:127–44.

Herskovits, Melville J. (1941) *The Myth of the Negro Past.* New York: Harper & Brothers.

Hickey, Raymond (forthcoming a) Ebb and flow: A cautionary tale of language change. In Teresa Fanego et al. (eds.), *English Historical Linguistics 2000: Selected Papers from the 11th International Conference on English Historical Linguistics.* Amsterdam: John Benjamins.

Hickey, Raymond (forthcoming b) Salience, stigma, and standard. In Laura Wright (ed.), *The Standardization of English.* Cambridge, UK: Cambridge University Press.

Hollien, Harry, and Ellen Malcik (1962) Adolescent voice change in Southern Negro males. *Speech Monographs* 29:53–8.

Holm, John (1984) Variability in the copula in Black English and its creole kin. *American Speech* 59:291–309.

Holm, John (1988) *Pidgins and Creoles: Volume 1, Theory and Structure*. Cambridge, UK: Cambridge University Press.

Holm, John (1989) *Pidgins and Creoles: Volume 2, Reference Survey*. Cambridge, UK: Cambridge University Press.

Horn, James (1979) Servant emigration to the Chesapeake in the Seventeenth Century. In Thad W. Tate and David Ammerman (eds.), *The Chesapeake in the Seventeenth Century: Essays on Anglo-American Society*. Chapel Hill: University of North Carolina Press, pp. 51–95.

Howren, Robert (1962) The speech of Ocracoke, North Carolina. *American Speech* 37:163–75.

Hudson, Amelia I., and Anthony Holbrook (1981) A study of reading fundamental vocal frequency of young black adults. *Journal of Speech and Hearing Research* 24:197–201.

Hudson, Amelia I., and Anthony Holbrook (1982) Fundamental frequency characteristics of young black adults: Spontaneous speaking and oral reading. *Journal of Speech and Hearing Research* 25:25–8.

Hyatt, Harry Middleton (1970–8) *Hoodoo-conjuration-witchcraft-rootwork*, vols. 1–5. Hannibal, MO: Western Publishing Co.

Ihalainen, O. (1994) The dialect of England since 1776. In Robert Burchfield (ed.), *Cambridge History of the English Language*. Cambridge, UK: Cambridge University Press, pp. 197–274.

Ingram, David (1976) *Phonological Disability in Children*. New York: Elsevier.

Ingram, David (1989) *First Language Acquisition: Method, Description, and Explanation*. Cambridge, UK: Cambridge University Press.

Jaffe, Hilda (1973) *The Speech of the Central Coast of North Carolina: The Carteret County Version of the Banks "Brogue"*. Publication of the American Dialect Society, No. 60. Tuscaloosa: University of Alabama Press.

Jespersen, Otto (1933) *Essentials of English Grammar*. Tuscaloosa: University of Alabama Press.

Jones, Jamila (2000) The vowel systems of African Americans in the Urban North. Paper presented at NWAVE 29. East Lansing: Michigan State University, October.

Johnson, Daniel M. and Rex R. Campbell (1981) *Black Migration in America: A Social Demographic History*. Durham, NC: Duke University Press.

Johnstone, Barbara (1996) *The Linguistic Individual: Self-Expression in Language and Linguistics*. New York/Oxford: Oxford University Press.

Johnstone, Barbara (forthcoming) Place, globalization, and linguistic variation. In Carmen Fought (ed.), *Identities and Place: Sociolinguistic Approaches*. Oxford: Oxford University Press.

Jun, Sun-Ah, and Christina Foreman (1996) Boundary tones and focus realization in African-American intonation. Paper presented at the 3rd joint meeting of the Acoustical Society of America and the Acoustical Society of Japan, Honolulu, HI, 6 December.

Kallen, Jeffrey L. (1989) Tense and aspect categories in Irish English. *English World-Wide* 10:1–39.

Kay, Marvin L., and Lorin Lee Cary (1995) *Slavery in North Carolina, 1748–1775*. Chapel Hill/London: University of North Carolina Press.

Keiser, Steve Hartman (2001) Demystifying drift: explaining linguistic change across speech islands. Paper presented at the Linguistic Society of America. Washington, DC, January.

Kochman, Thomas (1981) *Black and White: Styles in Conflict*. Chicago: University of Chicago Press.

Kretzschmar, William A., Virigina G. McDavid, Thomas K. Lerud, and Ellen Johnson (eds.) (1994) *Handbook of the Linguistic Atlas of the Middle and South Atlantic States*. Chicago: University of Chicago Press.

Kulikoff, Allan (1986) *Tobacco and Slaves: The Development of Southern Cultures in the Chesapeake, 1680–1800*. Chapel Hill: University of North Carolina Press.

Kurath, Hans (1949) *A Word Geography of the Eastern United States*. Ann Arbor: University of Michigan Press.

Kurath, Hans, and Raven I. McDavid, Jr. (1961) *The Pronunciation of English in the Atlantic States*. Ann Arbor: University of Michigan Press.

Labov, William (1966) *The Social Stratification of English in New York City*. Washington, DC: Center for Applied Linguistics.

Labov, William (1969) Contraction, deletion and inherent variability of the English copula. *Language* 45:715–62.

Labov, William (1972a) *Language in the Inner City: Studies in the Black English Vernacular*. Philadelphia: University of Pennsylvania Press.

Labov, William (1972b) *Sociolinguistic Patterns*. Philadelphia: University of Pennsylvania Press.

Labov, William (1985) The increasing divergence of black and white vernaculars: Introduction to the research reports. Unpublished manuscript, University of Pennsylvania.

Labov, William (1991) The three dialects of English. In Penelope Eckert (ed.), *New Ways of Analyzing Sound Change*. New York: Academic Press, pp. 1–44.

Labov, William (1994) *Principles of Linguistic Change: Internal factors*. Cambridge, MA/Oxford: Blackwell.

Labov, William (1998) Coexistent systems in African-American vernacular English. In Salikoko Mufwene, John R. Rickford, Guy Bailey, and John Baugh (eds.), *African American English: Structure, History, and Use*. London/New York: Routledge, pp. 110–53.

Labov, William, Sharon Ash, and Charles Boberg (2001) *Phonological Atlas of North American English*. Berlin: Mouton de Gruyter.

Labov, William, Paul Cohen, Clarence Robins, and John Lewis (1968) *A Study of the Non-Standard English of Negro and Puerto Rican Speakers in New York City*. United States Office of Education Final Report, Research Project 3288. Washington, DC: National Instite of Education.

Labov, William, and Wendell A. Harris (1986) De facto segregation of black and white vernaculars. In David Sankoff (ed.), *Diversity and Diachrony*. Philadelphia: John Benjamins, pp. 1–24.

Labov, William, Malcah Yaeger, and Richard Steiner (1972) *A Quantitative Study of Sound Change in Progress*. Philadelphia: US Regional Survey.

Lass, Norman J., Celest A. Almerino, Laurie F. Jordan, and Jayne M. Walsh (1980) The effect of filtered speech on speaker race and sex identifications. *Journal of Phonetics* 8:101–12.

Lefler, Hugh Talmage, and Albert Ray Newsome (1973) *North Carolina: The History of a Southern State*. Chapel Hill: University of North Carolina Press.

LePage, R. B., and Adreé Tabouret-Keller (1985) *Acts of Identity*. Cambridge, UK: Cambridge University Press.

Levine, Lewis, and Harry J. Crockett, Jr. (1966) Speech variation in a Piedmont community: Postvocalic *r*. *Sociological Inquiry* 36:204–26.

Lippi-Green, Rosina (1997) *English with an Accent: Language, Ideology, and Discrimination in the United States*. London/New York: Routledge.

Loman, Bengt (1967) *Intonation Patterns in a Negro American Dialect: A Preliminary Report*. Washington, DC: Center for Applied Linguistics.

Loman, Bengt (1975) Prosodic patterns in a Negro American dialect. In Håkan Ringbom, Alfhild Ingberg, Ralf Norrman, Kurt Nyholm, Rolf Westman, and Kay Wikberg (eds.), *Style and Text: Studies Presented to Nils Erik Enkvist*. Stockholm: Språkförlaget Skriptor AB, pp. 219–42.

Mann, Betty S., Ellen A. Williams, and R. S. Spencer, Jr. (1986). Hyde County roads. *High Tides* 7.2:2–28.

Martin, Danielle, and Sali Tagliamonte (1999) "Oh, it beautiful": Copula variability in Britain. Paper presented at NWAVE 28, Toronto, ON, 16 October.

Martin, Stefan Edmund (1992) Topics in the syntax of nonstandard English. PhD dissertation, University of Maryland.

Matarese, Maureen, and Matt Downs (2001) The ethnolinguistic role of interdental fricatives in English: A comparative analysis. Paper presented at NWAV 30. Raleigh, NC, 12 October.

McDavid, Raven I., Jr. (1948) Postvocalic /-r/ in South Carolina: A social analysis. *American Speech* 23:194–203.

McDavid, Raven I., Jr. (1958) The dialects of American English. In W. Nelson Francis (ed.), *The Structure of American English*. New York: Ronald Press, pp. 480–543.

McDavid, Raven I., Jr., and McDavid, Virginia G. (1951) The relationship of the speech of American Negroes to the speech of whites. *American Speech* 26:3–17.

McElhinney, Bonnie S. (1993) Copula and auxiliary contraction in the speech of white Americans. *American Speech* 68:371–99.

McIntosh, Angus (1983) Present indicative plural forms in the later Middle English of the North Midlands. In S. Grey-Douglas (ed.), *Middle English Studies Presented to Norman Davis in Honour of his Seventieth Birthday*. Oxford: Clarendon, pp. 235–44.

Mallinson, Christine, Walt Wolfram, and Jaclyn Fried (2001) Dialect accommodation in a bi-ethnic mountain ethnic community: More evidence on the earlier development of African American English. Paper Presented at the Southeastern Conference on Linguistics 64. Knoxville, TN, April.

Meechan, Marjory (1996) In search of the missing link: Copula contraction in Canadian English. Unpublished manuscript. Ottawa: University of Ottawa.

Migeod, F. W. H. (1911, 1913) *The Languages of West Africa*, 2 vols. London: Paul-Trench-Trübner.

Milroy, Lesley (1987) *Language and Social Networks*, 2nd edn. Cambridge, MA/Oxford: Blackwell.

Milroy, Lesley (1999) Standard English and language ideology in Britain and the United States. In Tony Bex and Richard Watts (eds.), *Standard English: The Widening Debate*. London/New York: Routledge, pp. 173–206.

Montgomery, Michael (1989) The roots of Appalachian English. *English World-Wide* 10:227–78.

Montgomery, Michael (1994) The evolution of verb concord in Scots. In A. Fenton and D. A. MacDonald (eds.), *Studies in Scots and Gaelic: Proceedings of the Third International Conference on the Languages of Scotland*. Edinburgh: Canongate Academic, pp. 81–95.

Montgomery, Michael (1997) Making the trans-Atlantic link between variety of English: The case of plural verbal *-s*. *Journal of English Linguistics* 25:122–41.

Montgomery, Michael (1998) In the Appalachians they speak like Shakespeare. In Laurie Bauer and Peter Trudgill (eds.), *Language Myths*. London: Penguin Books, pp. 66–76.

Montgomery, Michael (1999) Eighteenth-century Sierra Leone English: Another exported variety of African American English. *English World-Wide* 20:1–34.

Montgomery, Michael (2000) Isolation as a linguistic construct. *Southern Journal of Linguistics* 24:41–53.

Montgomery, Michael (forthcoming) The British and Irish antecedents of American English. In John Algeo (ed.), *Cambridge History of the English Language: vol. 6. American English*. Cambridge, UK: Cambridge University Press.

Montgomery, Michael, and Janet Fuller (1996) Verbal *-s* in 19th-century African-American English. In Edgar W. Schneider (ed.), *Focus on the USA*. Philadelphia: John Benjamins, pp. 211–30.

Montgomery, Michael, Janet Fuller, and Sharon DeMarse (1993) The black men has wives and sweet harts [and third person *-s*] jest like the white men: Evidence for verbal *-s* from written documents on nineteenth-century African-American speech. *Language Variation and Change* 5:335–57.

Montgomery, Michael, and Joseph S. Hall (forthcoming) *Dictionary of Smoky Mountain English*. Knoxville: University of Tennessee Press.

Morgan, Lucia A. (1960) The speech of Ocracoke, North Carolina: Some observations. *Southern Speech Journal* 25:314–22.

Mufwene, Salikoko S. (1991) Pidgins, creoles, typology and markedness. In Francis Byrne and Thom Huebner (eds.), *Development and Structures of Creole Languages: Essays in Honor of Derek Bickerton*. Amsterdam/Philadelphia: John Benjamins, pp. 123–43.

Mufwene, Salikoko S. (1996a) The founder principle in creole genesis. *Diachronica* 12:83–134.

Mufwene, Salikoko S. (1996b) The development of American Englishes: Some questions from a creole genesis perspective. In Edgar W. Schneider (ed.), *Focus on the USA*. Philadelphia: John Benjamins, pp. 231–64.

Mufwene, Salikoko S. (1999) The founder principle revisited: Rethinking feature selection in North American Englishes. Paper presented at the 10th International Conference on Methodology. Memorial University of Newfoundland, St Johns, August.

Mufwene, Salikoko S. (2001) *The Ecology of Language Evolution*. Cambridge, UK: Cambridge University Press.

Murray, J. (1873) *The Dialects of the Southern Counties of Scotland*. London: Philological Society.

Myers-Scotton, Carol (1998) A way to dusty death: The matrix language turnover hypothesis. In Leonora A. Grenoble and Lindsay J. Whaley (eds.), *Endangered Languages: Current Issues and Future Prospects*. Cambridge/New York: Cambridge University Press, pp. 289–316.

Myers-Scotton, Carol, and Janice L. Jake (forthcoming). Explaining aspects of codeswiching and their implications. In J. Nicol and T. Langendoen (eds.), *Bilingualism*. Malden, MA/Oxford: Blackwell.

Myhill, John (1988) Postvocalic /r/ as an index of integration into the BEV speech community. *American Speech* 63:203–13.

Myhill, John, and Wendell A. Harris (1986) The use of the verbal -*s* inflection in Black English Vernacular. In David Sankoff (ed.), *Diversity and Diachrony*. Philadelphia: John Benjamins, pp. 25–31.

Odlin, Terence (1989) *Language Transfer: Cross-Linguistic Influences in Language Learning*. Cambridge, UK: Cambridge University Press.

Orton, Harold, Wilfred J. Halliday, Michael V. Barry, Philip M. Tilling, and Martyn F. Wakelin (eds.) (1962–71) *Survey of English Dialects. The Basic Materials*, 4 vols. Leeds, UK: Edward Arnold.

Pederson, Lee A., Susan Leas McDaniel, Guy Bailey, Marvin H. Basset, Carol M. Adams, Caisheng Liao, and Michael Montgomery (eds.) (1986–92) *Linguistic Atlas of the Gulf States*, 7 vols. Athens, GA: University of Georgia Press.

Poplack, Shana, (ed.) (1999) *The English History of African American English*. Malden, MA/Oxford: Blackwell.

Poplack, Shana, and David Sankoff (1987) The Philadelphia story in the Spanish Caribbean. *American Speech* 62:291–314.

Poplack, Shana, and Sali Tagliamonte (1989) There's no tense like the present: Verbal -*s* inflection in Early Black English. *Language Variation and Change* 1:47–84.

Poplack, Shana, and Sali Tagliamonte (1991) African-American English in the diaspora: Evidence from old-line Nova Scotians. *Language Variation and Change* 3:301–39.

Poplack, Shana, and Sali Tagliamonte (1994) -*S* or nothing: Marking the plural in the African American diaspora. *American Speech* 69:227–59.

Poplack, Shana, and Sali Tagliamonte (2001) *African American English in the Diaspora*. Malden, MA/Oxford: Blackwell.

Powell, William S. (1977) *North Carolina: A History*. Chapel Hill: University of North Carolina Press.

Powell, William S. (1989) *North Carolina Through Four Centuries*. Chapel Hill: University of North Carolina Press.

Rickford, John R. (1985) Ethnicity as a sociolinguistic boundary. *American Speech* 60:99–125.

Rickford, John R. (1987) Are Black and White vernaculars diverging? *American Speech* 62:55–62.

Rickford, John (1991) Representativeness and reliability of the ex-slave materials, with special reference to Wallace Quarterman's recording and transcript. In Guy Bailey, Natalie Maynor, and Patricia Cukor-Avila (eds.), *The Emergence of Black English*. Philadelphia/Amsterdam: John Benjamins, pp. 191–212.

Rickford, John R. (1992) Grammatical variation and divergence. In Marinel Gerristen and Dieter Stein (eds.) *Internal and External Factors in Linguistic Change*. The Hague: Mouton, pp. 175–200.

Rickford, John R. (1996) Copula variability in Jamaican Creole and African American Vernacular English: A reanalysis of DeCamp's texts. In Gregory R. Guy, Crawford Feagin, Deborah Schiffrin, and John Baugh (eds.), *Towards a Social Science of Language. Vol. 1: Variation and Change in Language and Society*. Amsterdam: John Benjamins, pp. 357–72.

Rickford, John R. (1997) Prior creolization of AAVE? Sociohistorical and textual evidence from the 17th and 18th centuries. *Journal of Sociolinguistics* 1:315–36.

Rickford, John R. (1998) The Creole origins of African-American vernacular English: Evidence from copula absence. In Salikoko Mufwene, John R. Rickford, Guy Bailey and John Baugh (eds.), *African American English: Structure, History, and Use*. London/New York: Routledge, pp. 154–200.

Rickford, John R. (1999) *African American Vernacular English: Features, Evolution and Educational Implications*. Malden, MA/Oxford: Blackwell.

Rickford, John, Arnetha Ball, Raina Jackson Blake, and Naomi Martin (1991) Rappin on the copula coffin: Theoretical and methodological issues in the analysis of copula variation in African American Vernacular English. *Language Variation and Change* 3:103–32.

Rickford, John R., and Renee Blake (1990) Copula contraction and absence in Barbadian English, Samaná English and Vernacular Black English. *Berkeley Linguistics Society* 16:257–68.

Romaine, Suzanne (1982a) *Socio-Historical Linguistics: Its Status and Methodology*. Cambridge, UK: Cambridge University Press.

Romaine, Suzanne (1982b) What is a speech community? In Suzanne Romaine (ed.), *Sociolinguistic Variation in Speech Communities*. London: Edward Arnold, pp. 13–24.

Rydén, M., and S. Brorström (1987) *The Be/Have Variation with Intransitives in English*. Stockholm: Almqvist and Wiksell International.

Sabban, Annette (1984) Investigations into the syntax of Hebridean English. *Scottish Language* 3:5–32.

Sabino, Robin (1988) Word final vowels in Negerhollands: Linguistic change and contact. In Kathleeen Ferrara, B. Brown, Keith Walters, and John Baugh (eds.), *Proceedings of NWAVE 14*. Austin: Linguistic Department. University of Texas at Austin, pp. 310–18.

Sabino, Robin (1993) On onsets: Explaining Negerhollands initial clusters. In John Holm and F. Byme (eds.), *The Atlantic Meets the Pacific: Selected Papers from the Society for Pidgin and Creole Linguistics*. Philadelphia/Amsterdam: John Benjamins, pp. 37–44.

Sabino, Robin (1994a) First language transfer and universal processes in the acquisition of phonotactic structure. In Carol Blackshire-Belay (ed.), *Current Issues in Second Language Acquisition and Development*. Lanham, MD: University Press of America, pp. 7–28

Sabino, Robin (1994b) They just fade away: Language death and the loss of phonological variation. *Language in Society* 23:495–526.

Santa Ana, Otto (1991) Phonetic simplification processes in the English of the Barrio: A cross-generational study of the Chicanos of Los Angeles. PhD dissertation, University of Pennsylvania, Philadelphia.

Santa Ana, Otto (1996) Sonority and syllable structure in Chicano English. *Language Variation and Change* 8:3–91.

Sapir, Edward (1921) *Language, an Introduction to the Study of Speech*. New York: Harcourt Brace.

Saunders, William L. (ed.) (1886–90) *The Colonial Records of North Carolina*, 10 vols. Raleigh: State of North Carolina.

Saussure, Ferdinand de (1959) *Course in General Linguistics*. New York: McGraw-Hill.

Schilling-Estes, Natalie (1997) Accommodation vs. concentration: Dialect death in two post-insular communities. *American Speech* 72:12–32.

Schilling-Estes, Natalie (1998) Situated ethnicities: Constructing and reconstructing identity in the sociolinguistic interview. Paper presented at NWAV 27, Athens, GA, October.

Schilling-Estes, Natalie (2000a) Investigating intra-ethnic differentiation: /ay/ in Lumbee Native American English. *Language Variation and Change* 12:141–74.

Schilling-Estes, Natalie (2000b) Exploring morphological change: The *was/weren't* pattern in Smith Island English. Paper presented at NWAVE 29, East Lansing, MI, 7 October.

Schilling-Estes, Natalie, and Walt Wolfram (1994) Convergent explanation and alternative regularization patterns: *were/weren't* leveling in a vernacular English variety. *Language Variation and Change* 6:273–302.

Schilling-Estes, Natalie, and Walt Wolfram (1997) Symbolic identity and language change: A comparative analysis of post-insular /ay/ and /aw/. *University of Pennsylvania Working Papers in Linguistics* 4:486–521.

Schilling-Estes, Natalie, and Walt Wolfram (1999) Alternative models of dialect death: Dissipation vs. concentration. *Language* 75:486–521.

Schneider, Edgar W. (1983) The origin of the verbal *-s* in Black English. *American Speech*, 58:99–113.

Schneider, Edgar W. (1989) *American Earlier Black English: Morphological and Syntactic Variables*. Tuscaloosa: University of Alabama Press.

Schneider, Edgar W. (ed.) (1996) *Focus on the USA*. Philadelphia/Amsterdam: John Benjamins.

Schneider, Edgar W. (1997) Earlier Black English revisited. In Cynthia Bernstein, Thomas Nunnally, and Robin Sabino (eds.), *Language Variety in the South Revisited*. Tuscaloosa: University of Alabama Press, pp. 35–50.

Schneider, Edgar W., and Michael Montgomery (1999) On the trail of early nonstandard grammar: An electronic corpus of Southern U.S. antebellum overseers' letters. Paper presented at NWAVE 28, Toronto, October.

Schreier, Daniel M. (2001) Nonstandard grammar and geographic isolation: The genesis, structure, and development of Tristan da Cunha English. PhD dissertation, University of Fribourg.

Selby, Marjorie T., R. S. Spencer, Jr., and Rebecca Swindell (1976) Hyde County history: A Hyde County bicentennial project. Hyde County: Hyde County Historical Society.

Sharpe, Bill (1958) *A New Geography of North Carolina*, vol. 2. Raleigh, NC: Sharpe Publishing Co.

Shores, David L. (1984) The stressed vowels of the speech of Tangier Island, Virginia. *Journal of English Linguistics* 17:37–56.

Shores, David L. (1985) Vowels before /l/ and /r/ in the Tangier Dialect. *Journal of English Linguistics* 18:124–6.

Shores, David L. (2000) *Tangier Island: Place, People, and Talk*. Newark, DE: University of Delaware Press.

Silverman, Kimberly E. A., Mary E. Beckman, J. F. Pitrelli, Mari Ostendorf, Colin W. Wightman, P. J. Price, Janet Pierrehumbert, and Julia Hirschberg (1992) ToBI: A standard for labeling English prosody. In *Proceedings of the 1992 International Conference on Spoken Language Processing*. University of Calgary: Banff, Canada 867–70.

Simmons, Carolina Virginia (1907) The settlement and early history of Hyde County. In *Reports of the Public Schools of Washington, North Carolina, for the Seventh, Eighth, Ninth, and Tenth Years, 1903–1904, 1904–1905, 1905–1906,1906–1907*. Goldsboro, NC: Nash Brothers, pp. 106–14.

Singler, John V. (1989) Plural marking in Liberian settler English, 1820–1980. *American Speech* 64:4–64.

Singler, John V. (1991) Liberian settler English and the ex-slave recordings: A comparative study. In Guy Bailey, Natalie Maynor, and Patricia Cukor-Avila (eds.), *The Emergence of Black English*. Philadelphia/Amsterdam: John Benjamins, pp. 249–74.

Singler, John V. (1998a) What's not new in AAVE. *American Speech* 73:227–56.

Singler, John V. (1998b) The African-American diaspora: Who were the dispersed? Paper presented at NWAVE 27. Athens, GA, October.

Smitherman, Geneva (1994) *Black Talk: Words and Phrases from the Hood to the Amern Corner*. Boston: Houghton Mifflin.

Smitherman, Geneva (1998) Ebonics, *King*, and Oakland: Some folks don't believe fat meat is greasy. *Journal of English Linguistics* 26:97–107.

Spears, Arthur K. (1982) The Black English semi-auxiliary *come*. *Language* 58:850–72.

Spencer, R. S., Jr. (1982a) The Donnell family's Hyde County Civil War letters. *High Tides* 3.1:10–13.

Spencer, R. S., Jr. (1982b) Trouble on the Donnell farm. *High Tides* 3.1:14–18.

Spencer, R. S., Jr. (1984) *Hyde Remembers: Historic Bible and Family Records of Hyde County, North Carolina*. Charlotte, NC: Herb Eaton Historical Publishers.

Spencer, R. S., Jr. (1987) Early days on Mount Pleasant Ridge. *High Tides* 8.1:3–4.

Spencer, R. S., Jr. (2000) 1790–1860 slave owners – Some observations. *High Tides* 21.1:4–35.

Spencer, R. S., Jr., Ellen A. Williams, and Dorothy Roberts (1988) Early settlers and landowners of eastern Hyde County. *High Tides* 9.2:10–29.

Stack, Carol (1996) *Call to Home.* New York: Harper-Collins.

Statistics of the Population of the United States (1872) Washington, DC: Government Printing Office.

Stephenson, Edward A. (1977) The beginnings of the loss of postvocalic/r/ in North Carolina. In David L. Shores and Carole P. Hines (eds.) *Papers in Language Variations: SAMLA-ADS Collection.* Tuscaloosa: University of Alabama Press, pp. 73–92.

Stewart, William A. (1967) Sociolinguistic factors in the history of American Negro dialects. *The Florida FL Reporter* 5.2:11,22,24,26.

Stewart, William A. (1968) Continuity and change in American Negro dialects. *The Florida FL Reporter* 62:14–16, 18, 304.

Surprenant, Aimée M., and Louis Goldstein (1998) The perception of speech gestures. *Journal of the Acoustical Society of America* 104:518–29.

Sutcliffe, David (forthcoming) The voice of the ancestors: New evidence on 19th century precursors to 20th century AAVE. In Sonja Lanehart (ed.), *Sociocultural and Historical Contexts of African American Vernacular.* Philadelphia/Amsterdam: John Benjamins.

Syrdal, Ann K., and H. S. Gopal (1986) A perceptual model of vowel recognition based on the auditory representation of American English vowels. *Journal of the Acoustical Society of America* 79:1086–1100.

Tagliamonte, Sali (1991) A matter of time: past temporal verbal structures in Samaná and the ex-slave recordings. Ph.D. dissertation, University of Ottowa.

Tagliamonte, Sali (1997) Obsolescence in the English perfect? Evidence from Samaná English. *American Speech* 72:33–68.

Tagliamonte, Sali, and Jennifer Smith (1999) Old *Was*, new ecology: Viewing English through the sociolinguistic filter. In Shana Poplack (ed.), *The English History of African American English.* Malden, MA/Oxford: Blackwell, pp. 141–61.

Tarone, Elaine E. (1972) Aspects of intonation in vernacular white and black English speech. Unpublished doctoral dissertation, University of Washington.

Tarone, Elaine E. (1973) Aspects of intonation in Black English. *American Speech* 48:29–36.

Tarone, Elaine E. (1980) Some influences on the syllable structure of interlanguage phonology. *International Review of Applied Linguistics* 18:130–52.

Tarone, Elaine E. (1988) *Variation in Interlanguage.* London: Edward Arnold.

Thomas, Erik R. (1989) The implications of /o/ fronting in Wilmington, North Carolina. *American Speech* 64:327–33.

Thomas, Erik R. ([1989] 1993) Vowel change in Columbus, Ohio. *Journal of English Linguistics* 22:205–15.

Thomas, Erik R. (1996a) A comparison of variation patterns of variables among sixth-graders in an Ohio community. In Edgar W. Schneider (ed.) *Focus on the USA.* Philadelphia: John Benjamins, pp. 149–68.

Thomas, Erik R. (1996b) The role of individuation in sound change. Paper presented at the Southeastern Conference on Linguistics, College Station, Texas, 16 March.

Thomas, Erik R. (1999) A first look at African-American Vernacular English intonation. Paper presented at NWAVE 28, Toronto, ON, 16 October.

Thomas, Erik R. (2001a) *An Acoustic Analysis of Vowel Variation in New World English*. Publication of the American Dialect Society 85. Durham: Duke University Press.

Thomas, Erik R. (2001b) Instrumental phonetics. In J. K. Chambers, Peter Trudgill, and Natalie Schilling-Estes (eds.), *The Handbook of Language Variation and Change*. Malden, MA/Oxford: Blackwell, pp. 168–200.

Thomas, Erik R., and Guy Bailey (1998) Parallels between vowel subsystems of African American Vernacular English and Caribbean Anglophone creoles. *Journal of Pidgin and Creole Languages* 13:267–96.

Thomas, Erik R. and Jeffrey Reaser (2001) A perceptual experiment on the ethnic labeling of Hyde County, North Carolina, voices. Paper presented at SECOL 62, Knoxville, TN, April.

Thomason, Sarah Grey (forthcoming) *Language Contact*. Edinburgh: Edinburgh University Press.

Thomason, Sarah Grey, and Terrence Kaufman (1988) *Language Contact, Creolization and Genetic Linguistics*. Berkeley: University of California Press.

Torbert, Benjamin (forthcoming) Language history traced through consonant cluster reduction: The case of Lumbee English *American Speech* 76.

Trudgill, Peter (1990) *The Dialects of England*. Cambridge, MA: Blackwell.

Trudgill, Peter (1998) Third person singular zero: African-American English, East Anglian dialects and Spanish persecution in the low countries. *Folia Linguistica Historica* 18:139–48.

Trudgill, Peter (1999) New dialect formation and drift: The making of New Zealand English. Paper presented at the 10th International Conference on Methodology. Memorial University of Newfoundland, St Johns, August.

Trudgill, Peter, Daniel Schreier, Daniel Long, and Jeffrey P. Williams (forthcoming) On the reversibility of mergers: /w/, /v/ and evidence from lesser-known Englishes. *Folia Linguistica Historica*.

Viereck, Wolfgang (1988) Invariant *be* in an unnoticed source of American English. *American Speech* 63:291–303.

Walker, James A. (1999) Rephrasing the copula: Contraction and zero in Early African American English. In Shana Poplack (ed.), *The English History of African American English*. Malden, MA/Oxford: Blackwell, pp. 35–72.

Walton, Julie H., and Robert F. Orlikoff (1994) Speaker race identification from acoustic cues in the vocal signal. *Journal of Speech and Hearing Research* 37:738–45.

Wakelin, Martyn F. (1986) *The Southwest of England*. Amsterdam/Philadelphia: John Benjamins.

Waynick, Capus M. (1952) *North Carolina Roads and their Builders*. Raleigh: Superior Stone Company.

Weinreich, Uriel (1953) *Languages in Contact*. Mouton: The Hague.

Weinreich, Uriel, William Labov, and Marvin I. Herzog (1968) Empirical foundations for a theory of language change. In W. P. Lehmann and Yakov Malkiel (eds.), *Directions for Historical Linguistics: A Symposium*. Austin: University of Texas Press, pp. 95–188.

Welch, P. H. (1886) *Topography of Hyde County, N.C.* Norfolk, VA: John W. Barcroft.

Weldon, Tracey (1994) Variability in negation in African American Vernacular English. *Language Variation and Change* 6:359–97.

Welmers, William E. (1973) *African Language Structures*. Berkeley: University of California Press.

Williams, Ellen A. (1983) Lake Landing Historic District. *High Tides* 4.2:3–6.

Williams, Ellen A. (1988a) Early Hyde inhabitants, 1700 to 1717. *High Tides* 9.1:6–34.

Williams, Ellen A. (1988b) Early landowners and/or residents of the Swan Quarter and Heron Bay areas. *High Tides* 9.2:5–9.

Williams, Ellen A. (1989) *In the Name of God, Amen! Abstracts of Hyde County, North Carolina Wills. Probate 1709 through 1775.* Charlotte, NC: Herb Eaton Historical Publishers.

Williams, Ellen [Louise] A[midon], and Effron Avery Williams, Jr. (1999) Over the Creek: A community of Oyster Creek, Swan Quarter Township, Hyde County, North Carolina. *High Tides* 20:5–30.

Wimberly, Ronald C. and Libby V. Morris (1997) *The Southern Black Belt: A National Perspective.* Lexington, KY: TVA Rural Studies.

Winford, Donald (1992) Another look at the copula in Black English and Caribbean creoles. *American Speech* 67:21–60.

Winford, Donald (1997) On the origins of African American Vernacular English – a creolist perspective, Part I: The sociohistorical background. *Diachronica* 14:304–44.

Winford, Donald (1998) On the origins of African American Vernacular English – a creolist perspective, Part II: The features. *Diachronica* 15:99–154.

Winford, Donald (forthcoming) Creoles in the context of contact linguistics. In Glenn Gilbert (ed.) *Pidgin and Creole Linguistics in the 21st century.* Amsterdam/Philadelphia: John Benjamins.

Wolfram, Walt (1969) *A Linguistic Description of Detroit Negro Speech.* Washington, DC: Center for Applied Linguistics.

Wolfram, Walt (1974a) The relationship of Southern White Speech to Vernacular Black English. *Language* 50:498–527.

Wolfram, Walt (1974b) *Sociolinguistic Aspects of Assimilation: Puerto Rican English in New York City.* Washington, DC: Center for Applied Linguistics.

Wolfram, Walt (1980) Dynamic dimensions of language influence: The case of American Indian English. In Howard A. Giles, W. Peter Robinson, and Philip M. Smith (eds.), *Language: Social Psychological Perspectives.* Oxford/New York: Pergamon Press, pp. 377–88.

Wolfram, Walt (1984) Unmarked tense in American Indian English. *American Speech* 59:31–50.

Wolfram, Walt (1987) On the divergence of Vernacular Black English. *American Speech* 62:40–48.

Wolfram, Walt (1991) Re-examining the status of Vernacular Black English. *Language* 66:121–33.

Wolfram, Walt (1993) Identifying and interpreting variables. In Dennis R. Preston (ed.), *American Dialect Research.* Philadelphia/Amsterdam: John Benjamins, pp. 193–221.

Wolfram, Walt (1994a) On the sociolinguistic significance of obscure dialect structures: The [NP$_i$ CALL NP$_i$ V-ING] construction in African American Vernacular English. *American Speech* 69:339–60.

Wolfram, Walt (1994b). The phonology of a sociocultural variety: The case of African American Vernacular English. In John Bernthal and Nicholas Bankston (eds.), *Child Phonology: Characteristics, Aassessment, and Intervention with Special Populations*. New York: Thieme, pp. 227–44.

Wolfram, Walt (1996) Delineation and description in dialectology: The case of perfective *I'm* in Lumbee English. *American Speech* 70:5–26.

Wolfram, Walt (2000) Issues in reconstructing Earlier African American English. *World Englishes* 19:39–58.

Wolfram, Walt (2001) On constructing vernacular dialect norms. In Arika Okrent and John Boyle (eds.) *Chicago Linguistic Society 36, The Panels*. Chicago: University of Chicago, pp. 335–58.

Wolfram, Walt, and Dan Beckett (2000) The role of individual differences in earlier African American Vernacular English. *American Speech* 75:1–30.

Wolfram, Walt, Adrianne Cheek, and Hal Hammond (1996) Competing norms and selective assimilation: Mixing Outer Banks and Southern /ɔ/. In Jennifer Arnold, Renée Blake, Brad Davidson, Scott Schwenter, and Julie Solomon (eds.), *Sociolinguistic Variation: Data, Theory, and Analysis. Selected papers from NWAVE 23 at Stanford*. Stanford, CA: CSLI Publications, pp. 41–67.

Wolfram, Walt, Becky Childs, and Benjamin Torbert (2000) Tracing language history through consonant cluster reduction: Evidence from isolated dialects. *Southern Journal of Linguistics* 24:17–40.

Wolfram, Walt, and Donna Christian (1976) *Appalachian Speech*: Arlington, VA: Center for Applied Linguistics.

Wolfram, Walt, Donna Christian, and Deborah Hatfield (1986) The English of adolescent and young adult Vietnamese refugees in the United States. *World Englishes* 5:47–60.

Wolfram, Walt, and Clare J. Dannenberg (1999) Dialect identity in a tri-ethnic context: The case of Lumbee American Indian English. *English World-Wide* 20:179–216.

Wolfram, Walt, and Ralph Fasold (1974) *The Study of Social Dialects in the United States*. Englewood Cliffs, NJ: Prentice Hall.

Wolfram, Walt, Kirk Hazen, and Natalie Schilling-Estes (1999) *Dialect Change and Maintenance on the Outer Banks*. Publication of the American Dialect Society 80. Tuscaloosa: University of Alabama Press.

Wolfram, Walt, Kirk Hazen, and Jennifer Tamburro (1997) Isolation within isolation: A solitary century of African American English. *Journal of Sociolinguistics* 1:7–38.

Wolfram, Walt, and Natalie Schilling-Estes (1995) Moribund dialects and the endangerment canon: The case of the Ocracoke brogue. *Language* 71:696–721.

Wolfram, Walt, and Natalie Schilling-Estes (1996) Dialect change and maintenance in a post-insular island community. In Edgar W. Scheider (ed.) *Varieties of English Around the World: Focus on the USA*. Amsterdam/Philadelphia: John Benjamins, pp. 103–48.

Wolfram, Walt, and Natalie Schilling-Estes (1997) *Hoi Toide on the Outer Banks: The Story of the Ocracoke Brogue.* Chapel Hill/London: University of North Carolina Press.

Wolfram, Walt, and Natalie Schilling-Estes (1998) *American English: Dialects and Variation.* Malden, MA/Oxford: Blackwell.

Wolfram, Walt, and Natalie Schilling-Estes (forthcoming) Dialectology and linguistic diffusion. In Richard D. Janda and Brian D. Joseph (eds.), *Handbook of Historical Linguistics.* Malden, MA/Oxford: Blackwell.

Wolfram, Walt, Natalie Schilling-Estes, Kirk Hazen, and Chris Craig (1997) The sociolinguistic complexity of quasi-isolated Southern coastal communities. In Cynthia Bernstein, Thomas Nunnolly, and Robin Sabino (eds.), *Language Variety in the South Revisited.* Tuscaloosa: University of Alabama Press, pp. 173–87.

Wolfram, Walt, and Jason Sellers (1999) Ethnolinguistic marking of past *be* in Lumbee Vernacular English. *Journal of English Linguistics* 27:94–114.

Wolfram, Walt, Erik Thomas, and Elaine Weslee Green (2000) The regional context of earlier African American Speech: Reconstructing the development of African American Vernacular English. *Language in Society* 29:315–55.

Wolfram, Walt, Patricia Watson, Jeffrey Reaser, and Cathleen Hellier (1999) The Southern roots of Earlier African American English. Paper given at SECOL 60, Norfolk, VA. April.

Wright, Laura (1999) Depositions of sixteenth and seventeenth century Londoners deported to Virginia and the Bermudas: Third person singular present tense markers. Paper presented at NWAVE 28. Toronto.

Young, Richard, and Robert Bayley (1996) VARBRUL analysis for second language acquisition research. In Robert Bayley and Dennis R. Preston (eds.), *Second Language Acquisition and Linguistic Variation.* Philadelphia/Amsterdam: John Benjamin, pp. 253–306, October.

Zwicker, E., and E. Terhardt (1980) Analytical expressions for critical-band rate and critical width as a function of frequency. *Journal of the Acoustical Society of America* 68:1523–5.

Index